Study Guide

Diane Moczar

The Western World

1600s to the Present
VOLUME II

Anthony Esler

The College of William and Mary

Prentice Hall, Englewood Cliffs, New Jersey 07632

Project manager: **Benjamin D. Smith**
Production coordinator: **Peter Havens**
Acquisitions editor: **Steve Dalphin**
Assistant editor: **Jennie Katsaros**

Printed in the United States of America

10 9 8 7 6 5 4 3 2 1

ISBN 0-13-946740-8

Prentice-Hall International (UK) Limited, *London*
Prentice-Hall of Australia Pty. Limited, *Sydney*
Prentice-Hall Canada Inc., *Toronto*
Prentice-Hall Hispanoamericana, S.A., *Mexico*
Prentice-Hall of India Private Limited, *New Delhi*
Prentice-Hall of Japan, Inc., *Tokyo*
Simon & Schuster Asia Pte. Ltd., *Singapore*
Editora Prentice-Hall do Brasil, Ltda., *Rio de Janeiro*

CONTENTS

TO THE STUDENT

This Study Guide will help you master the material presented in <u>The Western World</u> by Anthony Esler. Please read this introductory section <u>carefully</u>; a little time spent in organizing your study program according to the suggestions given here should save you work and worry later on.

Step I: Getting to Know the Textbook

First, look through the history book with a few questions in mind. What time period is covered by this volume? What areas of the world will you be studying? What sort of material is included in the boxes? Skim the preface, introduction, chapter openings, time lines, and topical summaries at the end of each chapter. Can you get an idea of some of the historical developments that the author considers most important? Notice the index at the back of the book; you may need it to locate terms, people, and events as you are studying. Use the glossary to learn the meaning of unfamiliar terms. Try not to be daunted by the amount of material to be covered during the semester. The key to mastering it successfully is to develop a workable method of study.

Step II: Forming a Study Plan

Like any other project, the study of history requires budgeting your time and dividing the work into manageable segments. Here are a few hints for studying the textbook:
   A. <u>Skim before you study</u>. Look over the chapter you are working on to get a general idea of what it covers. Then break it into sections for careful reading.
   B. <u>Make sure you understand what you read</u>. If you do not know what a word means, look it up. Identify the main points the author is making and stop periodically to explain them to yourself in your own words. Since each chapter builds on material presented earlier in the book, lack of clear concepts at any point can spell disaster later on.
   C. <u>Ask, What? Where? When? Why? So What?</u> If you can answer these questions about any historical event, you know you have a good understanding of it. The answers to the first three queries define the subject--that is, describe it so that the description cannot apply to anything else--and situate it in time and place; the last

two deal with causality (why did a historical event happen?) and significance (what difference did it make? why do we spend time studying it?).

D. <u>Create your own version of the chapter material</u>. Take notes, write short summaries, make a list of dates and terms you need to remember, outline the chapter. Do whatever works best to get the material into your mind and memory, but do something that forces you to interact with the material in the book. Reading (and highlighting) are usually not enough.

E. <u>Identify problems</u>. Too often students wait until they are hopelessly at sea before seeking help with their studying. If you make it a point to keep up with the reading and study the material in manageable segments, you should immediately become aware when you do not understand something. As Socrates insisted, the highest wisdom can be to know that you do <u>not</u> know. Try to pinpoint exactly what is giving you trouble. If the problem is a real lack of comprehension, ask for help from your instructor. If, on the other hand, you have gotten behind in studying and are trying to cram three chapters at once, that is obviously a problem which only extra time and discipline (yours) can solve.

Step III: Using This Study Guide

It is a good idea to look over the pertinent chapter in the Study Guide before turning to your textbook, and return to it to review and test your knowledge when you have finished studying the textbook material. Every chapter in this Study Guide includes the five sections described here, each designed to exercise one of the skills needed in the study of history.

A. <u>Chapter Outline</u>. This is intended to be a guide for you in constructing your own outlines. Outlining requires active analysis and organization of the text material, and is a great help in learning and retaining information. Since doing it yourself is far more useful than studying a prepackaged outline, this section includes only a simplified schema of the text chapter that you can use as a framework for your own construction. You will want to fill in important points, details you need to remember, and perhaps themes your instructor has stressed in class.

B. <u>Read to Find Out</u>. This section raises the kind of questions you should be thinking about as you study your textbook chapter. After you have finished the chapter, go back to the questions and make sure you can answer them all. Write out the answers if it helps you.

C. <u>Multiple-Choice Questions</u>. After studying the textbook, test yourself with these questions covering some of the main points. Use the page references in the answer key to find out the answers to questions you missed. Make up a few additional questions of your own; this is another active learning exercise, and is good preparation for tests. You can also reformulate these questions along the lines of the tests your instructor tends to give; turn them into true-false or matching questions, for example.

D. Map Exercises. Do not neglect this section! Too many of us have only a vague notion of where important places are in the world, yet geography is often crucial to an appreciation of historical happenings. It matters very much not only where countries are, but what features of their terrain have affected the course of their history. The fate of a nation surrounded by water will differ significantly from that of a steppe region open to invasion from all sides. Depending on how retentive your visual memory is, you will need to spend more or less time on map study.

E. Essay Topics. This section includes several types of analytical questions designed to make you think beyond the facts, as a historian does, and consider the larger significance of what you are studying. You will find in these questions ideas for essays, term papers, and classroom discussion points, as well as topics likely to turn up on essay-question and short-answer tests. Some of the questions require summaries of broad developments, some focus on the significance of an event, and others ask you to make value judgments. Some Study Guide chapters will provide sample paragraphs or essay outlines to help you work on historical essay writing.

The methods of analytical reasoning, organization, memory, and study skills discussed briefly here are not limited to the study of history, but may be adapted to virtually any subject. If you develop these habits according to the suggestions given here, adapting them to your own needs and circumstances, you should find them useful in many areas of your life and work, not just in history courses. Good luck in making the most of them.

Chapter 15: The Critical Century

Outline

 A. The Crisis of the Seventeenth Century
  1. background
  2. military growth and development
   a. increased size of armies
   b. new weapons and use of gunpowder
   c. expansion of sea power
   d. consequences of military growth and expenditure
  3. wars and rebellions
   a. Thirty Years' War (1618-1648)
    1) causes
    2) occasion: defenestration of Prague
    3) early imperial successes
    4) problems
     a) armies living off land, independent of
    emperor's control
     b) neighboring countries fear imperial power,
    join in war
    5) intervention of Denmark and Sweden
    6) France declares war on Spain and Empire; invades
    Empire, 1636
    7) devastation of German lands, great loss of
    population
    8) Treaty of Westphalia
     a) France and Sweden main winners
     b) Habsburgs primary losers
     c) Calvinism and independence of German princes
     recognized in Holy Roman Empire
    9) general results of war
   b. rebellions
    1) France: the Fronde (1648-1653)
    2) England: the Puritan revolt, 1640s
    3) Spain: Castilian domination challenged in many
    areas
    4) United Provinces: merchant elite against House
    of Orange
    5) Poland: Ukrainian Cossack rebellion, 1648
    6) Russia: Cossack and peasant revolts, 1660s
  4. response of governments
   a. political alliances with country
   b. continued centralization
   c. administrative expansion
   d. standing armies
   e. emergence of nation-states of ancient regime

5. economic problems
   a. relative economic stagnation in 1600s
   b. considerable decline in population growth
   c. economic results of wars and rebellions
   d. famines and plague
   e. Little Ice Age affects agriculture 1640s, 1650s
6. the witch craze c. 1550-1650
   a. reflects crisis of the times
   b. types of people accused
   c. church and state courts execute tens of thousands
   d. theories on causes

B. Seventeenth-Century Society
   1. aristocracy
      a. failure to limit power of monarch leads to alliance with government
      b. maintains dominant social position through royal patronage and government jobs
      c. variety of landowning classes in different countries
      d. new sophistication of court life
   2. local communities
      a. discrepancies in wealth divide peasants
      b. Reformation clergy undermine local belief systems
      c. aristocrat leaders of rural society often absent at court
      d. increased royal regulation of local life, including providing of social services
      e. local reactions to outside intrusions
         1) peasant and urban revolts
         2) workers' rebellions
         3) religious disturbances

C. Absolute Monarchy
   1. France
      a. characteristics of French absolutism
      b. architects of the system
         1) Henry IV (r. 1589-1610)
            a) works with minister Sully for prosperity of France
            b) reestablishes royal authority over nobles and other subjects
         2) Louis XIII (r. 1610-1643)
            a) regency of Marie de Medicis
            b) Cardinal Richelieu increases royal power
      c. The Sun King: Louis XIV (r. 1643-1715)
         1) regency of Anne of Austria
         2) Cardinal Mazarin and victory over Fronde
         3) character of Louis XIV
         4) revocation of Edict of Nantes, 1685

5) method of governing
   a) full-time king
   b) expands royal control, curtails independent authority
   c) attempts to control Catholic Church in France
   d) builds Versailles
6) economic policies
   a) Colbert
   b) principles of mercantilism
   c) development of natural resources
   d) increased trade
   e) development of colonies
   f) results
7) preparations for war
   a) Louvois
   b) Vauban
   c) great buildup of army
8) early successes
   a) War of Devolution (1667-1668)
   b) Dutch War (1672-1678) and territorial gains
9) later wars
   a) War of the League of Augsburg (1688-1697)
   b) War of the Spanish Succession (1702-1714)
   c) great loss of life, colonies, money, economic stability
2. the Habsburg Empire
  a. decline of Spain under Philip II and successors
       1) much wealth from empire escapes royal control
       2) inflation
       3) wars of Philip II
       4) declining prosperity, revolts
       5) costs of Thirty Years' War
       6) huge national debt
       7) defeats on land and sea
  b. loss of Habsburg control of Holy Roman Empire
  c. forge new empire on Danube
       1) based on Austria, Bohemia, Hungary, Lombardy
       2) Leopold I drives Turks out of Hungary; annexes country, 1683
       3) acquires Lombardy, 1713

          4) consequences of new Habsburg strategy
              a) increased power in east
              b) revived prestige and leverage in Holy
      Roman Empire
3. rise of Prussia
    a. the Hohenzollern dynasty
        1) extent of possessions
        2) imperial electors
    b. Frederick William (r. 1640-1688), the Great
Elector
        1) builds up army
        2) efficient centralized administration
        3) makes use of Junkers for army and
        government posts
    c. Frederick I (r. 1688-1713) given title of
king
4. Russia under Peter the Great (1682-1725)
    a. character of Peter
    b. goals for Russia
    c. background of early seventeenth-century
chaos in country
    d. Romanov dynasty in power, 1613
        1) national recovery under first three
        Romanovs
        2) position of serfs
        3) Orthodox Church
            a) reforms of Nikon
            b) reaction: Old Believers
        4) Romanov encouragement of skilled
        foreigners in Russia
        5) recovery of territory from Poland and
        Sweden
    e. accession of Peter the Great, 1682
        1) acquires sole power
        2) European tour, 1697
        3) returns home to implement Western ideas
        4) westernizes court
        5) brutal suppression of rebellion
    f. governmental measures
        1) demands government service of all
            a) peasants in military or labor force
            b) nobles in regiments or government
        officials
        2) government structures reorganized
        3) expanded taxation
        4) control of Church
        5) economic measures
            a) expand trade and production
            b) exploit mines

g. wars
1) unsuccessful with Turks
2) Great Northern War with Sweden
a) victory at Poltava, 1709
b) acquisition of Baltic territory
h. St. Petersburg: "window on the West"
D. Constitutional Government
1. England
a. the Stuart dynasty, 1607-1688
1) absolute rulers
2) opposed by (mostly Puritan) gentry
a) opposition to taxation and wars
b) hostile to Church of England
c) fear reestablishment of Catholicism
b. Oliver Cromwell
1) parliamentary opposition to Charles I
2) Civil War (1642-1649)
a) Cromwell and the New Model Army
b) defeat of Cavalier army and capture of
king
3) trial and execution of king, 1649
4) Cromwellian Commonwealth (1649-1660)
a) rallying of opposition to Charles II
b) brutality of Cromwell in Ireland
c) religious and political divisions among
rebels
d) Cromwell becomes military dictator
e) disaffection of citizens with Puritan
measures
c. restoration of Charles II (r. 1660-1685)
d. James II (r. 1685-1688), Catholic
1) anti-Catholic sentiments aroused
2) "Glorious Revolution," 1688
a) triggered by birth of James III,
another Catholic king
b) engineered by political faction,
Whigs
c) Mary (sister of James II) and William
of Orange land with Dutch army in
England
e. William III (r. 1689-1702), Mary II (r.
1689-1696)
1) Whigs insist on Bill of Rights
a) increased political power of
Parliament
b) enunciation of some rights of
(Protestant) citizens
2) result: loose government alliance of
crown and aristocrats

2. the Dutch Republic
   a. golden age of Netherlands
   b. more citizen participation in government than elsewhere
   c. sources of Dutch economic prosperity
      1) shipbuilding
      2) manufacturing of luxury and other goods
      3) finance
      4) trade
   d. political structure
      1) compromise between urban autonomy and noble domination
      2) the seven provinces: medieval-style republics
      3) urban patriciate represented by Jan de Witt and Jan van Oldenbarneveldt
      4) aristocracy by House of Orange
         a) more fanatically Calvinist
         b) more eager for war
   e. seventeenth-century power struggle
      1) Oldenbarneveldt, architect of truce with Spain, executed by Maurice of Nassau who brings Netherlands into Thirty Years' War
      2) peace and control by De Witt after 1648, until his murder by mob, 1672
      3) triumph of William of Orange and centralized authority, limited by:
         a) lack of autocratic tradition
         b) absence of powerful bureaucracy
         c) urban mercantile economic power
         d) provincial loyalties
         e) citizen participation in urban political life

Read to Find Out

1. Why is the seventeenth century considered a critical period in history?
2. What were some of the crises of the seventeenth century?
3. What changes occurred in warfare and military and naval technology during this period?
4. What and when was the Thirty Years' War?
5. What were some of the causes of the war and what were its main results?
6. What countries came out of the war most profitably?

7. What were the effects of the war on the states of the Holy Roman Empire?

8. How would you characterize the midcentury rebellions? What did they have in common and in what ways did they differ?

9. What general policies did the European monarchies follow to increase their power during this century?

10. How would you describe the seventeenth century in terms of economic, demographic, and public health factors?

11. What was the witch craze, in which countries did it mainly occur, and what were some of the probable causes?

12. How did the position of the aristocracy change in the course of the century?

13. How did governmental and other regulation of people increase in the seventeenth century?

14. What were some signs of resistance to social and political changes at this time?

15. What was the most common type of government in seventeenth-century Europe?

16. What is the definition of absolutism?

17. How would you sum up the development of absolute monarchy in France from Henry IV to Louis XIV?

18. Who were some of the powerful government ministers who promoted this trend?

19. What were the main features of the career of Richelieu?

20. Who were the intendants?

21. What was the Fronde and how did it end?

22. How would you summarize the various aspects of the long reign of Louis XIV?

23. Who were Colbert and Louvois and how did they contribute to the rule of the Sun King?

24. What are the main tenets of mercantilism?

25. What were the reasons why Louis XIV waged war and which of his early limited wars were successful?

26. Which of his wars proved disastrous and why?

27. What was the main issue in the War of the Spanish Succession and how was it resolved?

28. What is meant by the new Habsburg Empire?

29. What lands did the seventeenth-century Habsburg realm include and how were they acquired?

30. What characterized the organization of the Empire?

31. Who were the Hohenzollerns and how did they rise to power?

32. What means did they take to unify their lands?

33. Who were the Junkers and what was their role in the governmental system of the Hohenzollerns?
34. What was the political situation before the accession of Peter the Great?
35. Who were the Romanovs and when did they first come to power in Russia?
36. What was the zemsky sobor and how long did it last?
37. Who was Nikon and what was a result of his reforms?
38. What were the main goals of Peter the Great and how did he achieve them?
39. Why did he make an extended trip to western Europe?
40. What were the main results of his reign for Russia?
41. How would you summarize the history of the Stuart dynasty in England?
42. What problems did they face in trying to rule the country?
43. What role did the Puritans play in opposing the king and what were their reasons for doing so?
44. Which English king was executed and when?
45. Who was Oliver Cromwell and what were the main events in his career?
46. Why has the name of Cromwell remained infamous in Ireland?
47. What were some features of the Cromwellian Commonwealth and how did it end?
48. Who was Charles II and why was he welcomed back to England?
49. Why were the Whigs dissatisfied with James II?
50. What role did religious hostility play in the Glorious Revolution?
51. Who came to power in England in 1688 and what were the results of the change in government?
52. Why is the seventeenth century known as the golden age of the Dutch Republic?
53. What two groups competed for political dominance in the Netherlands and who were some of the leaders of each faction?
54. For what reasons did the triumph of the House of Orange not lead to an absolute monarchy in Holland?

Multiple-Choice Questions

1. The seventeenth century may be described as a period of
    a. crisis and resolution
    b. unmitigated disaster
    c. peace and tranquillity
    d. regression in thought and technology

2. Seventeenth-century armies and navies
a. became much smaller than in earlier centuries
b. developed in size, tactics, use of new equipment
c. were larger but used medieval weapons
d. were disbanded because of absence of wars

3. The Thirty Years' War was all of the following except
a. the last great religious war
b. the first general European war
c. a total disaster for the German states
d. a great victory for the Habsburgs

4. The development of centralized, modern nation-states
a. continued unchallenged throughout the century
b. was abandoned in favor of decentralization
c. encountered armed resistance in many areas around mid-century
d. had universal support from all classes

5. Most of the witchcraft persecutions occurred
a. in Catholic Spain and Italy
b. in areas marked by Reformation conflict
c. in Russia
d. because of royal patronage of witches in some countries

6. The old struggle between monarchs and aristocracy was resolved in the seventeenth century by
a. alliances and partnerships between rulers and nobles
b. the elimination of the aristocracy
c. the destruction of monarchy
d. the rise of democracy

7. All classes began to feel
a. neglected by the new central governments
b. a sense of equality
c. increasingly regulated by government
d. a new share in independent local self-government

8. Absolutism means
a. the same thing as totalitarianism
b. that a hereditary monarch is the source of political authority in a state
c. bureaucratic control by city governments
d. total control by a noble over his lands

9. Assertion of royal authority in France required
   a. frequent meetings of the Estates General
   b. dismantling the bureaucracy
   c. a military dictatorship
   d. taming the aristocracy

10. All of the following were true of Louis XIV **except**
    a. he was lazy and incompetent
    b. he was served by talented ministers
    c. he worked to build French prosperity
    d. he involved France in several wars

11. The new Habsburg Empire
    a. recreated the old one as it was in the sixteenth century
    b. succeeded in gaining absolute control over the Holy Roman Empire
    c. was concentrated on non-German lands ruled from Vienna
    d. was limited to Austria

12. The Hohenzollern dynasty
    a. declined in the course of the seventeenth century
    b. remained a powerful but provincial family
    c. proved inept at government
    d. rose to great power through its possessions, military, and centralized government

13. Among the problems faced by Russia at this period were
    a. overpopulation
    b. the wealth and independence of the middle class
    c. too much urban growth
    d. general backwardness, underdevelopment, foreign invasion

14. Peter the Great did all of the following except
    a. develop a powerful bureaucracy
    b. foster traditional Russian Christianity
    c. promote rapid economic development
    d. build a new capital

15. Reasons for the English revolution include
a. desire of Parliament for the restoration of Catholicism
b. the ambitions of a descendant of Queen Elizabeth
c. Puritan political and religious opposition to the king
d. an invasion by the Irish

16. The power struggle that followed the execution of Charles I ended in
a. the accession of a new Tudor king
b. the dictatorship of Oliver Cromwell
c. the triumph of parliamentary monarchy
d. the coronation of Cromwell as king

17. The overthrow of the Catholic King, James II
a. was the result of a great popular revolution
b. was caused by the Tories
c. was imposed by Louis XIV
d. resulted from a coup engineered by the Whigs

18. The accession of William and Mary marked
a. a stage in limitation of royal power by an increase in power of Parliament
b. a return to absolutism
c. the beginning of a revolt by those Englishmen who did not want to be ruled by a Dutchman
d. the start of a democratic regime

19. Political tensions in the Dutch Republic occurred between
a. Dutch and Flemings
b. townspeople and agricultural workers
c. the merchant elite and the House of Orange
d. pro-French and pro-English factions

20. By the end of the seventeenth century, the ultimate winner of the Dutch political struggle was
a. Jan van Oldenbarneveldt
b. William of Orange
c. Jan de Witt
d. Louis XIV

Answer Key

1. a, 450-451
2. b, 451-452
3. d, 452-56
4. c, 456-457
5. b, 457-459
6. a, 459-461
7. c, 461-462
8. b, 462
9. d, 464-465
10. a, 465-469
11. c, 469-470
12. d, 470-471
13. d, 471-472
14. b, 472-473
15. c, 474-475
16. b, 475-477
17. d, 477-478
18. a, 478
19. c, 478-480
20. b, 480-481

Map Exercises

1. From studying Map 15.1, page 454, would you say that the
Thirty Years' War was truly a general European conflict? How
many different states can you count that were directly
involved? Where was most of the fighting concentrated? In
England, where was the Civil War mostly fought? Where is
Drogheda and what happened there? Why would the Irish
support Charles II?

2. On Map 15.2, page 467, locate the states with which
Louis XIV went to war as discussed in the chapter. How did
his earlier wars alter the borders of France? What
territorial changes occurred as a result of the War of the
Spanish Succession? With what states did Peter the Great
wage war? Where is Poltava and what is its significance?
What was the importance to Peter of the territory he gained
on the Baltic?

3. On Map 15.3, page 479, locate Brandenburg-Prussia and
East Prussia. What powerful dynasty controlled these areas,
and what was its capital? What other areas did it rule? How
has the Habsburg Empire changed? Locate the non-German areas
in which the Habsburgs were asserting imperial control.
Where is Lombardy?

Essay Questions

1. Discuss the various crises of the seventeenth century and the way in which each was resolved. Can you make any comparisons with twentieth-century crises?

2. In what ways did new military capabilities cause havoc in the seventeenth century? Would Europe have been better off if warfare had remained restricted and small scale as in the Middle Ages? How did military power become "a force for order" as mentioned in the chapter?

3. Summarize the what, when, why, and so what of the Thirty Years' War, or do a biographical sketch of one of the important figures involved in the war such as Wallenstein or Gustavus Adolphus.

4. Consider the benefits and drawbacks of the intrusion of centralized government into the local affairs of people all over Europe. Do you think that benefits outweighed drawbacks? Give reasons for your answer.

5. Explore the principles of mercantilism and contrast them with free market economics. Is any form of mercantilism practiced by nations in today's world?

6. Peter the Great is still a controversial figure in modern Russia. What arguments could be made that he was a historical disaster? How could you argue that he significantly benefited his people?

7. James II was blamed for issuing declarations of religious toleration, particularly of Catholics. On the other hand, the Bill of Rights of 1689 limits some rights to "those subjects which are Protestants." In what ways did an anti-Catholic mentality affect the course of the English Revolution?

8. In the absence of centralized government, what do you think accounts for the national unity eventually achieved by the Dutch Republic? What role do you think material prosperity played?

Chapter 16: The Birth of the Modern Mind

Outline

    A. Political Thought
      1. the concept of sovereignty
        a. traditional meaning: highest level of authority within an institution
        b. Jean Bodin: supreme authority over whole body politic; necessary to hold nation together
        c. Thomas Hobbes: <u>Leviathan</u>
          1) brutality of state of nature
          2) social contract: surrender all power to government
          3) result: ultimate governmental authority over everything in state
      2. constitutionalism
        a. Levelers
          1) ideas
          2) suppressed by Cromwell
        b. John Locke
          1) works
          2) theories
            a) state of nature and humans not brutal
            b) social contract to preserve natural rights
            c) result: limited government by consent of people
            d) right to revolution against illegitimate government
            e) free society requires private property, toleration of dissent
    B. The Arts
      1. baroque style
        a. emotional impact
        b. used by Catholic Reformation
        c. adopted by absolute rulers
        d. characteristics
        e. baroque painters
          1) Rubens
          2) Velásquez
          3) Murillo
          4) Caravaggio
          5) Gentileschi
        f. sculpture

g. music
  1) ballet
  2) opera
     a) Monteverdi
     b) Lully
h. architecture
2. classical style
  a. definition of classicism
  b. theorists
  c. contrasts with baroque style
  d. painting
     1) le Brun
     2) Poussin
     3) Lorrain
  e. drama
     1) Corneille
     2) Racine
  f. poetry
     1) Dryden
     2) Milton
3. middle-class art
  a. bourgeois taste
  b. religious works
     1) Cornelius Jansen
     2) John Bunyan
  c. secular prose
  d. Molière and bourgeois drama
  e. painting: Dutch realism
     1) Franz Hals
     2) Judith Leyster
     3) Vermeer
     4) Rembrandt
C. Science
  1. early modern explanations of natural phenomena
     a. belief in non-Christian supernatural beings
     b. astrology
     c. alchemy
     d. occultists
        1) number symbolism
        2) Cabala
  2. knowledge of ancient science
     a. ancient Greek natural science
     b. medical theories
     c. Ptolemaic cosmology
  3. early modern pioneers of scientific progress
     a. Paracelsus
     b. Paré

4. the scientific revolution
   a. meaning of the term
   b. new emphasis on natural science
   c. the new scientists
      1) Nicolaus Copernicus (1473-1543)
         a) fields of study
         b) heliocentric theory
      2) Johannes Kepler (1571-1630)
         a) assistant to Tycho Brahe
         b) accepts Copernican theory
         c) adds three laws of planetary motion
      3) Galileo Galilei (1564-1642)
         a) discoveries in physics
         b) astronomical observations with
   telescope: sunspots, rings of Saturn, etc.
         c) espouses heliocentricism, conflict with
   Catholic authorities
      4) Isaac Newton (1642-1727)
         a) career
         b) development of calculus
         c) invention of reflecting telescope
         d) contributions in optics
         e) law of universal gravitation
   d. other scientific thinkers
      1) Giordano Bruno
      2) William Gilbert: magnetism
      3) Andreas Vesalius: anatomy
      4) William Harvey: circulation of blood
      5) Gerolamo Cardano: algebra
      6) Descartes: geometry
      7) Leibniz: calculus
D. Philosophy
   1. René Descartes (1596-1650)
      a. founder of modern philosophy
      b. rationalism and systematic doubt
   2. Baruch Spinoza (1632-1677)
      a. attempts at logical system of ethics
      b. pantheism
   3. Gottfried Wilhelm Leibniz (1646-1716)
      a. logician and mathematician
      b. theory of independent monads, interacting
   only because of harmony decreed by God
   4. Francis Bacon (1561-1626)
      a. emphasis on new beginning in knowledge
      b. stresses empiricism and experiment
      c. exalts status of scientists
      d. see science as means of progress and
   conquest of nature

E. The Seventeenth-Century Craze for Science
   1. popularity of natural science in education
   2. spread of scientific knowledge through printing
   3. formation of scientific societies
      a. Accademia dei Lincei, Rome, 1603
      b. Royal Society of London, 1660
      c. Académie des Sciences, Paris, 1666
   4. the new world-view
      a. experimental method
      b. quantitative logic of mathematics replaces Aristotelian logic
      c. leads to materialist view of universe, with space and time its basic dimensions
      d. revival of atomism
         1) real qualities of matter those of atoms
         2) sense perceptions only in mind of observer, not objective
      e. expanded view of size of universe
      f. mechanical cosmos, distant and aloof creator

Read to Find Out

1. What two rival schools of political philosophy developed during the seventeenth century?
2. How would you summarize the argument of Thomas Hobbes's <u>Leviathan</u>? How does it differ from political principles based on Christianity?
3. What is meant by social contract theory?
4. Who were the Levelers and what were some of their main ideas? Why were they so controversial?
5. How would you sum up the arguments of John Locke?
6. What concepts did Locke have in common with Hobbes and how did they differ?
7. How did Locke view human nature, and how did his view contrast with that of Hobbes?
8. Why did Locke insist on property ownership as a prerequisite for active participation in government?
9. How did baroque art reflect the spirit of the Catholic Reformation and the new absolutism?
10. What were some characteristics of the baroque style?
11. Who were some famous baroque painters and what distinguishes their work as baroque?
12. What are favorite themes of the great baroque painters?
13. Who was Artemisia Gentileschi and what are some features of her art?
14. What are some examples of baroque music and what new forms of musical entertainment emerged from it?

15. What are some examples of baroque architecture and what impressions does it arouse in the viewer?
16. How does seventeenth-century classical art differ from baroque?
17. How did the training of classical artists in various fields influence their art? What standards were they attempting to meet?
18. Who were some of the French classical painters?
19. What great French dramatists wrote plays in the classical style?
20. Who were some of the English writers in the classical style and who was the greatest of them?
21. How would you describe the kind of visual art and literature middle-class people enjoyed?
22. Who were some of the writers who satisfied this taste, and what sort of works did they write?
23. What are the prime examples of the type of pictures middle-class people liked and bought?
24. Who were Franz Hals, Judith Leyster and Jan Vermeer, and why was their work popular?
25. Who was the greatest artist of the Dutch golden age?
26. How would you describe the various approaches that early modern people took in trying to understand nature and the universe?
27. How did the work of early modern doctors, alchemists, astrologers, and technical workers contribute to the development of a new scientific paradigm?
28. To what does the term scientific revolution refer?
29. Who was Nicholas Copernicus and what was his main scientific contribution?
30. What did Kepler add to the Copernican theory?
31. What were Galileo's contributions to physics?
32. What phenomena did his use of the telescope allow him to observe for probably the first time in history?
33. Why is Isaac Newton considered the major figure of the scientific revolution?
34. What is his great discovery and how did he formulate it?
35. For what is William Harvey famous?
36. What developments in mathematics occurred during the seventeenth century?
37. How did the scientific revolution affect philosophical thinking?
38. How would you describe the philosophical approach of Descartes?
39. What were some of the ideas of Spinoza and how were they at odds with both Judaism and Christianity?

40. What do the monods represent in the thought of Leibniz, and does he account for the operation of the universe?
41. What did Francis Bacon stress as the best way of reaching truth?
42. What is the difference between induction and deduction?
43. What did Bacon see as the future results of the new science?
44. In what ways was the seventeenth-century fascination with science expressed?
45. How were the findings of the scientists disseminated?
46. How would you describe the salient features of the new world view at the end of the seventeenth century?

Multiple-Choice Questions

1. The conflict in political theory in the seventeenth century was between
   a. oligarchy and monarchy
   b. republicanism and democracy
   c. absolutism and constitutionalism
   d. anarchism and autocracy

2. Thomas Hobbes argued for
   a. a Christian commonwealth
   b. a Christian monarchy
   c. secular absolutism
   d. democracy

3. The Levelers proposed all of the following except
   a. the restoration of the Stuarts
   b. universal manhood suffrage
   c. elimination of property requirements for voting
   d. toleration for Protestant sects

4. John Locke thought government should be based on
   a. the will of the sovereign
   b. traditional laws and customs
   c. the Magna Carta
   d. the consent of the governed

5. Baroque art was characterized by
   a. light, movement, color, emotion
   b. restraint and lack of ornament
   c. strict adherence to classical rules
   d. geometric abstraction

6. Baroque music included compositions for
   a. Puritan processions
   b. piano and orchestra
   c. ballet and opera
   d. twelve-tone scale

7. The classical style was seriously cultivated
   especially in
   a. the Netherlands
   b. France
   c. Russia
   d. Italy

8. The greatest English poet of the seventeenth
   century was
   a. Racine
   b. Shakespeare
   c. Milton
   d. Locke

9. Middle-class people of the seventeenth century
   enjoyed art and literature that was
   a. realistic, moralistic, adventurous
   b. abstract and abstruse
   c. full of mythological allusions
   d. pessimistic and amoral

10. Seventeenth-century Dutch painting was popular
    because of its
    a. avant-garde character and shocking subject
    matter
    b. realistic and homely scenes
    c. grandiose scenes of court life
    d. emphasis on classical Greek and Roman
    divinities

11. Early modern people looked for explanations of
    natural phenomena through all of the following
    means except
    a. occultism
    b. astrology
    c. ancient science
    d. innovative scientific instruments and
    experiments

12. All of the following were components of the
scientific revolution except
a. an emphasis on deduction from Aristotelian
premises
b. invention of new scientific instruments
c. use of the experimental method
d. formulation of natural laws in mathematical
terms

13. The great controversy that marked the beginning of
the scientific revolution was between
a. Bacon and Pascal
b. heliocentrism and geocentrism
c. Hobbes and Locke
d. Newton and Descartes

14. Newton is considered the major figure of the
scientific revolution because of
a. his religious skepticism
b. his heliocentric theory
c. the law of universal gravitation
d. his anatomical studies

15. Descartes is known for
a. relying on the senses to attain knowledge
b. doing experiments
c. neglecting mathematics
d. philosophical rationalism

16. Leibniz claimed that interaction in the universe
of monads was
a. established by divine decree
b. due to natural causality
c. a theory he got from Voltaire
d. impossible

17. Francis Bacon's attitude toward experimental
science may be described as
a. pessimistic
b. the same as Pascal's
c. an optimistic glorification
d. lacking in enthusiasm

18. All of the following are true of the scientific
world of the seventeenth century except
a. scientific knowledge was spread through
printing
b. scientists lacked prestige and an audience for
their works
c. new scientific societies were founded
d. some scientists wrote in vernacular languages

19.   The late seventeenth-century view of the nature of things may be characterized as
a. materialistic
b. Neoplatonic
c. increasingly spiritualized
d. derived from ancient sources

20.   To Blaise Pascal, the new worldview seemed
a. enchanting
b. the same as the old worldview
c. frightening
d. irrelevant

Answer Key

1. c, 485
2. c, 487
3. a, 487-488
4. d, 488-490
5. a, 490-491
6. c, 494
7. b, 495
8. c, 495-496
9. a, 496-497
10. b, 497
11. d, 499-500
12. a, 502-507
13. b, 502-505
14. c, 505-506
15. d, 507-508
16. a, 508
17. c, 508
18. b, 508-510
19. a, 510
20. c, 510

Essay Questions

1.   Imagine a dialogue between Thomas Hobbes and John Locke. What objections would each make to the arguments of the other? On what points might they both agree? Evaluate the arguments and give your own opinion. Which view of human nature do you support?

2.   Discuss Locke's point that only property owners should have an active share in government. Consider reasons for and against this idea and draw a conclusion.

3. Write a biographical essay on one of the baroque artists mentioned in the text, such as Caravaggio, Velasquez, or Gentileschi. What elements of their art classifies their style as baroque?

4. Compare a seventeenth-century painting in the classical style with a baroque painting and discuss the differences between them.

5. Analyze the features of "middle-class" art as described in the chapter. Do today's middle classes enjoy avant-garde classical music, expressionist painting, modern architecture? If not, what art, music, and literature do they like? Is there a general lack of enthusiasm on the part of ordinary people today for the culture of their own time, and if so, why?

6. Considerable research has recently been done on medieval science, especially on the contribution of late scholastic thinkers who seem to have anticipated the work of later scientists such as Newton. If this topic interests you, you might want to investigate the work done in mathematics, physics, and other fields by Roger Bacon, Nicholas of Oresme, Thomas Bradwardine, Robert Grossteste, and others. Gordon Leff's Paris and Oxford Universities in the Thirteenth and Fourteenth Centuries (1975) has useful information on these thinkers.

7. What role does belief, rather than direct knowledge, play in what we accept as our worldview? Do we know that atoms exist or that the earth orbits the sun because we have evidence or because scientists tell us these things are so? Compare the authorities accepted by early modern people with those we accept.

8. Galileo got in trouble with the Inquisition largely because he insisted on teaching heliocentrism as a fact rather than a theory, although even his friends remained unconvinced that he had proved it. When did it become possible to refer to heliocentrism as a proven fact? Or has relativity theory made it impossible to prove even now?

9. If Descartes knew that he was thinking, where did he get the information he was thinking about if not ultimately from his senses? This would be the objection of Aristotle, for whom all knowledge begins with the senses, and expresses the position of philosophical realism as opposed to Descartes's idealism (meaning the primacy and independence of thought over sensible reality). Analyze this question, and consider where ideas ultimately come from.

Chapter 17: Western Imperial Expansion

Outline

A. Beginnings of Western Imperialism
  1. the non-Western world
     a. Islamic zone
     b. India and Southeast Asia
     c. China and East Asia
     d. Africa
     e. the Americas
     f. Pacific islanders
  2. Western knowledge of non-Western world
     a. earliest contacts
     b. medieval travelers and merchants
     c. obstacles to contacts
     d. sources of information
        1) ancient writers
        2) popular tales
        3) inaccurate maps
  3. motives for imperial expansion
     a. desire for gain
     b. missionary zeal
     c. craving for fame and glory
  4. technological means of Western expansion
     a. improvements in shipbuilding
     b. new navigational aids
     c. breakthroughs in map making
     d. advances in military technology
  5. other Western advantages
     a. business organization
        1) joint-stock companies
        2) efficient business and financial techniques
     b. governmental organization
     c. traditional Western competitiveness and militarism
  6. phases and forms of imperialism
     a. phases
        1) old imperialism, 1492-1776
        2) new imperialism, 1870s to post-1945
     b. participants
        1) pioneers: Portugal and Spain
        2) later imperialist nations
           a) Holland
           b) France
           c) England

c. forms of imperialism
  1) settlement empire
    a) establishment of colonies and European institutions
    b) most common in New World
  2) trading empire
    a) more common in Asia and Africa
    b) trading posts and treaties
    c) Portuguese and Dutch in Southeast Asia
    d) French and English in India
B. First Global Empires
  1. the Iberians
    a. defeat of Ottoman Turks, obstacle and threat to European expansion
    b. rise of Portugal
      1) Prince of Henry the Navigator (1394-1460)
        a) fosters research center to expand knowledge, improve ships and maps
        b) goals: alliance with Christian African ruler against Turks, control African gold mines
        c) success of search for gold
      2) goal of Henry's successors
        a) find sea route around Africa
        b) Bartolomeu Dias reaches Cape of Good Hope, 1488
      3) Vasco da Gama (c. 1460-1524)
        a) reaches India, 1498
        b) losses in ships and men
        c) great profit on cargo of spices
      4) expansion of trading empire
        a) Brazil
        b) Indian Ocean main center of empire
      5) problems
        a) small size of Portugal compared with empire
        b) great costs involved
        c) lack of Portuguese expertise in business
        d) competition from other countries
    c. Spain
      1) greatest imperial state of sixteenth century
      2) Christopher Columbus (1451-1506)
        a) character and career to 1492
        b) voyages to the New World
      3) Ferdinand Magellan (1480-1521)
        a) circumnavigation of globe
        b) death of Magellan, survival of one ship

        4) the Native American empires
          a) the Aztecs
            1) characteristics of society and culture
            2) large-scale human sacrifice
            3) conquest by Hernán Cortés, 1519
          b) the Incas
            1) type of society and governmental
          organization
            2) conquered by Pizarro, 1532
        5) further Spanish exploration
        6) organization of Spanish Empire
          a) colonial administration
          b) economic policies and organization
        7) colonial society
          a) first European women settlers and their
        position
          b) class structure
          c) decline of Native American population,
        largely through disease
        8) seventeenth-century decline of Spanish power
  2. other imperial powers
      a. the Dutch Empire
        1) commercial and seafaring experience of Dutch
        2) trading empire developed by private
      businessmen under government charters
        3) spheres of activity
          a) supplant Portuguese in Indonesia
          b) South Africa
          c) Java
          d) failure to monopolize slave trade and
           to capture Brazil and Angola
          e) American colonies
        4) problems
          a) small size of Netherlands
          b) wars with rivals
      b. the French Empire
        1) obstacles to early French imperialism
        2) Canada
          a) founding of Montreal by Jacques Cartier
          b) founding of Quebec by Samuel de Champlain
        (c. 1600)

          3) seventeenth-century expansion
            a) encouragement by Richelieu of Canadian and Caribbean colonies
            b) Colbert and the royal mercantilist empire
          4) French explorers
            a) Father Marquette and La Salle explore Mississippi
            b) claim land for France, but few settlers
          5) other imperial ventures
            a) West Africa and Madagascar
            b) India
      c. the British Empire
        1) sixteenth-century efforts
          a) voyages of exploration
          b) unsuccessful attempt to found American colony
          c) piracy and attacks on settlements of other countries
        2) seventeenth-century successes
          a) joint-stock companies and other private groups
          b) first permanent English settlements in New World: Jamestown, 1607; Plymouth, 1620
          c) colonial expansion in North America for religious and commercial motives
          d) Caribbean colonies
          e) continued activity of pirates
          f) the East India Company and its ventures
        3) English colonial society
          a) women colonists and their roles
          b) development of town life in northern American colonies, plantations in south
          c) friction with Indians
C.   Expansion of Russia
   1. size of territory between Moscow and the Pacific
   2. characteristics of the land and people
   3. the Cossacks
     a. relations with Russian authorities
     b. vanguard of Russian eastward expansion
     c. under Ivan the Terrible, conquest by Cossacks of western Siberia
   4. seventeenth-century Russian exploration and territorial claims
     a. result: more land claimed than by any other European monarch on Eurasian continent

        b. few Russian settlers
        c. little government structure or order
        d. largest country in world by time of Peter the
Great
D. Benefits for Europe from Imperialism
    1. luxury goods from Asia
        a. types
        b. effect on European economy and society
            1) stimulates domestic production of similar
            products
            2) new customs derive from popularity of new
            products, e.g., tea and coffee
    2. the African slave trade
        a. reasons for use of African slaves
        b. countries involved in the slave trade
        c. estimates of number of slaves in the Americas
    3. goods from the Americas
        a. fish
        b. tobacco
        c. sugar
    4. Latin American gold and silver
        a. much of Spain's intake flows out to merchants and
bankers elsewhere in Europe
        b. inflationary effect
        c. some classes profit, wage workers suffer from
higher prices
E. Global Impact of Imperialism
    1. transfer of crops and animals from one continent
    to another
    2. demographic changes
        a. decline in native population of Americas
        b. arrival of African slaves
        c. European settlers
    3. economic impact
        a. European manufactured goods reach Africa and
           America
        b. positive effects on native cultures
        c. negative effect of undermining native economic
development
    4. impact of ideas
        a. Christianity
        b. obstacles to spread of Christianity
            1) persecution of Christian community in
            Japan
            2) difficult terrain and diseases new to
            Europeans in Africa
            3) Puritan hostility to Indians in North America

                c. successful missionary ventures
                    1) French Jesuits in Canada
                    2) Franciscan missions in California
                    3) widespread conversion and cultural influence of
                    Christianity in Latin America
            5. emergence of European global predominance

Read to Find Out

1. What areas of the world were unknown, or imperfectly
known, to Europeans of the late fifteenth and early
sixteenth centuries?
2. From what sources did Europeans derive what knowledge
they had of other lands and peoples?
3. What were the three main motives for Western imperial
expansion in the early modern period?
4. Why did this expansion not begin in an earlier age?
5. How would you summarize the advantages the Western world
possessed that enabled it to embark on imperial expansion?
6. What were the major Western technological advances of
this period?
7. How did the Western mentality influence Europeans in the
direction of imperial adventure?
8. What is meant by the old imperialism and the new
imperialism?
9. What two forms did the old imperialism generally take?
10. Who were the first peoples to develop global   empires?
11. What significance did the decline of the Ottoman
Empire have for European expansionism?
12. What advantages did Portugal possess in its pursuit
of transoceanic expansion?
13. Who was Prince Henry the Navigator and for what is
he most famous?
14. What were his two goals in pursuing the naval
development of Portugal? Did he attain them?
15. What was the main objective of later Portuguese
rulers and how did they attain it?
16. Who was Vasco da Gama and how would you sum up his
career and main achievement?
17. What eventually became the main area of Portuguese
overseas commercial concentration?
18. How many voyages did Columbus make, and what was the
extent of his exploration of the New World?

19. What was the great accomplishment of Magellan's expedition?
20. What areas of the New World did the Spanish conquer under Cortés and Pizarro?
21. How would you describe the Aztec Empire when the Spaniards encountered it? Why did many tribes support the Spaniards?
22. In what ways did the economy of the Spanish Empire operate on mercantilist principles?
23. What was the main cause of the deaths of so many Native Americans after contact with Europeans?
24. What were some reasons for the decline in the power of Spain in the seventeenth century?
25. What factors made the Dutch well qualified for developing and managing a trading empire?
26. In what ways did the Dutch Empire differ from that of Portugal?
27. What were the main centers of Dutch overseas commerce?
28. What led to the decline of the Dutch Empire by the end of the seventeenth century?
29. When did France begin its overseas expansion and who were the governmental figures who encouraged it?
30. Who were some of the French explorers and what territories did they claim for France?
31. Where were French trading centers in Asia?
32. What characterized English imperial involvement in the sixteenth century?
33. How did English imperialism develop during the seventeenth century? What different groups of people were involved in it?
34. What were the first permanent settlements in North America? What were some of the later settlements in America and the Caribbean?
35. How and where did the English acquire a commercial position in East Asia?
36. In what major way did Russian expansion differ from that of the other imperialist nations?
37. What was the result of Russia's push eastward by the end of the seventeenth century?
38. What types of goods did Europeans import from Asia and the Americas, and how was European culture affected by some of the new imports?
39. How did the African slave trade develop, what countries were involved, and what approximate figures do we have for the number of slaves brought to the Americas?

40. What effects did the influx of precious metals have on the economy of Spain? On that of the rest of Europe?
41. What were some of the beneficial ecological effects of Western expansion? Some demographic effects?
42. What were some negative results of Western expansion on the economic development of the colonized areas?
43. What Christian religion had the most success in making converts and in what colonial territories?

Multiple-Choice Questions

1. In the fifteenth century, the world beyond the West was
   a. lacking in culture and civilization
   b. largely uninhabited
   c. about to overwhelm the West
   d. imperfectly known to Westerners

2. The motives that led Europeans to undertake their great voyages may be summarized as
   a. a mixture of spiritual and secular ambitions
   b. natural cruelty
   c. pure philanthropy
   d. greed alone

3. The great European expansion of the fifteenth, sixteenth, and seventeenth centuries was due in part to all of the following except
   a. a new combination of sails
   b. the new spirit of peaceful cooperation among Europeans
   c. new navigational instruments
   d. improved maps

4. The two forms taken by the old imperialism were
   a. mercantilism and private enterprise
   b. royal colonies and charter colonies
   c. trading empires and settlement empires
   d. temporary colonies and permanent colonies

5. Before European states could turn their attention and resources toward empire building, they had to deal with the threat posed by
   a. the Arabs
   b. Russian westward expansion
   c. the new Mongol imperium
   d. the Ottoman Turks

6. Sixteenth-century imperialism was dominated by
   a. Spain and England
   b. France and Portugal
   c. Spain and Portugal
   d. the Netherlands

7. The main Portuguese imperial objective was
   a. trade with India and Southeast Asia
   b. permanent colonies on the North American coast
   c. control of the Mediterranean islands
   d. finding a passage through North America to Asia

8. All of the following are true of the Spanish Empire in
   the Americas except that
   a. it was governed by a combination of royal
   representatives and local assemblies
   b. its economy was run by private companies with no
   government control
   c. the native population declined primarily due to
   disease
   d. the Spanish government passed laws protecting the
   Indians

9. The principles of seventeenth-century mercantilism
   included
   a. government involvement in and regulation of colonial
   activity
   b. a laissez-faire economic policy
   c. rejection of imperialism
   d. disapproval of permanent settlements abroad

10. The decline of both the Portuguese and Dutch empires
    was due in part to
    a. disillusionment with lack of profits
    b. the small size of Portugal and Holland
    c. defeat of both by Spain
    d. revolts of conquered native peoples

11. Early French colonies survived in
    a. Brazil
    b. Florida
    c. Canada and the Caribbean
    d. New Amsterdam

12. Sixteenth-century English explorers
    a. founded lasting colonies in the Americas
    b. discovered and worked gold mines
    c. were peaceful traders
    d. were pirates who preyed on the ships of other
    countries

13. By 1700, England
    a. had fallen further behind the other imperial powers
    b. had given up the attempt to establish an empire
    c. had been conquered by France
    d. had an extensive colonial network centered in the New World

14. Russia by the early eighteenth century had
    a. joined the ranks of the great imperial naval powers
    b. developed a vast Eurasian empire
    c. broken up into small republics
    d. been invaded again by the Mongols

15. The first Asian products sought by the early European seafarers were
    a. spices and luxury goods
    b. gold and slaves
    c. timber and cotton
    d. furs and fish

16. Precious metals from the New World
    a. remained in banks in Spain
    b. spread throughout Europe, causing a depression
    c. spread throughout Europe, causing inflation
    d. had little effect on the European economy

17. One important ecological consequence of European imperialism was
    a. a decrease in colonial food production
    b. an exchange of food plants with the New World and increased food production
    c. a refusal by Europeans to try unfamiliar foods
    d. the inability of European plants and animals to thrive in the New World

18. The population shifts brought about by imperialism resulted in
    a. an increase in Native American populations
    b. depopulation of Europe
    c. increased isolation of ethnic groups
    d. a great diversity and mingling of peoples in the Americas

19. An important economic result of imperialism was
    a. the emergence of a global market
    b. a decline in long-distance trade
    c. a great increase in Asian demand for western goods
    in the seventeenth century
    d. the growth of economic provincialism

20. The Western religion that had the most success in
    making converts, particularly in the Americas, was
    a. Puritanism
    b. Deism
    c. Catholicism
    d. Lutheranism

Answer Key

    1. d, 515-517
    2. a, 517-519
    3. b, 519-520
    4. c, 520-521
    5. d, 522
    6. c, 522-531
    7. a, 522-524
    8. b, 529-531
    9. a, 529
   10. b, 531
   11. c, 532
   12. d, 532-533
   13. d, 534-535
   14. b, 535
   15. a, 536
   16. c, 538-539
   17. b, 539-540
   18. d, 539-540
   19. a, 540-542
   20. c, 540

Map Exercises

1. On Map 17.1, page 518, trace the routes of the Portuguese
explorers described in the chapter. How far down the coast of
South America did Columbus get? Locate the main Asian trading
posts of the Western imperial powers. Why are those in India
located on the coast and not in the interior? Trace the route of
Magellan's circumnavigation of the globe. What was the longest
distance he would have sailed without sighting land? Where did he
meet his death? Which areas of North America were claimed by the
French and which by the English?

2.   On Map 17.2, page 530, locate the main areas in Africa from which slaves were obtained. What were their primary destinations in the New World? What is meant by the triangular trade mentioned in the chapter? Follow its general route on the map.

3.   On Map 17.3, page 541, observe the distribution of overseas territories among the major imperial powers. Does the map show evidence of the decline of the Portuguese and Dutch empires discussed in the chapter? Which European countries appear to control the most territory, and of the areas controlled, which ones were the most lucrative for the imperialists?

Essay Questions

1.   Describe the process by which Europeans gradually acquired more accurate knowledge of other parts of the world. What persons mentioned in the chapter played a key role in the advancement of geographical knowledge, and what were their specific contributions? What technology was developed that facilitated exploration?

2.   Discuss the qualities and experience that enabled some European peoples to become particularly successful at early empire building. What accounted for the subsequent decline of some of these same empires? By 1700, which imperial nations had become most successful and why?

3.   Summarize the great onslaught on Europe, by land and sea, of the Ottoman Turks. What were the stages in Western repulsion of the Turks and what were some of the famous battles in this struggle?

4.   Investigate the "Black Legend" of unique Spanish cruelty, referred to in the chapter. An analysis of the historiography of the Legend may be found in Philip Powell's Tree of Hate (1971), as well as more recent works. Aspects of Spanish colonialism such as education of the Indians (including girls), treatment of slaves, and so on, can be found in The Spanish Struggle for Justice in the Conquest of America by Lewis Hanke and The Spanish Empire in America by C.H. Haring.

5. Read an account of some of the adventures of the early Spanish settlers, such as Cabeza de Vaca's epic three-year trek through the Southwest of the modern United States and his friendship with the Indians. Or explore the life of a woman in Spanish America, such as the seventeenth-century poet Juana de la Cruz.

6. Information on the lives of North American Indian women in the colonial period is sparse. One young Mohawk woman, whose story is known through the French missionaries who befriended her, is Kateri Tekakwitha. Look up one of the recent accounts of her life.

7. Look up the most recent theories on what happened to the Lost Colony, the doomed sixteenth-century English settlement on the North Carolina coast.

8. One of the Jesuits who worked with the African slaves arriving at the port of Cartagena, Father Sandoval, has been called the first abolitionist because of his anti-slavery writings. His more famous colleague, Peter Claver, spent forty-four years of his life ministering to and caring for thousands of individual slaves. Investigate the abolitionist movement beginning with the seventeenth century.

Chapter 18: The Old Regime: States, Classes, Communities

Outline

    A.   European Geography in 1700
        1. similarity of physical features to those of ancient times
        2. expansion of civilized zone
        3. new political divisions based on nation-state system
    B.   Overview of the Eighteenth Century
        1. contrasting themes in middle period of modern history
            a. politics
            b. foreign policy
            c. the Enlightenment
            d. agricultural and industrial changes
            e. emergence of new ideologies and thought patterns
            f. revolution
        2. the great European powers
            a. France
               1) political power
               2) prosperity
               3) reign of Louis XV, 1715-1774
                  a) character
                  b) state ministry of Cardinal Fleury (1653-1743) and national stability
                  c) influence of Madame de Pompadour
                  d) political problems of reign
            b. Great Britain
               1) strongest naval and imperial state
               2) last Stuart ruler, Queen Anne (r. 1702-1714)
                  a) Act of Union, 1707
                  b) no surviving children
               3) Hanoverian dynasty
                  a) George I (r. 1714-1717) and George II (r. 1717-1727)
                  b) defeat of last Stuart attempts to regain throne
                  c) monarchs support Whigs
                  d) Robert Walpole (1676-1745), first prime minister and architect of cabinet system
                  e) rise of power of Parliament
             c. Austria
               1) multinational character of Danubian Empire
               2) Charles VI (r. 1711-1740) and the Pragmatic Sanction, 1713

       d. Prussia
         1) rivalry with Austria
         2) strong military power
         3) eighteenth-century rulers
           a) Frederick I (r. 1688-1713) acquires title of king
           b) Frederick William I (r. 1713-1740), the Soldier King
           c) Frederick II the Great (r. 1740-1786)
       e. Russia
         1) least developed of European great powers
         2) entrance into European affairs under Romanovs
           a) Peter the Great (r. 1682-1725) and Russian modernization
           b) period of political intrigue and weak rulers, 1715-1741
           c) Elizabeth I (r. 1741-1726) and regained power of service nobility
           d) political and economic regression
   3. other European states
       a. decline of Spain, Portugal, and other older Mediterranean states
       b. Sweden
       c. Poland
       d. the Netherlands
C.   The Eighteenth-century Power Structure
   1. characteristics of royal government
       a. absolutism
       b. royal ministers of state
       c. royal bureaucracies
   2. resistance to royal power by claimants to traditional rights and privileges
       a. churches
       b. hereditary aristocracies
       c. urban business oligarchies
       d. local governmental and judicial institutions
       e. national assemblies
   3. general balance among elements of power structure
D.   Eighteenth-Century Society
   1. variation in wealth and power of aristocracy, but general social predominance
   2. growth of wealth and influence of middle classes
       a. various sources of prosperity
       b. values and social outlook
   3. urban workers and their problems

4. the peasantry
   a. general disappearance of serfdom in western Europe, survival of traditional duties and restrictions
   b. continuation of serfdom in central and eastern Europe
5. position of women
   a. influence of Renaissance and Reformation attitudes toward women's place in society
   b. decline in legal rights
   c. effect of emergence of wage labor on types of work done by women
6. community life
   a. importance of the family
      1) variations in size
      2) family life among different classes
   b. the village
      1) variations in physical structure
      2) collective decision making on common issues
      3) enforcement of shared values
      4) conservatism of peasantry
   c. city life
      1) size
      2) physical characteristics
      3) classes represented
      4) centers of community culture
         a) guilds
         b) taverns, coffeehouses, salons
      5) traditional morality
7. the Jewish community
   a. characteristics of early modern Jewish communities
      1) self-governing
      2) the ghettos
      3) generally peaceful coexistence within larger society
   b. functions in eighteenth-century society
      1) migration from eastern Europe to capitalist centers in western Europe
      2) administrative, financial, commercial activities
   c. general increase in assimilation

Read to Find Out

1. What were some of the characteristics of Europe in 1700?
2. What were some of the main political, economic, and social features of eighteenth-century history?

3. What was the greatest of the European powers in the eighteenth century and what were its main advantages?
4. Who was Cardinal Fleury and what was his historical importance?
5. Who were Madame de Pompadour and Madame du Berry?
6. What foreign dynasty began to rule in Britain during this century and how did it happen that they came to power?
7. Who was Robert Walpole and why was he important?
8. How did the English Parliament function, and who were the Whigs and the Tories?
9. What is the cabinet system?
10. What was the Danubian Empire and what were some of the problems it presented to its rulers?
11. What was the Pragmatic Sanction and why was it necessary?
12. How can the history of Prussia during this period be summarized?
13. How would you describe the political development of Russia at this time?
14. What were some major difficulties by the successors of Peter the Great?
15. What had happened to the power of the formerly great European states of the previous century?
16. How would you summarize the European political power structure of the eighteenth century? What was its center in all of the major states?
17. How did royal ministers and bureaucracies function in carrying out royal policies?
18. What centers of resistance to royal power existed, and on what principles did they base their resistance? Why did the existence of such centers not make centralized government impossible?
19. What contrasts were there in the lives of different groups of Europeans in the eighteenth century?
20. What is the difference between the concept of caste, order, or estate, and that of social class?
21. How would you describe the eighteenth-century aristocracy and its variations in wealth and power in different parts of Europe?
22. How would you characterize the world of the bourgeoisie?
23. What differences in position and degree of affluence existed among urban workers?
24. About what percentage of Europeans were peasants at this time?
25. What was a major difference between the status of peasants in eastern and western Europe?

26. How did Renaissance and Reformation ideas affect eighteenth-century views on women's nature and place in society?
27. How did the type of work done by women change during this period?
28. In what ways was the family central to the structure and functions of all classes of society?
29. How would you describe village life, and what were some factors that tended to make peasants more conservative than other members of society?
30. What were some variations in physical environment and the life of different classes in the cities of this period? In what ways were the lives of urban dwellers dependent on each?
31. In what ways did the lives of European Jews begin to change in the eighteenth century?
32. What important functions did the Jews perform in many areas of European society during this period?
33. What stimulated a trend toward assimilation among the Jews?
34. What was the Hasidic movement?

Multiple-Choice Questions

1. Europe in 1700
    a. was geographically much different from ancient times
    b. had the same national boundaries as in 1200
    c. saw the development of completely new methods of farming
    d. was marked by the expansion of Western expansion throughout the continent

2. All of the following are true of Louis XV except that
    a. he had a competent state minister in Cardinal Fleury
    b. he was greatly influenced by Madame de Pompadour
    c. he was as dedicated and hard-working as Louis XIV
    d. he had problems with the nobility and the parlements

3. The accession of the Hanover dynasty in Britain had the effect of
   a. increasing the power of Parliament and party government
   b. reducing the power of the prime minister
   c. abolishing the cabinet system
   d. increasing the power of the king over Parliament

4. Robert Walpole was
   a. a famous English writer
   b. promoter of the South Sea Bubble
   c. England's first prime minister
   d. an opponent of the cabinet system

5. The Danubian Empire was
   a. the rule of Hungary over its neighbors
   b. a multinational realm ruled by the Habsburgs
   c. the central European equivalent of the Hanseatic League
   d. the new German Empire centered on Prussia

6. The Hohenzollern dynasty was known for
   a. seizing power in Austria
   b. recognizing local independence and self-government within its territory
   c. its defeat by France
   d. building up the political and military power of Prussia

7. The immediate successors of Peter the Great
   a. continued his reforms and state-building policies
   b. were unable to prevent political and economic stagnation in Russia
   c. divided Russia into many independent states
   d. intensively exploited the resources of Russian Siberia

8. In the eighteenth century, Spain, Portugal, Sweden, Poland, and Holland
   a. were no longer great powers
   b. were known as the Big Five most powerful states
   c. had all been partitioned and removed from the map of Europe
   d. united in a powerful coalition

9. At the center of the eighteenth-century political power structure was usually
    a. the Church
    b. the merchant oligarchy
    c. the monarchy
    d. the nobility

10. To carry out government policies, rulers relied on
    a. the traditional aristocracy
    b. local governmental structures
    c. the military
    d. state ministers and bureaucrats

11. Resistance to the exercise of royal power was
    a. generally nonexistent
    b. centered in several traditionally powerful groups and institutions
    c. limited to the aristocracy
    d. rarely expressed

12. A feature of the early modern class structure was
    a. a completely new social hierarchy
    b. that it was still composed only of priests, knights, and peasants
    c. a classless society was emerging
    d. the increasing importance of the middle classes and the urban working class

13. Peasants in early modern Europe
    a. were among the most conservative elements of society
    b. were constantly involved in social revolutions
    c. made up a small percentage of the population
    d. were mostly serfs in western Europe and free in eastern Europe

14. The areas in which early modern women were allowed to work
    a. had greatly expanded since the Renaissance
    b. were more limited than before
    c. no longer existed
    d. were the same as in the Middle Ages

15. The basic unit of preindustrial society was
    a. the isolated individual
    b. the commune
    c. the family
    d. the manor

16. The family in the eighteenth century
    a. was structurally the same throughout Europe
    b. varied in importance according to social level
    c. was much less important than in earlier times
    d. was disintegrating because of easy divorce

17. The eighteenth-century city was
    a. hardly more than a village
    b. composed only of slums
    c. inhabited only by the wealthy
    d. a large community of different classes living
    in very diverse neighborhoods and conditions

18. Relations among social classes and economic groups
    in the cities was characterized by
    a. endemic class warfare
    b. complete separation of spheres of activity and
    interest
    c. interaction and interdependence
    d. the complete subjugation of the lower classes
    by the upper classes

19. The Jewish community at this period was
    a. beginning to be assimilated in the states in
    which it prospered
    b. mostly located in eastern Europe
    c. subject to more persecution in western Europe
    than before
    d. unimportant to the political and economic life
    of European states

20. Among the areas in which Jews were active at this
    time were all of the following except
    a. owning real estate
    b. trade
    c. estate managers
    d. governmental administrators

Answer Key

    1. d, 548
    2. c, 552
    3. a, 554-555
    4. c, 554-555
    5. b, 555
    6. d, 556
    7. b, 557-558

8. a, 558
9. c, 558-563
10. d, 559-560
11. b, 560-562
12. c, 563-564
13. a, 568, 573
14. b, 569-570
15. c, 571-572
16. c, 571-572
17. d, 573-574
18. c, 574
19. a, 574-575
20. a, 574-575

Map Exercises

1. On Map 18.1, page 551, locate the five major powers discussed in the chapter. Compare the borders of France with those shown on maps in earlier chapters and determine in what ways they changed after the reign of Louis XIV. What does the map show about the growth of the Prussian state by 1715? In what way is the new Britain geographically different from the England of earlier maps?

2. Which of the French provinces shown on Map 18.2, page 561, had been part of the Angevin Empire in the early Middle Ages? Where is Aquitaine and what famous queen is associated with it? Which provinces would you expect to be vulnerable to attack or annexation by neighboring states and why?

Essay Questions

1. Views of the seriousness and competence of Louis XV differ widely among historians, as do estimates of his ministers and his reign as a whole. Historians seem to agree on the great influence wielded by Madame de Pompadour, but disagree on the question of whether or not it was a benefit or a disaster for France. Look into the latest historiography on this controversial king and his reign, and draw some conclusions.

2. How does the cabinet system as established by Walpole compare to the governmental system of the United States? What are points of similarity and difference?

3.   Compare the Danubian Empire of the Habsburgs with any earlier empire you have studied, such as the Roman Empire or the empire of Charlemagne. What advantages resulting from Habsburg rule can you envision for the subjects of the Empire, and what imperial policies would you expect to cause trouble for the dynasty? How did the Romans handle similar problems in a multinational empire?

4.   Analyze the basic political and social equilibrium that existed in most European states in the early eighteenth century, in spite of political rivalries, social antagonisms, and economic tensions. Discuss what you think were the most important elements in maintaining balance and order within states at this time.

5.   In what ways did the guilds still benefit their members and how were they increasingly at odds with the new economic order that was emerging? Can you think of ways in which the guild system could have been modified to meet changing conditions while still protecting workers?

6.   Notice the description of the twentieth-century model of society on page 571 and compare it with the eighteenth-century model. What drawbacks and advantages do you see in each model? Which appears to you as more fulfilling for human nature and psychologically satisfying?

Chapter 19: The Old Regime: Dynastic Wars and World Empire

Outline

    A.   International Affairs in the Eighteenth Century
1. wars
2. Western expansion
    a. Asia
    b. North America
    c. Africa
    d. Australia
3. reasons for international conflict
    a. reason of state
    b. imperial rivalries
        1) nations involved
        2) role of mercantilist economics
4. attempts to attain balance of power
    a. lack of imposed political unity such as that of Roman Empire
    b. decline in international role of papacy
    c. Hugo Grotius and international law
    d. theoretical peace plans
    e. actual goals of great powers and means of attaining them
5. role of warfare in modern history
    a. function
    b. benefits for material progress
6. foreign policy
    a. diplomats and their tactics
    b. eighteenth-century armies
        1) composition
        2) campaign strategy
        3) discipline
        4) warships and naval tactics

    B.   Wars of the Eighteenth Century
1. the War of the Austrian Succession (1740-1748)
    a. causes
        1) character and goals of Frederick II (r. 1740-1786)
        2) accession of Maria Theresa (r. 1740-1780)
        3) goals and involvement of many European states

        b. course of the war
            1) tactics of Frederick and conquest of
        Silesia
            2) strategy of Maria Theresa
                a) plea to Hungarian nobles, 1741
                b) other diplomatic tactics
            3) peace treaties
                a) between Austria and Prussia, 1745
                b) Treaty of Aix-la-Chapelle, 1748
        c. results
            1) recognition of Maria Theresa's right to
        the Austrian throne
            2) recognition of Prussian conquest of
        Silesia
    2. The Seven Years' War (1756-1763)
        a. causes
            1) the Diplomatic Revolution
            2) European antagonisms
            3) colonial rivalries
        b. course of the war on the continent
            1) military brilliance of Frederick II
            2) Russia switches sides
            3) new willingness of Britain to make peace
        after fall of Pitt
        c. the war in the colonies
            1) strategies of Pitt and Choiseul
            2) the war in North America (French and
        Indian War)
                a) British victories
                b) deaths of Wolfe and Montcalm at Quebec
            3) India
                a) tactics of Clive and Dupleix
                b) British triumph
            4) other overseas territories
                a) Caribbean
                b) West Africa
        d. the Peace of Paris, 1763
    3. wars with the Turks
        a. Ottoman control of southeastern Europe and
        southern Russia
            1) goals of Catherine the Great
            2) naval defeat of Turks in the Aegean, 1770
            3) Russian victories in Balkans and Crimean
        peninsula
        b. Treaty of Kuchuk Kainerji (1774) and
        subsequent Russian acquisitions
            1) Russia gains north shore of Black Sea and
        the Crimea
            2) Russian rights to passage through
        Dardanelles and Bosporus

4. partitions of Poland
    a. weakness of Polish monarchy
    b. first partition, 1772
        1) proposed by Frederick II, who takes Polish territory in 1771
        2) Russian annexation of White Russia
        3) Austrian occupation of Galicia
        4) result: Poland loses one-third of its territory, half its population
    c. second partition, 1790s
    d. third partition (1795) and disappearance of Poland from map of Europe
C. Overseas Empires
    1. eighteenth-century changes in nature of Eastern and Western colonies
        a. New World colonies become valuable trading partners
        b. increased attraction of Asian trading posts for ambitious Europeans
    2. character of expansion in this century
        a. no major acquisitions of new territories
        b. continued expansion of existing imperial zones
    3. features of European presence in different areas
        a. Africa
            1) few Europeans
            2) great influence on continent through slave trade
            3) possible detrimental effects of European trade goods on local economy
        b. Asia
            1) European countries represented
            2) geographical areas of concentration
            3) influence on local populations
        c. Latin America
            1) older, settled colonies
            2) features of urban and rural life
        d. North America
            1) British expulsion of Indians
            2) British colonies dominated by Europeans
            3) economic variations among colonies
            4) degree of local self-government
    4. the world market
        a. changing character of global trade
            1) great expansion in eighteenth century
            2) increased demand for overseas products by Europeans, for European products by colonists
            3) great growth in proportion of foreign trade to total European commerce

      b. transatlantic exchange of goods
         1) speculation and investment disasters
         2) the sugar boom
         3) triangular trade routes
   5. colonial society
      a. styles of European life in the colonies
      b. differences and tensions between Europeans
         born in colonies and those from mother
         country
      c. preservation by slaves of African culture
         and traditions
         1) music
         2) useful agricultural techniques
      d. Indian life

Read to Find Out

1. How would you summarize the main features of
international relations in the eighteenth century?
2. How would you define <u>raison d'état</u> (reason of
state)?
3. In what way did imperial rivalries affect the
relations of the European states in the eighteenth
century?
4. What was the significance of mercantilist economic
policies for colonial development?
5. What is meant by the balance of power? How was a
balance of power maintained in earlier ages? What were
some ways of enforcing such a balance in the eighteenth
century?
6. How does the twentieth-century view of warfare
differ from that of the eighteenth century? In what
ways was war an ordinary instrument of political and
economic survival in earlier ages, and how was it
beneficial in some areas?
7. How did the conduct of diplomacy and warfare change
in the eighteenth century? What were some new features
of military and naval organization and strategy?
8. In what areas of the West did wars develop in the
middle of the eighteenth century?
9. How would you summarize the causes and effects of
the War of the Austrian Succession? What were some of
the tactics that allowed Maria Theresa to survive and
keep her throne?
10. Who was the great Austrian foreign minister of this
period?

11. What two great central European powers were antagonists in the eighteenth century, and how would you contrast the personalities of their rulers?
12. In what two main arenas was the Seven Years' War fought? What were the causes of hostility in each case?
13. What was the Diplomatic Revolution and how and why did it come about?
14. What was the result of the Seven Years' War in Europe?
15. Who was William Pitt and what were his goals for Britain?
16. Who was the duc de Choiseul?
17. By what techniques did Britain defeat France outside Europe in the course of the Seven Years' War?
18. Where was the battle of the Plains of Abraham and why was it important?
19. What areas of Europe did the Ottoman Empire still control in the eighteenth century? What goals of the Russian monarchs involved attacks on Turkish-held territory?
20. What were the results of the Treaty of Kuchuk Kainerji and the Russian annexations of 1784?
21. What were the stages in the obliteration of Poland as an independent state? What countries were involved in the process? How many partitions of Poland were there, and when did they occur?
22. How would you sum up the situation of the European overseas empires in this century?
23. In what ways did imperial expansion differ from that of the previous two centuries?
24. In what main colonial areas did Europeans settle permanently and where did they reside temporarily in the pursuit of wealth and advancement?
25. What roles did the Dutch East India Company and the British East India Company play in the expansion and maintenance of imperialist ventures during this century?
26. What type of society had developed in the older Spanish and Portuguese colonies of the New World?
27. How would you characterize the life of the thirteen North American British colonies during this century? Were they similar in lifestyle and economic base? In what ways were they more independent than Englishmen in the mother country?
28. What is meant by the world market and when did it first emerge?

29. For what reasons did foreign trade gain great prominence in the economic life of the eighteenth-century European nations?
30. What is meant by a financial "bubble" and what examples occurred during this period?
31. Why was sugar such an important international trade commodity at this time? Where was it mainly cultivated?
32. What is meant by triangular trade routes?
33. In what ways did the various peoples who came to inhabit the Americas seek to preserve their native cultures and traditions?
34. What useful agricultural techniques did African slaves bring to farm work in America?

Multiple-Choice Questions

1. In the eighteenth century, wars were fought for all of the following reasons except
   a. the imposition of one religion on all of Europe
   b. reason of state
   c. imperial ambitions
   d. dynastic struggles

2. The most powerful eighteenth-century imperial nations were
   a. Spain and Portugal
   b. Portugal and Holland
   c. Britain and France
   d. Spain and Britain

3. Mercantilism envisioned colonies as
   a. economically independent of the mother country
   b. part of a closed economic system
   c. free manufacturing and trading partners
   d. liabilities for the mother country

4. A way of enforcing at least minimal international order through alliances was
   a. the restoration of the Roman Empire
   b. a willingness to submit to papal arbitration
   c. the enforcement of the legal system of Grotius
   d. the balance of power

5. Warfare in the eighteenth century was
   a. rarely resorted to
   b. seen as essential to the pursuit of political and economic goals
   c. viewed as the greatest of evils
   d. renounced by all states in favor of peaceful negotiations

6. Both armies and navies in this century
   a. decreased in size
   b. were staffed entirely by volunteers
   c. increased in size and destructive capacity
   d. were larger but used medieval weapons

7. Faced with the refusal of neighboring states to abide by the Pragmatic Sanction, Maria Theresa did all of the following except
   a. surrender to Prussia
   b. appeal in person to the Hungarian nobility
   c. rally the Bohemians to her side
   d. enlist the aid of Wenzel von Kaunitz

8. All of the following were factors in the outbreak of the Seven Years' War except
   a. Austrian desire to regain Silesia from Prussia
   b. the Diplomatic Revolution
   c. imperial rivalry between Britain and France
   d. the revolt of the American colonies

9. Results of the Seven Years' War included
   a. the triumph of Britain over France in Canada and India
   b. the restoration of Silesia to Austria
   c. reduction of Prussia to the size of Hanover
   d. the decline of British naval power

10. During the eighteenth century, the Ottoman Empire
    a. mounted its greatest offensive against Europe
    b. lost previously conquered territory to Russia
    c. lost control of Greece
    d. surrendered Istanbul to the Persians

11. The partitions of Poland
    a. were due to the aggression of Poland against Prussia
    b. involved France and Hungary
    c. began at the suggestion of Frederick II
    d. only lasted until the Polish monarchy was restored in 1796

12. In the eighteenth century, the presence of Europeans from the imperialist nations
a. was less evident in the non-Western world than in earlier centuries
b. greatly influenced African, Asian, and New World societies
c. had little impact on the lands they visited
d. was rare in the non-Western world except for Africa, where Europeans were numerous

13. In North America,
a. the most numerous and prosperous colonies were Spanish and French
b. British colonialism had largely failed
c. few British settlers stayed for long
d. the British colonies were the largest

14. Foreign trade in the eighteenth century
a. remained small in scale and unprofitable
b. declined due to the continuing economic depression
c. dealt exclusively with luxury products
d. greatly increased due to colonial development and demand for overseas products

15. The most profitable of the New World plantation crops in the eighteenth century was
a. sugar
b. tobacco
c. rice
d. corn

16. The triangular trade involved
a. three countries on the Baltic
b. European manufactured goods, African slaves, New World products
c. three central European currencies
d. goods from three continents, but not slaves

17. Colonists in the New World attempted to
a. go home as soon as possible
b. create a completely different way of life in their new land
c. reproduce the style of life they had had in the Old World
d. imitate Native American lifestyles

18. Colonists born in the New World increasingly
    a. identified completely with the interests and
    views of people in the country they had left
    b. developed new attitudes and resentments toward
    the mother country
    c. rejected all of their European heritage
    d. became indifferent to political issues

19. Africans who were brought to the New World
    a. abandoned their African culture and traditions
    b. kept some features of their native culture and
    ways of working
    c. kept up their native songs and dances but no
    agricultural techniques
    d. did not have a distinctive way of working on
    the land

20. Native Americans in North America
    a. were expelled from land claimed by the British
    b. lived in close proximity with the English
    settlers
    c. were integrated into colonial society
    d. had been systematically exterminated by the end
    of the eighteenth century

Answer Key

    1. a, 581-582
    2. c, 583
    3. c, 583-584
    4. d, 584-585
    5. b, 585-586
    6. c, 586-587
    7. a, 588-589
    8. d, 590-594
    9. a, 591,594
   10. b, 594-595
   11. c, 595-596
   12. b, 598-600
   13. d, 600
   14. d, 600-601
   15. a, 601
   16. b, 601-602
   17. c, 602-603
   18. b, 603
   19. b, 603
   20. a, 600, 603

Map Exercises

1. On Map 19.1, page 588, locate the boundaries of Prussia and Austria. How has the territory of Prussia expanded compared with its size on the maps in earlier chapters? Where is Silesia and what is its significance for the relations between these two countries? Where is Hungary, and how far would Maria Theresa have had to travel to make her personal appeal to the nobles at Pressburg (Pozsony)? Trace some of the rapid marches of Frederick II as described in the chapter.

2. On Map 19.2, page 592, compare the boundaries of the five major powers with those shown on Map 18.1, Europe in 1715, in the previous chapter. What are the main changes that have occurred since 1715? What are the borders of the Ottoman Empire? How large is Poland on this map, compared with Austria, Prussia, and European Russia?

3. On Map 19.3, page 596, trace the partitions of Poland as described in the chapter. Compare the size of the country after each of the divisions. What has happened to Poland by 1795? What country gained the most Polish territory from the partitions? What state gained least?

4. On Map 19.4, page 597, what changes have occurred in territories previously held by France? How has the British Empire increased? Has European penetration into the Indian subcontinent progressed compared with maps of the region in earlier chapters?

Essay Questions

1. Write a summary of the various causes of the eighteenth-century wars, including the partitions of Poland and Russia's campaigns against the Turks. Compare these wars and their causes with the wars of the twentieth century. What are similarities and differences?

2. Consider the concepts of reason of state and balance of power. Do they still operate in the politics and international relations of modern states? Are there any workable substitutes for these principles in the affairs of nations?

3. A number of recent works have focused on the efforts of the Jesuit missionaries in colonial Paraguay to save the Guarani Indians from exploitation by competing imperialist powers. See the video <u>The Mission</u> for an idea of the situation on the South American borderlands, and consult such works as <u>The Lost Paradise: The Jesuit Republic in South America</u> by Philip Caraman (1975).

4. Would the indigenous cultures encountered by the Europeans in Africa and the Americas have evolved economically and politically, or would they have declined and vanished, like many of their predecessors? This is a question impossible to answer with any degree of certitude, but it would be interesting to look into the dynamics of Aztec, Inca, and West African societies for clues to their strengths and weaknesses in the pre-colonial period.

Chapter 20: The Enlightenment: The Age of Reason

Outline

A. The Enlightenment Mentality
1. the philosophes
2. definition of Enlightenment
3. influenced by Scientific Revolution; influences French Revolution
4. major Enlightenment thinkers
    a. Voltaire (1694-1778)
        1) career
        2) themes of writings
    b. Pierre Bayle (1647-1706)
    c. Montesquieu
    d. Diderot
    e. general goals of philosophes
5. role of the salons
    a. characteristics
    b. the French salonières
        1) Julie d'Espinasse
        2) Madame Necker
        3) Madame de Geoffrin
    c. British salonières
        1) Fanny Burney
        2) Hannah More
        3) Elizabeth Montagu
6. Enlightenment attitudes and ideas
    a. cultural and social background
    b. cosmopolitanism
    c. belief in operation of universal principles in arts and society
    d. faith in reason, as understood by philosophes
        1) great influence of scientific method
        2) belief in nature as standard of truth and right
        3) "natural religion" instead of Christianity
        4) doctrine of progress
        5) perfectibility of human nature
        6) goal of human thought and activity: human welfare and happiness in this life
    e. social thought: subversive critiques
        1) Voltaire's attacks on religion and other targets

    2) the <u>Encyclopedia</u>
      a) ideas of Diderot and d'Alembert
      b) features and purpose of work
f. new political ideas
  1) influence of Locke's theories on natural
rights and social contract
    2) Montesquieu and <u>The Spirit of the Laws</u>
      a) idea of governmental checks and balances
      b) method of studying government
    3) Rousseau's <u>Social Contract</u>
      a) idea of the general will
      b) use of force to compel acceptance
g. new theories of economics
    1) the physiocrats: François Quesnay (1694-1774)
      a) rejection of mercantilist view of sources
      of wealth
      b) only real wealth is that produced by earth
      c) abolition of tariffs and taxes on
      industry; imposition of tax on land and
      produce
      d) method of presenting economic ideas
      quantitatively and in graphs
    2) free-market economics: Adam Smith (1723-1790)
      a) <u>The Wealth of Nations</u>
      b) source of wealth: human labor
      c) idea of division of labor
      d) law of supply and demand
      e) the invisible hand and the free market
h. new humanitarian ideas
  1) repudiation of Christian charity and
individual philanthropy to relieve suffering
  2) emphasis on reform or abolition of
circumstances that cause suffering
    3) sources of new reformism
      a) Enlightenment belief in progress and human
      perfectibility
      b) sentimentalism
    4) types of reforms proposed
      a) legal
      b) Cesare Beccaria (1738-1794): principles of
      penal theory and criminal justice
      c) opposition to serfdom
      d) William Wilberforce (1759-1833): leader of
      antislavery crusade
      e) opposition to war: Abbé de Saint-Pierre
      and proposal for Senate of Europe

        i. ideas on women and the family
            1) acknowledgement by some thinkers of women's intelligence, desirability of women's education
            2) scientific view of women's rationality as conditioned or limited by physical nature
            3) sentimental emphasis on family life and motherhood
            4) philosophes' views on contributions of family to society
        j. religion
            1) deism
            2) atheism
                a) Julien de la Mettrie
                b) Baron d'Holbach
            3) Pietism: emotional Christian reaction to deism in Germany
            4) Methodism in Britain
                a) John Wesley (1703-1791)
                b) emotional preaching to poor
        k. philosophy
            1) David Hume (1711-1776)
                a) affirms sense knowledge
                b) denies possibility of knowledge of causality
                c) therefore denies that either existence or nonexistence of God can be proven
            2) Immanuel Kant (1724-1804)
                a) mind imposes structure on reality
                b) things in themselves are unknowable
            3) morality for Hume and Kant
                a) agree on natural human decency
                b) Hume: human benevolence and morality lead to socially useful action and happiness
                c) Kant: categorical imperative
B.   Enlightened Absolutism
    1. definition: absolute power directed to "enlightened" goals
        a. differences from earlier absolutism
            1) enlightened despots claim to be imbued with new spirit
            2) benefit from new image
        b. some sincere adoption of "enlightened" ideas by some rulers
    2. Frederick the Great
        a. character and personality
        b. Prussian nationalism

c. nature of his reign
  1) traditional Hohenzollern aims and methods
    a) reliance on and favoritism of Junkers
    b) ignoring of aspirations of middle class,
needs of peasantry
  2) reputation for enlightenment
    a) drains swamps
    b) encourages immigration
    c) introduces new crops, supplies peasants
     with equipment
    d) some religious toleration, except for Jews
    e) legal reforms
    f) development of Prussian civil service
3. Maria Theresa (r. 1740-1780)
  a. devotion to Catholicism and Habsburg dynasty, not
        to "enlightened" ideas
  b. character
  c. lasting reforms
    1) reduction of power of aristocracy
    2) increases taxes on Church
    3) eases burdens on serfs
4. Joseph II (r. 1765-1790)
  a. takes on ideas and spirit of Enlightenment
  b. further undermines aristocratic power
    1) use of middle-class administrators
    2) reduction of aristocratic power over peasantry
  c. religious policies
    1) tolerates Protestants and Jews
    2) confiscates and regulates affairs and property
of Catholic Church
    3) temporarily abolishes serfdom
    4) widespread resentment and hostility generated
by highhanded and unpopular measures
5. Catherine the Great (r. 1762-1796)
  a. early life and rise to power
  b. literary and intellectual activities
  c. early reform projects
  d. the Pugachev rebellion and reversal of policies
concerning serfs
  e. limited reform measures
6. other enlightened despots
  a. Charles III (r. 1759-1788) of Naples and Spain
    1) usual absolutist policies
    2) fights Church, expels Jesuits from Spain
  b. Leopold II (r. 1765-1790) of Tuscany
    1) applies Beccaria's ideas to penal system
    2) applies physiocratic economic principles
  c. Gustavus III (r. 1771-1792), king of Sweden
    1) economic reform, religious toleration
    2) struggle against nobles

C.   Eighteenth-Century Culture
1. culture of pleasure in general
2. pleasures of the mind
   a. attraction of scientific feats
      1) popularity of hypnotism practiced by
      Anton Mesmer
      2) the Montgolfier hot-air balloon
3. sensuality and sentimental love stories
4. atmosphere of contrivance and artifice
5. art
   a. neoclassicism
      1) models and rules derived from ancient
      classical art
      2) examples
   b. rococo art
      1) artificial, frivolous, pleasing to the
      senses
      2) difference from baroque art
      3) characteristics
      4) examples
   c. middle-class realism
      1) different view of the age
      2) examples and features of bourgeois art
      3) Chardin (1699-1779)
6. literature
   a. middle-class drama
   b. epistolary novels
      1) Fielding
      2) Richardson
   c. first real English novel: <u>Robinson Crusoe</u> by
   Daniel Defoe (1660-1731)
   d. women writers
7. popular culture
   a. survival of traditional forms of
entertainment
   b. oral literature
      1) ballads and epics
      2) plays (commedia dell'arte), puppet shows,
      religious plays
   c. printed works
      1) adventure stories and humorous works
      2) religious catechisms and spiritual books
      3) occult and how-to books
8. music
   a. importance of music in eighteenth-century
life
   b. broadening of taste for more complex music
      1) opera houses
      2) virtuoso concerts

            c. composers
                1) Johann Sebastian Bach (1685-1750)
                    a) climax of baroque music
                    b) types of music written
                    c) harmony and counterpoint
                2) George Frideric Handel (1685-1759)
                    a) popular operas
                    b) oratorios such as <u>Messiah</u>
                3) Joseph Haydn (1732-1809)
                    a) develops symphony form
                    b) modern symphony orchestra
                4) Wolfgang Amadeus Mozart (1756-1791)
                    a) child prodigy
                    b) variety of works produced
    9. Goethe as epitome of Enlightenment
        a. the German Enlightenment and eighteenth-
           century flowering of German literature
                1) philosophers: Leibniz and Kant
                2) drama and criticism: G.E. Lessing (1729-
                1781)
                3) drama and poetry: Friedrich von Schiller
                (1759-1805)
        b. career of Johann Wolfgang von Goethe (1749-
        1832)
                1) life
                2) great variety of literary works
                    a) <u>The Sorrows of Young Werther</u>
                    b) <u>Iphigenia on Tauris</u>
                    c) <u>Wilhelm Meister's Apprenticeship</u>
                    d) <u>Faust</u>
                3) scientific writings and travel books
                4) autobiographical works
        c. belief in order and harmony of universe

<u>Read to Find Out</u>

1. What different ideologies and social theories had
their roots in Enlightenment thought?
2. How would you define the term <u>Enlightenment</u>, and
what time period does it include?
3. Who was Voltaire and in what way does he express the
Enlightenment spirit?
4. What were the main targets of his barbed criticism?
5. In what ways were the philosophes different from
traditional philosophers? What were their main
interests?

6. How did the ideas of the philosophes undermine eighteenth-century society and its values, and by what means were the new ideas spread among various classes?

7. How would you describe a salon and its function? Who were some of the celebrated salonières?

8. How would you sum up the central beliefs of the Enlightenment?

9. What is meant by cosmopolitanism?

10. How was the idea of natural laws controlling the physical world applied to society and culture?

11. What was the Enlightenment concept of reason?

12. How did the Scientific Revolution affect the trend of Enlightenment thought?

13. What were some scientific discoveries of the eighteenth century?

14. How did nature and progress become substitutes for revealed religion? How would you characterize the "religion of humanity"?

15. What role did Voltaire, Diderot, and d'Alembert play in developing and diffusing the Enlightenment critique?

16. What were the main political ideas of Montesquieu and what method did he use to develop them?

17. What did Rousseau mean by the social contract?

18. In his system, what would happen to people who resisted the general will?

19. Who was François Quesnay and how would you summarize his economic theory? In what ways did it differ from mercantilism?

20. What was Quesnay's <u>Economic Table</u> and what was its significance for later economists?

21. Who was Adam Smith and what were his main economic theories? How did they differ from those of Quesnay?

22. What is meant by free-market economics, the division of labor, and the invisible hand?

23. How did the new humanitarianism differ from Christian charity?

24. With what types of reforms were the new humanitarians especially concerned?

25. In what ways did the views of eighteenth-century scientists on women differ from those of other thinkers?

26. How would you summarize the reasons given by Enlightenment thinkers for emphasizing the importance to society of family life and motherhood?

27. What was deism?

28. Who were some eighteenth-century atheists?

29. What was Pietism and where did it flourish?
30. Who was John Wesley and what was Methodism?
31. How would you summarize the philosophical theories of David Hume?
32. What is philosophical idealism and how is it expressed in the theories of Kant?
33. On what Enlightenment attitude did Hume and Kant agree?
34. Why did the philosophes advocate enlightened absolutism instead of democracy?
35. What distinguished an enlightened absolute monarch from earlier, unenlightened, absolute monarchs?
36. Why is Frederick the Great considered an enlightened despot? What facets of his character seem to be at odds with Enlightenment attitudes?
37. How did the character and approach to reform of Maria Theresa differ from those of her son, Joseph II?
38. How would you summarize the career and rise to power of Catherine the Great? Why is she known as an enlightened despot? What reforms did she carry through?
39. Who were some enlightened despots of the lesser European powers during the eighteenth century?
40. What were some of the characteristics of the art and literature of this period?
41. What is meant by neoclassicism and what are some examples of the style?
42. What is rococo art, what are its main features, and how does it differ from the neoclassical style?
43. What are the general characteristics of middle-class realism, and what are some examples from art and literature?
44. What was the first real English novel and what explains its broad appeal to readers?
45. How would you describe popular culture in the eighteenth century?
46. Who were some of the great composers of music in this age, and who would you say was the greatest of them?
47. In what ways does Goethe epitomize the Enlightenment mentality?

Multiple-Choice Questions

1. The Enlightenment was the period when
   a. electricity was widely used
   b. confidence in the use of reason alone to solve all human problems was widespread
   c. Hinduism had an increasing influence on Western thinkers
   d. Christian philosophy was most popular

2. Voltaire was known for all of the following except
   a. reverence for Catholicism and established institutions
   b. his writings on many subjects
   c. his acid wit and scathing criticisms
   d. his difficulties with the authorities

3. The philosophes were
   a. academic philosophers
   b. neo-scholastic logicians
   c. unsystematic thinkers who wrote on social and political questions
   d. royal bureaucrats

4. The ideas of Enlightenment thinkers were discussed and spread in
   a. scholarly journals
   b. rural taverns
   c. universities
   d. salons

5. The laws governing the natural world discovered during the Scientific Revolution
   a. had no influence on the philosophes
   b. were used by the philosophes to support their claim that human society and behavior were regulated by natural laws
   c. were repudiated by eighteenth-century scientists
   d. were accepted as applying to the material world but not to human society

6. The Enlightenment view of human nature was that
   a. it is perfectible through progress
   b. it is totally depraved
   c. its best time was in the past
   d. it cannot be changed

7. Goals of the Enlightenment critique as exemplified in the Encyclopedia included
   a. the presentation of objective summaries of all areas of knowledge
   b. the support of royal foreign policy and mercantilism
   c. attacking religion and exalting science and reason
   d. educating the public in classical literature and art

8. Montesquieu's political theory held that
   a. society should be governed by the general will
   b. absolutism was the best form of government
   c. the basic powers of government should be separated and balanced against each other
   d. the judicial branch should control the executive and legislative branches

9. For Rousseau, the state should be governed by
   a. property-owning citizens
   b. a king
   c. an enlightened despot
   d. the general will

10. For the physiocrats,
    a. national wealth was based on precious metals
    b. physical education was very important
    c. trade tariffs and taxes on industry should be increased
    d. real wealth is that produced by the earth

11. For Adam Smith, the source of real wealth was
    a. human labor
    b. a favorable balance of trade
    c. the same as that proposed by the physiocrats
    d. the supply of gold and silver

12. Smith believed that a prosperous society would result from
    a. wise government regulation of the marketplace
    b. the free operation of the law of supply and demand
    c. a return to traditional handicraft techniques
    d. economic control by the workers

13. Humanitarian reform proposals included all of the following except
    a. legal and penal reforms
    b. opposition to serfdom and slavery
    c. massive support for the charitable work of religious orders
    d. schemes to prevent war

14. Eighteenth-century thinkers viewed the family as
    a. an oppressive and outmoded institution
    b. irrelevant to Enlightenment society
    c. another medieval survival to be overthrown
    d. vital to the emergence of a better future society

15. Deism held that
    a. God did not exist
    b. God created the world but took no further interest in it
    c. Christianity was the only true religion
    d. there is no God except the world soul

16. Pietism and Methodism were both
    a. emotional forms of Christianity developed in reaction to rationalism
    b. forms of deism
    c. new philosophical schools
    d. schools of painting

17. All of the following ideas are associated with Immanuel Kant except
    a. the categorical imperative
    b. philosophical idealism
    c. that the mind can know the essences of things
    d. that the mind imposes innate categories on sense perceptions

18. Frederick II is considered an enlightened despot because
    a. he played the flute
    b. he was ruthless and cynical
    c. he strengthened the aristocracy and maintained serfdom
    d. he implemented legal, agricultural, and other reforms

19. In contrast to the limited and practical reforms of Maria Theresa, those of Joseph II
    a. were more successful
    b. were less successful and aroused resentment
    c. were less ideologically motivated
    d. did not achieve any results

20. Catherine the Great's claim to enlightenment was based largely on
    a. her interest in Enlightenment ideas and culture, combined with very limited actual reforms
    b. the large-scale reform program she implemented in Russia
    c. her activities before she got to Russia
    d. a false account of her reign by Diderot

21. Rococo art
    a. was more formal than neoclassicism
    b. followed rigid rules and ancient models
    c. was lighter and more frivolous than neoclassical art
    d. was represented by Hogarth and Chardin

22. Middle-class art in the eighteenth century was characterized by
    a. abstract design
    b. realism and moralism
    c. formalism
    d. rococo decoration

23. Music in the eighteenth century
    a. was unpopular
    b. produced no great composers
    c. is no longer appreciated
    d. represents one of the great ages of Western music

24. Goethe epitomized the Enlightenment because of all of the following except
    a. his conviction of the basic chaos and disorder within human nature and the world
    b. his wide-ranging accomplishments and writings
    c. his cosmopolitanism
    d. his scientific interests

Answer Key

    1. b, 609
    2. a, 609-612, 618
    3. c, 612
    4. d, 612-614
    5. b, 614-616
    6. a, 616-617
    7. c, 617-618
    8. c, 618
    9. d, 618-620
   10. d, 620
   11. a, 620-621
   12. b, 620-621
   13. c, 621-622
   14. d, 622-623
   15. b, 623
   16. a, 623-624

17. c, 624
18. d, 626-627
19. b, 627-628
20. a, 628-629
21. c, 631-632
22. b, 632-633
23. d, 633-634
24. a, 634-635

Map Exercises

1. On Map 20.1, page 625, locate the major states that had enlightened despots for rulers. Which of this group was the most effective reformer? The most powerful monarch? Which major countries were not ruled by enlightened despots? What were the less powerful enlightened absolutist states mentioned in the chapter, who were their rulers, and where were their capitals?

Essay Questions

1. Write a biographical sketch of any political or cultural figure mentioned in the chapter. The biography of Maria Theresa by Edward Crankshaw, listed in the reading list, is a very readable account of one of the most important woman rulers.

2. Which goal of the philosophes do you think was more successful: the discrediting of traditional society and institutions through mockery and criticism, or the implementation of a new social order? How much agreement was there among the philosophes as to what the new order should be like and how it should be attained? What were major points of disagreement among the major thinkers?

3. Discuss the eighteenth-century salon, using contemporary descriptions of some of the gatherings. Does anything in our modern style of entertaining correspond to the salon? Does it seem to you an attractive institution? Boring? Irrelevant? Impractical in modern circumstances?

4. If medieval people, like the ancient Hebrews, saw obedience to God's will as their highest duty, does that exclude human happiness and welfare in this life, if God wills the good of human society? Medieval thinkers did not think so, and were passionately interested in political theory, education, and other humanistic pursuits. Granting some similarities between earlier humanism and that of the Enlightenment, there are major differences in mentality beginning in the eighteenth century. Reread the chapter

section on "Nature, Humanity, and Progress" and formulate the concepts that seem to be new to Western thought.

5. Were the Enlightenment scientists correct in their view that women's way of thinking is partially conditioned by their anatomy? Does everyone's body have an effect on the mind, or is thinking independent of anatomy and physiology?

6. If David Hume cannot be sure of causality, how does he know there is any real thing causing the impressions his senses are receiving? Aristotle and his medieval disciples insisted there is nothing in the intellect that is not first in the senses, which give the basic (and real) knowledge of things that is the foundation for further intellectual activity. If you are interested in philosophy, construct a dialogue between Hume or Kant and Aristotle on the question of how the mind knows and what the eighteenth-century philosophers are substituting for classical realism.

Chapter 21: Beginnings of Revolutionary Change

<u>Outline</u>

   A.   The Agricultural Revolution
      1. traditional rural way of life
      2. agricultural improvements
         a. outmoded practices
         b. seventeenth-century Dutch innovations
         c. eighteenth-century English pioneers
            1) Jethro Tull (1674-1741)
              a) replenishing soil with enriching crops
              b) invention of seed drill
              c) horse-drawn hoe
            2) Lord Charles Townshend's successful use of crop rotation
            3) Robert Bakewell and selective stock breeding
      3. impact on peasant society
         a. enclosure for grain cultivation drives peasants off land
            1) yeomen freeholders almost disappear
            2) tenants lose leases, become laborers
            3) desertion of villages for cities
         b. some peasant farmers adapt new techniques
         c. decline of less productive small farms, growth in middle-sized and large farms
         d. greatly increased productivity reduces threat of famine
   B.   Population Growth
      1. checks on population growth in earlier times
      2. causes of rise in eighteenth century
         a. decrease in death rate
            1) decline in civilian deaths in war
            2) disappearance of bubonic plague
            3) increased food supply
         b. increase in birth rate
            1) decline in power of lords and guild masters to regulate or delay marriages
            2) possibility that more jobs led to larger families
            3) possible influence of new emphasis on family life
      3. consequences of population growth
         a. problem of excess children
         b. attachment to and love for children

       c. economic demand stimulates industrial growth
       d. political advantages of large French population

C.   The Industrial Revolution, c. 1760-1830
    1. definition
    2. characteristics and importance
    3. economic reorganization
       a. shift from guild labor to cottage industry
       b. use by capitalists of peasant labor: proto-industrialism
    4. technical development
       a. earlier invention of complex machines
       b. new source of power needed
    5. causes of the Industrial Revolution
       a. material factors
          1) availability of raw materials
          2) available labor force
       b. economic factors
          1) economic demand
          2) capital investment
          3) technological development
          4) the industrial entrepreneur
    6. beginnings in England
       a. all important factors present by mid-1700s
          1) coal and iron resources
          2) agricultural revolution had produced laborers
and demand for goods
          3) wealth available for consumption and
investment
          4) technical ingenuity encouraged
             a) liberal patent law
             b) weak mercantilist restrictions on industry
          5) entrepreneurial initiative stimulated by
flexible social system
       b. the cotton textile industry
          1) textile work employed larger percentage of
British workers than any other trade
          2) woolen cloth manufacture predominant in
cottage industry
          3) increased popularity of cotton
             a) advantages of cotton fabrics
             b) legal protection of domestic industry
against certain cotton imports
          4) problem of accelerating production to meet
demand
          5) new inventions
             a) John Kay's flying shuttle
             b) Richard Hargreaves's spinning jenny

                    c) Richard Arkwright's water frame, installed
              in first factories
                    d) Richard Crompton's "mule"
                    e) Edmund Cartwright's power loom
                    f) Eli Whitney's cotton gin
                    g) other new techniques
                    h) initial worker hostility to new technology
            c. the steam engine crucial to all industries
                1) Britain: leading European coal producer
                2) new processes for smelting and using iron
                3) James Watt's steam engine
        7. women in the Industrial Revolution
            a. employed mills and mines
            b. machines bring both loss of jobs in some areas
        and new jobs in others
            c. factory work
                1) women considered more adaptable to working
                machines than men
                2) often treated brutally by foremen
            d. hardships of family life in slum tenements,
        especially for mothers working long hours
            e. probably easier life for young single women
        8. impact of the Industrial Revolution
            a. major consequences beyond eighteenth century
                1) technological transformation of modern life
                2) new social problems and urban blight
            b. some perception in the eighteenth century
                of possible later consequences
    D. Political Revolution
        1. pressures throughout society
            a. against three top orders of society
                1) discontent aroused by some royal policies
                2) financial pressures on aristocracy, pressure
                from royal bureaucrats
                3) attacks on worldly clergy
            b. commercial and professional middle classes
                1) resent aristocratic claims
                2) adopt Enlightenment ideas
            c. peasant grievances
                1) enclosures in western Europe
                2) tightening of serfdom in eastern Europe
                3) royal taxation, noble exactions
            d. urban discontent
        2. Pugachev's Rebellion, 1773-1774
            a. background of other European peasant revolts
            b. Emelian Pugachev (1726-1775)
                1) rallies disparate group of malcontents
                2) claims to be murdered husband of Catherine
                3) announces abolition of serfdom

    c. brief ravages of Pugachev's band; defeat
3. urban uprisings
    a. revolt in Geneva, 1780s
        1) original feud between merchant elite and
        burgher middle class
        2) appeal of burghers to urban masses
            a) lower classes appeal to ideas of Rousseau,
        demand share in political power
            b) organize discussion groups, seize control
        of streets
        3) revolt quickly suppressed
    b. Britain
        1) Gordon Riots in London, 1780
            a) caused by efforts to reform anti-Catholic
        laws
            b) anti-Catholic riots for three days
        2) John Wilkes (1727-1797)
            a) disputes with king and Parliament
            b) support of Londoners, demonstrations
            c) vindication of Wilkes, 1782: becomes mayor
        of London, member of Parliament
4. aristocratic opposition to royal power
    a. various forms of resistance, various degrees of
success
    b. Russia
        1) struggle of nobles against state service
        imposed by Peter the Great
        2) requirement rescinded by Peter III, 1762
        3) murder of Peter connived by court nobles and
        guards, accession of Catherine the Great
        4) Charter of Nobility granted by Catherine,
        1785, giving great powers and privileges to
        nobility
    c. Swedish aristocratic struggle against Gustavus
III (r. 1771-1792)
        1) king imposes written constitution, 1772,
        increasing royal power
        2) continued attacks on aristocratic land,
        offices, privileges
        3) assassination of Gustavus III, 1792
5. bourgeois political agitation
    a. Austrian Netherlands
        1) attempt by Joseph II to impose autocratic
        regime
        2) commercial oligarchs organize secret societies
        3) two provinces declare independence, 1789
        4) attempt frustrated by internal quarrels and
        foreign invasion

        b. Britain
            1) radicals support American and French
            revolutions
            2) radical political proposals and leadership of
            workers' political societies
            3) William Pitt the Younger invokes treason and
            sedition laws to suppress meetings, exile leaders
    E.   Revolts in the Americas
         1. North America
            a. characteristics of British colonies
                1) prosperity
                2) self-government
            b. new British policies after 1763
                1) strengthen mercantilist control
                2) suppress smuggling
                3) quartering of troops
                4) new taxes and customs duties
            c. American opposition
                1) draw on radical Enlightenment political ideas
                2) influence of Locke's political theories
                3) formation of violent subversive organizations
                4) outbreaks of violence and skirmishes with
            British soldiers
                5) Continental Congress of 1774
            d. the American Revolution, 1775-1783
                1) Lexington and Concord, 1775
                2) Declaration of Independence, 1776
                3) leadership of George Washington (1732-1799)
                4) assistance from France
                5) key American victories
                    a) Saratoga, 1777
                    b) Yorktown, 1781
            e. formation of the new government
                1) Articles of Confederation, 1780s
                    a) no real authority over states
                    b) unequal to postwar problems
                2) the Constitution of the United States
                    a) social contract (from Locke)
                    b) separation of powers (from Montesquieu)
                    c) various limitations of powers
                    d) Bill of Rights
         2. South America
            a. sources of discontent
                1) creole resentment of colonial ruling class
                2) grievances of Amerindians and Africans
                3) mestizo and mulatto discontent

          b. improvement in conditions in late eighteenth
      century
                1) economic revival
                   a) increase in gold and silver production
                   b) discovery of gold and diamonds in Brazil
                   c) expansion to interior
                2) political reform
                   a) measures taken by Charles III to improve
                      colonial government
                   b) lower taxes and other economic benefits
                3) suppression of Jesuits disastrous for Indians
          c. development of radical ideas
                1) influence of Enlightenment theories
                2) news of American Revolution fuels political
                ambitions
          d. revolutions
                1) Peruvian Indian uprising, 1780
                   a) led by Tupac Amarú, descendant of last Inca
                   b) temporary success, then defeat
                2) Brazilian revolt, 1789
                   a) Joaquim José de Silva Xavier, "the
                Toothpuller"
                   b) failure of revolt, execution of Xavier
                3) Haiti
                   a) Toussaint L'Ouverture (1743-1803)
                   b) revolt inspired by French revolutionary
                decree abolishing slavery
                   c) model constitution written for Haiti
                   d) French capture of Toussaint L'Ouverture by
                treachery, death in prison
                   e) success of Haitian revolution by 1804

Read to Find Out

   1. What is meant by the agricultural revolution and when did
   it occur?
   2. What were some reasons why the agricultural revolution
   occurred when it did?
   3. Who were some of the pioneers involved in the development
   of new agricultural methods?
   4. What were some effects of agricultural change on peasant
   society?
   5. What were some causes for the slow European population
   growth before the eighteenth century?
   6. What were some causes for the growth in population
   starting in the eighteenth century?
   7. What were some consequences of population growth?

8. What was the Industrial Revolution and about when did it begin?
9. What is meant by protoindustrialism?
10. What was needed for manufacturing to advance from protoindustrialism to the Industrial Revolution?
11. How would you summarize the causes of the Industrial Revolution?
12. Why did the Industrial Revolution begin in England?
13. In what industry did the revolution first take hold and why?
14. What were some of the important inventions that contributed to the revolution, and who were some of the inventors?
15. What new power source was developed for use in industry and on what two resources did it depend?
16. Who was James Watt and what was his contribution to the Industrial Revolution?
17. What were some effects of the Industrial Revolution on the lives of women?
18. What were some positive and negative consequences of the Industrial Revolution?
19. Who was Emilian Pugachev and how would you describe his leadership of the revolt he led, its causes and its results?
20. Where did urban violence erupt during this period?
21. Who was John Wilkes and what were some features of his political career?
22. What were some examples of aristocratic resistance to royal power and in what countries did they occur?
23. What role did the middle classes play in reform movements and revolutionary agitation in the eighteenth century?
24. What were the causes of the American Revolution?
25. How were the various classes in the American colonies mobilized and united in opposition to British policies?
26. What and when was the First Continental Congress and what role did it play in the outbreak of the Revolution?
27. How would you describe the course of the American war against Great Britain, its leaders, and the main factors in its ultimate success?
28. What were the defects of the Articles of Confederation?
29. What were the main problems faced by the Constitutional Convention in drawing up the United States Constitution, and how were they resolved?
30. In what way did the Constitution incorporate the most radical political ideas of the eighteenth century?
31. In what ways did the condition of the Latin American colonies improve in the course of the eighteenth century?

32. What were the negative effects of the suppression of the Jesuit order and its missionary activities in Latin America?

33. What Indian uprisings occurred in Latin America during this period and who were their leaders?

34. Who was Toussaint L'Ouverture and how would you summarize his tragic career and its consequences for Haiti?

Multiple-Choice Questions

1. The agricultural revolution included all of the following elements except
    a. rotation of crops
    b. improved animal breeding
    c. increased threat of famine due to risky experimental farming techniques
    d. an increase in enclosures and displacement of peasants

2. Population growth in the eighteenth century was probably caused by
    a. the discovery of vitamins
    b. massive immigration from the Near East
    c. the new popularity of polygamy
    d. a decline in the death rate and rise in the birth rate, due to multiple causes

3. Protoindustrialism is a term for
    a. intensive development of the putting-out system
    b. the eighteenth-century guild organization
    c. large-scale farm production based on new techniques
    d. the rise of urban factories

4. The key factor in transforming protoindustrialism into modern industrialization was
    a. the growth of cottage industry
    b. new sources of power
    c. the invention of machines
    d. the development of metallurgy

5. All of the following were important factors in the Industrial Revolution except
    a. increased demand for goods
    b. new technology
    c. sufficient raw materials, labor, and capital investment
    d. the role of committees of guild members in organizing new industries

6. The Industrial Revolution began
   a. in the textile industry in France
   b. in seventeenth-century Holland
   c. in the textile industry in England
   d. with the invention of the cotton gin

7. The most significant invention of the Industrial Revolution was
   a. Watt's steam engine
   b. the spinning jenny
   c. Newcomen's steam engine
   d. the flying shuttle

8. The political power structure of the eighteenth century was challenged by
   a. massive peasant revolts only
   b. all classes of society
   c. very little opposition
   d. only the professional classes

9. Emilian Pugachev and John Wilkes were
   a. leaders of lower-class protest movements
   b. pioneers of the Industrial Revolution
   c. actors
   d. radical poets

10. Aristocratic discontent was expressed
    a. rarely
    b. only by legal means
    c. in both violent and nonviolent action
    d. only in court intrigues

11. Causes of the American Revolution included
    a. lack of colonial prosperity and land ownership
    b. an illiterate populace prone to class warfare
    c. British prohibition of elected assemblies in America
    d. revolutionary propaganda and discontent with new British policies

12. Reasons for the success of the American Revolution included all of the following except
    a. a larger American army
    b. the assistance of France
    c. American familiarity with battlefield terrain
    d. American superiority in ships and professional soldiers

13. The Articles of Confederation
a. provided for a workable and efficient United States government
b. imposed authoritarian centralized government on the states
c. were an ineffective means of government, unequal to postwar problems
d. were an improvement over the Constitution

14. The United States Constitution embodied all of the following except
a. divine right principles
b. compromises between large and small states
c. separation of powers
d. the ideas of Locke

15. Latin American colonial society in the eighteenth century
a. lacked class distinctions
b. included various social classes, each with its own grievances
c. was much more stable and contented than North American colonial society
d. had achieved self-government

16. In the later eighteenth century, the Latin American colonies experienced
a. a worsening of economic and political conditions
b. aggression by the North Americans
c. a series of natural disasters
d. an economic revival and political reform

17. The suppression of the Jesuits
a. greatly improved the condition of the Indians
b. eliminated the slave trade
c. left the Indians, formerly protected by the missionaries, vulnerable to slavery and exploitation
d. had no effect in Latin America

18. The revolt of Tupac Amarú
a. was inspired by Enlightenment ideology
b. was unsuccessful
c. achieved lasting reforms
d. changed the government of Peru

19. The revolt of Joaquim José de Silva Xavier
     a. was an ideologically motivated struggle for
     Brazilian independence
     b. aimed at reforms in the dental profession
     c. was limited to an attempt to gain land for the
     peasants
     d. succeeded in abolishing slavery

20. Toussaint L'Ouverture was
     a. a Caribbean adventurer and pirate
     b. the French governor of Haiti
     c. a radical pamphleteer
     d. leader of the ultimately successful Haitian slave
     revolt

Answer Key

    1. c, 641-643
    2. d, 644-645
    3. a, 648
    4. b, 648
    5. d, 648-650
    6. c, 650-652
    7. a, 652
    8. b, 655
    9. a, 655-657
    10. c, 657-658
    11. d, 658-660
    12. d, 661-662
    13. c, 662
    14. a, 662-664
    15. b, 664
    16. d, 664
    17. c, 664
    18. b, 665
    19. a, 665
    20. d, 665

Map Exercises

1. On Map 21.1, page 646, which areas shown have the greatest
population density? Are these the same areas in which the
Industrial Revolution first occurred? What connections could
there be between population density and industrial development?
How does eastern European population size and concentration
compare with that of western Europe?

2. Compare the manufacturing centers shown on Map 21.2, page 649, with the population map on page 646. What country shows the greatest manufacturing activity, and in what regions? What factors explain regional concentration of industry? How does industry in eastern and southern Europe compare with that in the northern and western parts of the continent?

3. On Map 21.3, locate the battle sites mentioned in the chapter. Where did the Revolution begin? What were the most decisive battles, and where did the British surrender? Which colonies produced the military and political leaders of the Revolution? In what region were the most radical revolutionaries located?

Essay Questions

1. Summarize the changes in farming practices that constituted the agricultural revolution and evaluate the effects of the new methods and techniques, including the consequences for the poorer peasants. What role did the agricultural revolution play in population growth during the eighteenth century?

2. Modern economists hold that Malthus's calculations were wrong, since food production is capable of a much greater and more rapid rate of increase than he thought. Look up modern views of Malthus and discuss this issue; consult the recent works of Julian Simon and Jacqueline Kasun.

3. Summarize the reasons why the Industrial Revolution occurred first in England. Which of the many factors involved do you consider most important?

4.   Write a biographical sketch of any of the revolutionary leaders mentioned in the chapter, such as Toussaint L'Ouverture, Pugachev, or one of the American revolutionaries.

Chapter 22: The French Revolution and Napoleon's Empire

Outline

A.   Causes of the French Revolution
1. radical philosophical criticism
     a. negative attacks undermine public confidence
in existing institutions
     b. new theories of reform
     c. Enlightenment ideas infiltrate all classes
2. social problems
     a. the social structure
     b. classes and their grievances
        1) the peasantry
            a) resentment of traditional payments and
     obligations
            b) pressures generated by population
     growth and agricultural revolution
        2) the urban poor
            a) reasons for discontent
            b) bring pressure for drastic measures
        3) the bourgeoisie
            a) social resentment of upper classes
            b) ambitious professionals enter politics
        4) the aristocracy
            a) pressures of inflation
            b) social antagonisms
            c) opposition to monarchy
3. economic and financial problems
     a. economic decline of 1770s and 1780s
        1) effects of commercial treaty with Britain
     1786
        2) bad harvest of 1788
        3) rise in food prices, bread riots in 1789
        4) rural violence and the Great Fear
     b. government financial crisis
        1) inadequate tax revenue
        2) expenses of court, reforms, wars
        3) tripling of national debt, huge interest
     payments leads to bankruptcy

4. political crisis
   a. reign of Louis XVI (1774-1792)
      1) indecisive character of king
      2) reforming ministers
         a) Jacques Turgot
         b) Jacques Necker
         c) Archbishop Etienne Charles de Loménie de Brienne
      3) opposition to proposed reforms
         a) Parlement de Paris
         b) court intrigues to dismiss reforming ministers
      4) the Assembly of Notables, 1787
         a) aristocratic opposition to tax reform and "royal tyranny"
         b) insistence on calling of Estates General

B. Stages of the French Revolution
  1. prelude: aristocratic challenge to royal authority during the 1780s
  2. stage 1: "the creative period" (1789-1791)
   a. the Estates General, May 1789
      1) composition of Third Estate
         a) few businessmen
         b) virtually no members of lower classes
      2) political ideology of Third Estate
         a) sources
         b) influential pamphlet of Sieyès
      3) controversy over voting
      4) the National Assembly
         a) the Tennis Court Oath
         b) acceptance by king
         c) Declaration of the Rights of Man, August 1789
   b. the situation in Paris
      1) radicals form new city government
      2) the National Guard under Lafayette
      3) the Bastille, July 14, 1789
         a) attack by mob, casualties
         b) symbolism
      4) March on Versailles, October 1789
         a) attack on National Assembly and palace
         b) royal family brought to Paris

c. measures taken by Assembly
    1) aristocratic privileges renounced
    2) assault on Catholic Church
        a) confiscation of church land, 1789
        b) Civil Constitution of the Clergy, 1790: clergy declared civil servants
        c) oath of allegiance required, refused by most clergy
    3) Constitution of 1791
        a) constitutional monarchy
        b) administrative and judicial reorganization of country
d. abortive attempt of royal family to flee country, June 1791
    1) captured at Varennes
    2) prisoners of Assembly
3. stage 2: constitutional monarchy (September 1791 to August 1792)
    a. increasing political radicalism
        1) the Jacobin clubs
        2) pamphleteering and propaganda
        3) popular revolutionary activities
    b. factionalism in Legislative Assembly
        1) the Jacobins
            a) program
            b) Jacobin leaders: Maximilien Robespierre
        2) the Girondins
            a) the Rolands
            b) political ideas
            c) demands for revolutionary crusade outside France
        3) other groups
            a) the enragés
            b) followers of Hébert
    c. growing foreign opposition to Revolution
        1) the émigrés
        2) Prussian and Austrian talk of intervention to save royal family
    d. French declaration of war on Austria and Prussia, spring 1792
        1) French defeats
        2) Jacobin seizure of Hôtel de Ville
            a) the Paris Commune
            b) mob attack on Tuileries
        3) actions of Legislative Assembly
            a) suspends monarchy
            b) dissolves Assembly
            c) calls for new elections, new government

4. stage 3: the Reign of Terror (1792-1794)
   a. the September Massacres
      1) radical takeover in Paris
      2) thousands of prisoners slaughtered
   b. extremist control of National Convention
      1) abolition of monarchy
      2) the Committee of Public Safety
         a) Carnot
         b) Saint-Just
         c) Danton
         d) Robespierre
   c. policies of Committee
      1) goals: defense against foreign invasion and domestic enemies
         a) counterrevolutionary peasant uprising in the Vendée, 1793
         b) widespread dissatisfaction and opposition to Revolution
      2) measures taken by Committee
         a) universal male military service
         b) mobilization of civilians in war effort
         c) regulation of prices and wages
         d) victories of revolutionary armies abroad
      3) the Terror in France
         a) mass executions of alleged opponents
         b) savage repression of Vendée rebellion
         c) execution of Louis XVI, January 1793
         d) execution of Marie-Antoinette, October 1793
         e) confiscation of land and execution of nobles
         f) abolition of Catholic Church, establishment of Cult of Reason
         g) execution of priests
         h) purges and execution of other revolutionaries
      4) Thermidorian reaction, July 1794
5. stage 4: the Directory (1794-1799)
   a. the Constitution of 1795 and the five-man Directory
   b. period of reaction
      1) clergy allowed to return to parishes
      2) concessions made to Vendée peasants
      3) reemergence of some aristocrats, revival of royalist sentiment

   c. economic situation
    1) rise in food prices, misery of poor
    2) profiteering and speculation
    3) greed and immorality of new elite
   d. foreign war
    1) victories of French armies
    2) development of French empire through annexations and satellite republics
    3) spread of French revolutionary ideas
C. Development of Ideologies
  1. socialism
   a. François-Noël Babeuf (1760-1797)
   b. the Conspiracy of Equals
    1) Babeuf's demands
     a) economic equality
     b) suppression of private property
    2) attempt to overthrow Directory, 1796
     a) advocate strong central committee; use of propaganda and violence
     b) betrayal and execution of Babeuf
   c. influence of tactics and ideas on development of socialism
  2. feminism
   a. role of women in French Revolution
   b. concessions of revolutionaries to women's demands for political reasons
   c. feminist tracts
    1) Declaration of the Rights of Woman by Olympe de Gouges
    2) Vindication of the Rights of Woman by Mary Wollstonecraft
  3. French Revolution as model for later ideological revolts
   a. early years become model for later bourgeois liberals
   b. radical sans-culottes activism sets pattern for later revolutionaries
   c. Vendée uprisings become model for counterrevolutions
   d. imposition of radical ideology by force influences subsequent revolutionaries
  4. wars of French Revolution as models for modern total war
D. Napoleon Bonaparte (1769-1821)
  1. character and personality
  2. career
   a. education and military training
   b. military advancement during Revolution
  3. marriage to Josephine de Beauharnais

4. advancement under Directory
   a. pacification of Paris mob in 1795
   b. campaigns against Austrians in Italy, 1796
   c. peace of Campo Formio, 1797
   d. Egyptian campaign
   e. coup d'état, 1799
5. the Consulate (1799-1804) and Empire (1804-1815)
   a. military campaigns against coalitions
      1) Treaty of Amiens, 1802
      2) naval defeat of French at Trafalgar, 1805
      3) French victories at Austerlitz, 1805; Jena, 1806; Friedland, 1807
      4) meeting with Czar Alexander I at Tilsit, 1807
      5) defeat in Spain; invasion of Russia, 1812
      6) the Battle of the Nations, 1813
      7) Waterloo, 1815
   b. Napoleon's military advantages and tactics
   c. goal of world empire
   d. domestic policies
      1) restoration of autocratic monarchy
      2) creation of new nobility
      3) concordat with Catholic Church
      4) centralized national bureaucracy
      5) Napoleonic Code
      6) the Bank of France and currency reform
      7) other economic programs
      8) education
         a) creation of lycée system
         b) University of France: educational centralization
      9) censorship and secret police
   e. great popularity of Napoleon
   f. rule of Napoleonic Empire
      1) relatives on thrones of satellites
      2) divorces Josephine; marries Marie-Louise in order to have heir
      3) abolition of Holy Roman Empire, establishment of Confederation of the Rhine
      4) other territorial rearrangements and confiscations
6. downfall of Napoleon
   a. Britain only great power to resist Napoleon
      1) Napoleon's Continental System, 1806
      2) British reaction
      3) costs to both sides

        b. increasing opposition within Empire
        c. costly Peninsular Wars
        d. disastrous campaign of 1812 in Russia
        e. Wars of National Liberation in German states
        f. exiled to Elba after Battle of the Nations
        g. escape and return in 1815
        h. the Hundred Days
        i. Waterloo and final exile on St. Helena
    7. variety of judgments on Napoleon
        a. opinions of his contemporaries
        b. assessments of later historians

Read to Find Out

1. Why is the French Revolution considered such a key event in Western history?
2. What role did Enlightenment ideas play in the outbreak of the Revolution?
3. What were some of the social problems in eighteenth-century France?
4. In what ways were all social classes affected by social and economic tensions?
5. What factors were involved in the economic decline of the 1770s and 1780s?
6. What role did rumor and hearsay play in the early eruption of revolutionary violence?
7. Why was the French national debt so high in the 1780s and how did it affect the government?
8. How would you characterize Louis XVI?
9. Who were some of the competent ministers of the king, what reforms did they propose, and why were they unable to achieve them?
10. What role did the Parlement of Paris play in neutralizing reform proposals?
11. What was the Assembly of Notables and what action did it take?
12. Into what stages do historians divide the course of the French Revolution?
13. What was the Estates General, and where and when was it called to meet by Louis XVI?
14. Did the delegates of the third estate represent all of the lower and business classes, or were they a type of elite?
15. How did the Estates General become the National Assembly?

16. What was the Tennis Court Oath?
17. What was the Bastille and why was it attacked by the Parisian mob?
18. What was the March on Versailles and how did it end?
19. What happened on the night of August 4?
20. How did the National Assembly attack the Catholic Church and what were some results of the measures taken by the Assembly?
21. How did the Constitution of 1791 limit royal power, and what changes did it make in governmental administration?
22. Why did the French Revolution not end in 1791?
23. What were some of the radical political factions and which one became dominant?
24. Why did revolutionary France declare war on Austria and Prussia?
25. What was the Paris Commune?
26. What was the Committee of Public Safety, who were some of its prominent figures, and what actions did it take when it came to power?
27. Where and why did opposition to the Revolution begin to emerge in the 1790s?
28. How did the Reign of Terror come to eliminate its own leadership?
29. What was the Thermidorian reaction?
30. What was the Directory and how would you describe its policies and the characteristics of its members?
31. Why were the poor worse off under the Directory than before the Revolution?
32. Where were the French armies victorious and what political and other measures were imposed on the new French empire?
33. Who was Babeuf and what was the Conspiracy of Equals?
34. What were Babeuf's main proposals and how did they influence later historical developments?
35. Who were two feminist writers of this period?
36. In what ways did the French Revolution set precedents and provide models for later revolutionaries?
37. Who was Napoleon Bonaparte and how would you describe his origins and early career?
38. How was Napoleon able to rise to prominence in the revolutionary period?
39. What were some of Napoleon's major campaigns and what were their results?

40. How could you describe some of the military tactics of Napoleon and how can his phenomenal success be explained?
41. In what ways did Napoleon's regime resemble the traditional monarchy?
42. What were some legal, economic, and educational innovations of the Napoleonic era?
43. How did Napoleon attempt to conquer British resistance to his imperial ambitions?
44. What elements were involved in the downfall of Napoleon?
45. What were the Hundred Days?
46. What and when was the Battle of Waterloo?
47. What are some of the different assessments given by historians of Napoleon and his place in history?

Multiple-Choice Questions

1. Historians agree that the French Revolution was
   a. directly caused by Enlightenment ideas
   b. a classic example of class warfare
   c. of no great significance for Western history
   d. a historical turning point and prototype for later revolutions

2. The philosophes contributed to the outbreak of the Revolution by
   a. insisting on direct democracy and universal suffrage
   b. undermining confidence in traditional institutions and proposing new political theories
   c. forming the Jacobin clubs
   d. assassinating public figures

3. The eighteenth-century French peasantry was
   a. conservative and traditionalist
   b. the most radical element in the population
   c. generally content with their lot
   d. the backbone of the Jacobin organization

4. In addition to social and political tensions, the 1770s and 1780s were marked by the additional stress of
   a. war with Britain
   b. economic problems and governmental bankruptcy
   c. another epidemic of bubonic plague
   d. drastic climatic change

5. Faced with aristocratic political opposition and increasing social and economic problems, Louis XVI
   a. acted decisively to restore royal authority
   b. fled the country
   c. agreed to call the Estates General
   d. refused to dismiss reforming ministers

6. At the meeting of the Estates General,
   a. the first and second estates maintained their voting advantage
   b. the king dissolved the session after three weeks
   c. little was accomplished
   d. the third estate took control and organized the National Assembly

7. The fall of the Bastille
   a. freed many political prisoners
   b. had a mainly symbolic significance
   c. was accomplished without bloodshed
   d. had little psychological impact

8. The National Assembly did all of the following except
   a. confiscate the lands of the Catholic Church
   b. make priests civil servants
   c. set up a constitutional monarchy
   d. maintain existing provincial administrative organization

9. After the establishment of the constitutional monarchy in 1791,
   a. political factions became increasingly polarized and active
   b. the Revolution was over
   c. political controversy ceased
   d. the country entered a new period of peace and prosperity

10. All of the following are true of the period of National Convention government except
   a. the monarchy was abolished
   b. France was engaged in foreign war
   c. the Committee of Public Safety lost power and was dissolved
   d. domestic enemies were executed

11. The Reign of Terror ended with
    a. the liberation of the king and queen
    b. the death of Robespierre in the month of Thermidor
    c. a coup d'état by the enragés
    d. the defeat of France by Austria

12. Under the Directory,
    a. one-man rule was restored
    b. the new French empire was dismantled
    c. reaction, corruption, and economic problems occurred
    d. Jacobin policies were pursued more zealously

13. The ideas of Babeuf and his fellow conspirators were
    a. influential in the development of modern socialism
    b. based on laissez-faire principles
    c. accepted and implemented by the Directory
    d. models of capitalist theories

14. Olympe de Gouges and Mary Wollstonecraft were
    a. friends of Marie Antoinette
    b. followers of Babeuf
    c. mistresses of Louis XV
    d. eighteenth-century feminists

15. The French Revolution influenced all of the following later developments except
    a. bourgeois liberal constitutional theories
    b. organized violent political activism
    c. mobilization of entire countries for total war
    d. a return to traditional authoritarian regimes

16. Napoleon Bonaparte first rose to prominence due to
    a. his naval training
    b. his military successes
    c. membership in the Girondin club
    d. the influence of Josephine

17. After his coup d'état of 1799, Napoleon
    a. built up an empire during several years of successful military campaigns
    b. made a lasting peace with all his enemies
    c. renounced foreign conquest
    d. engineered a series of stunning naval victories

18. Compared with the government of earlier French rulers, the regime of Napoleon was
a. unorganized and inefficient
b. less repressive
—c. more centralized, and exercised more control over citizens
d. committed to freedom of the press and political activity

19. After Trafalgar, Napoleon attempted to defeat Britain by
a. invasion
b. naval battles
c. assassinating key British leaders
—d. the Continental System

20. Between 1807 and 1813, Napoleon's main problems were
a. domestic revolts led by the Jacobins
—b. nationalist uprisings in the countries conquered by France
c. invasions by the British
d. rebellions in France's American colonies

21. When Napoleon returned from Elba
—a. he was greeted with popular enthusiasm and support
b. the French resisted his attempt to regain the throne
c. he was immediately recaptured
d. he was unable to raise a new army

Answer Key

1. d, 669-671
2. b, 670-671
3. a, 672
4. b, 673
5. c, 674
6. d, 677
7. b, 678
8. d, 679-680
9. a, 680-681
10. c, 682-684
11. b, 684
12. c, 684-685
13. a, 685-686
14. d, 686-687
15. d, 687-688
16. b, 689
17. a, 690-692
18. c, 692-693

19. d, 693
20. b, 693-694
21. a, 694

Map Exercises

1. On Map 22.1, page 675, locate sites mentioned in the chapter. In what direction is Versailles? Where was the Bastille? What revolutionary activity was connected with the Hôtel de Ville and where is it located? Where is the Tuileries Palace and what events took place there?

2. On Map 22.2, page 676, trace the early campaigns of the revolutionary armies. What foreign country did they first occupy? What route did the Austrian and Prussian armies take in invading France? How far did they get within French borders?

3. On Map 22.3, page 688, locate the sites of Napoleon's major victories. Where is Trafalgar and what happened there? Which occupied territories were ruled by members of Napoleon's family? How were the other parts of the empire ruled? What happened to the Papal States in Italy? Where did rebellion against the French first break out and why? Trace the route of Napoleon's invasion of Russia, and locate Borodino. What important battle occurred near Leipzig? Where is the island of Elba, and what was the route of Napoleon's march from the southern coast of France to Paris when he escaped? Where is Waterloo and what happened there?

Essay Questions

1. As discussed in the chapter, recent historiography of the French Revolution has considerably revised earlier interpretations of the event, including the former emphasis on class antagonisms. You might want to read Simon Schama's enjoyable narrative history of the Revolution, Citizens (on the reading list at the end of the chapter), which persuasively contrasts the progressivism and reforming zeal of the old regime with the destructiveness of the Revolution. Other works, such as Donald Sutherland's The Chouans, have focused on the opposition to the Revolution found in all areas of France and among all social classes in the 1790s. Even today the French are divided on the question of whether the Revolution was a good thing or a bad thing for France. Read some of the new work and see what you think. A good film to view in this connection is Danton, which presents the dramatic confrontation between Danton and Robespierre, and the reasons for their conflict.

2. The role of women in the French Revolution has received more attention from historians in recent years. Olwen Hufton's article, "Women in Revolution 1789-1796," in Past and Present, November 1971, is a good introduction to this topic. After you have read it, decide whether Madame Defarge in Dickens's A Tale of Two Cities is a historically plausible character.

3. The influence of ideology on the outbreak of the Revolution and the means by which revolutionary ideas were spread has been treated in several recent works. Fire in the Minds of Men: Origins of the Revolutionary Faith by James Billington (1980) discusses the proliferation of revolutionary and occult organizations in the late eighteenth century and the role of many of them, such as the French Masonic lodges, in disseminating revolutionary programs. Read the relevant chapters of this book and write a summary of the material.

4. Write an essay on Napoleon, concentrating either on his military genius and tactics, a detailed description of one of his battles, or the reasons for his defeat at Waterloo.

5. Develop an assessment of the historic role of Napoleon, either as the continuator of the French Revolution or the man who ended it. Include an explanation of how he differed, if you think he did differ, from earlier enlightened despots. Cite evidence for the points you make.

Chapter 23: Growth of Industrial Society

<u>Outline</u>

A. Britain
    1. advantages for growth of industry
        a. steam power
        b. flexibility of British industrial society
        c. Bank of England and investment
        d. domestic and foreign markets
        e. British entrepreneurs and inventors
    2. British predominance in industrialization throughout
    nineteenth century
B. European States
    1. general British influence
    2. differences from British industrial development
        a. importance of agriculture
        b. role of guilds
        c. less capital investment
        d. conservative peasantry
        e. less dynamic bourgeoisie
        f. lower demand for goods
    3. industrialization as regional phenomenon in Europe
        a. 1815-1850: concentration in resource-rich areas
            1) Belgium
            2) northern France
            3) western Germany
            4) some parts of Austrian Empire
        b. 1850-1914: spread to other European areas
    4. benefits from earlier British experience
        a. latecomers draw on more developed technology
        b. importation of machinery, workers, entrepreneurs
    from Britain
    5. characteristics of European industrialization in
    some areas
        a. mobilization of artisan handicraft production
            1) meets bourgeoisie demand for quality goods
            2) less expensive, but slows spread of
            industrialization
        b. continental dependence on heavy industry requires
    large-scale business and government investment

C. The Americas
1. time period of industrialization
2. American advantages
   a. natural resources
   b. rich agricultural lands
   c. growing skilled labor force
   d. stimulus of British technology, capital, trade
   e. expanding society and transportation
   f. role of steamship
   g. communications
3. industrial growth in North America
   a. concentration in New England, 1820s to 1850s
   b. agricultural raw materials from south and west
   c. later westward spread of industry
   d. growth of newer industries
   e. more rapid growth of industrial output of New World than of Europe
4. Latin America
   a. less rapid development
   b. emphasis on raw materials and agricultural production
   c. some growth of industry and transportation in 1880s, in most areas not until twentieth century
D. Growth and Change in Industrialization
1. power sources
   a. early reliance on water power and coal
   b. development of electrical generator
      1) first uses of electricity
      2) applications by end of century to transportation, lighting, industrial power, communications
   c. internal combustion engine
      1) invented in 1860s
      2) pioneering countries: France and Germany
      3) uses
2. new products
   a. steel
      1) demand
      2) inventors and their work
      3) great importance of steel in industry by end of nineteenth century
   b. industrial chemicals
      1) German research and development
      2) variety of products
         a) medicines
         b) photographic equipment
         c) improvements in existing products
         d) invention of aniline dyes
         e) dynamite

      f) chemical fertilizer
      g) plastic
  3. transportation and communication
    a. railroads
      1) earliest steam locomotives
      2) great expansion of railroad building
      3) effects
    b. steamboats
      1) early experimental steamers
      2) oceangoing vessels
      3) Suez and Panama canals
    c. the telegraph
      1) first U.S. telegraph line
      2) undersea cables
    d. trolleys and automobiles
    e. Alexander Graham Bell and the telephone
    f. Guglielmo Marconi and radio
  4. agricultural technology
    a. mechanical reapers and threshers
    b. chemical fertilizers
    c. food processing innovations
      1) use of beets for sugar
      2) new method of distilling grain
    d. spread of new technology and information to
agrarian population
  5. engineering
    a. key profession in large-scale industrial
development
    b. rise in status of engineering
    c. great variety of engineering enterprises
E.   Economic Organization
  1. free enterprise
    a. historical roots
    b. traditional limits
    c. nineteenth-century campaign for free trade
and freedom of contract
      1) Britain
        a) Richard Cobden and John Bright
        b) Manchester Anti-Corn Law League
        c) repeal of corn laws, 1846
      2) continental Europe
        a) slower pace of free enterprise movement
        b) strong mercantilist tradition; fear of
British competition
        c) German Zollverein
        d) French commercial treaty with Britain;
other tariff agreements

2. problems with free enterprise system
   a. industrial combination: "monopoly capitalism"
   b. costs of ruthless competition and bankruptcies
   c. periodic depressions
   d. proposed solutions
      1) less competition, more cooperation
      2) monopoly control exercised by industries
   e. modern big business
      1) individuals and family dynasties
      2) joint-stock companies
      3) sources of investment capital
   f. basic nineteenth-century types of industrial combination
      1) corporate amalgamation
         a) sometimes use of holding company
         b) horizontal amalgamation
         c) vertical amalgamation
         d) examples
      2) the cartel
         a) no mergers involved
         b) agreement by rival firms to eliminate competition
         c) possible provisions of agreements
         d) national and international cartels
3. attitudes toward corporate giantism and cartel power
   a. hostility to monopoly power in Britain and United States
   b. more positive attitude in European countries
   c. role of state in business regulation
      1) financing of German and Russian railroads
      2) tariff protection and commercial treaties
      3) control of labor unrest
4. consequences of business growth
   a. stimulates economic growth
   b. opportunities for individual entrepreneurs
5. economic integration
   a. traditional patterns of integration
   b. limits in earlier ages
   c. limits imposed by mercantilism
   d. economic rationalization in France during Revolution
   e. spread to other countries
   f. nineteenth-century examples of increasing integration
      1) customs unions
      2) British establishment of gold standard

        g. free trade promotes interdependence
        h. export of industrial technology from developed to less developed societies
        i. flow of capital across frontiers
        j. labor migration
        k. international agreements
           1) railways
           2) international river navigation
           3) communications
           4) health and disease
           5) slave trade
        l. advantages and disadvantages

E.   Class Conflict
    1. dominance of the middle classes
        a. middle-class morality
        b. the business elite
        c. admiration of success and moneymaking
        d. not dominant in high political circles
        e. increasingly seen as natural leaders of society
    2. the working classes
        a. exploitation of men, women, children
        b. factory conditions
           1) long hours
           2) dangerous working conditions
           3) miserable lodging
    3. the aristocracies
        a. general decline in noble and ecclesiastical prestige
        b. clergy
           1) still wield moral and spiritual influence
           2) control of institutions eroded
        c. nobility
           1) continued large-scale land ownership
           2) political and social leadership
           3) reactions to changing conditions
        d. the peasantry
           1) majority of European population
           2) increasing loss of rural culture and traditions
           3) negative image in nineteenth century
           4) changing agrarian conditions
              a) increase in peasant land ownership
              b) abolition of serfdom in Austria, Prussia, Russia
              c) influence of market economy
              d) varying reactions of peasants to new economic situation
              e) causes of social and cultural homogenization of countryside

F.   Population Changes
      1. continued population growth in nineteenth century
         a. great variation among states
            1) rapid growth in Britain and Ireland
            2) little change in French population
            3) population of united Germany helps new nation rival France and Britain
            4) Russia and United States show greatest growth
         b. causes
            1) some increase in birth rates
            2) more significant decrease in death rates, with some exceptions
            3) improved nutrition
               a) more food available
               b) ease of transport of food in cases of scarcity
            4) better sanitation, housing, clothing
            5) medical breakthroughs
               a) anesthesia and antiseptics
               b) vaccination
               c) Pasteur's work on microbial infection
               d) Koch's work on tuberculosis
            6) better hygiene
      2. migration
         a. relocation of large numbers of people within Europe
         b. temporary migration
         c. large-scale migration to the Americas
            1) motives
               a) religious or political freedom for some
               b) economic motivation in most cases
            2) results
               a) loss to Europe
               b) some advantage for overcrowded areas
               c) contribution of migrants to new homelands
      3. urban populations
         a. migration to new industrial cities
         b. city growth facilitated
            1) existence of railroads
            2) mechanized agriculture
         c. living conditions
            1) slum tenements
            2) lack of hygiene
            3) rampant disease
         d. advantages of city life
         e. life of the elite

    f. women
       1) in the countryside
       2) in the cities
          a) lower paid industrial work
          b) sweatshop labor
          c) service work
          d) other professions
       3) dilemma of combining work with care of family and children
       4) idealization and relative seclusion of middle-class and upper-class women
       5) exceptional women
          a) Florence Nightingale
          b) George Sand
  g. youth
       1) increased isolation
          a) decline of family businesses and farms
          b) necessity of leaving home to find work
          c) public education contributes to isolation of age group
          d) conscription
       2) difficulties of transmitting traditional values to youth
          a) lack of restraints from parents, clergy, local authorities
          b) influence of peer pressure
       3) consequences
          a) drastic changes in values and way of life
          b) distress of elders
          c) receptivity of youth to new ideologies

Read to Find Out

1. How did the economy and society of Britain favor the increased expansion of business activity in the nineteenth century?
2. In what ways did economic conditions on the continent differ from those in Britain?
3. Where did industrialization first develop in Europe?
4. How were other countries able to profit from the earlier industrial progress of Britain?
5. How did government and high finance come to play a greater role in European business than in Britain?
6. When did industrialization spread to North America?
7. What advantages did the Americas have for industrial growth?

8. What role did Britain play in the growth of industry in both North and South America?

9. By what means were the various economic regions of the United States integrated?

10. What characterized industrial development in Latin America?

11. What sources of industrial power were utilized in the nineteenth century, and what two new ones came into use?

12. How was steel developed and why was there a great demand for it?

13. What were some new chemical products of this period and what effects did they have on the economy and on daily life?

14. What were some of the effects of the expansion of railroads?

15. How was ocean transport revolutionized by 1914?

16. What new methods of communication were developed, and who were their inventors?

17. In what ways did agriculture change during the nineteenth century?

18. Why did engineering become so important, and how did the status of engineers change?

19. In what ways was business activity controlled prior to the Industrial Revolution?

20. What were the arguments of the free trade crusaders, and what results did they achieve in Britain and on the continent?

21. What was the Zollverein?

22. What is meant by industrial combination?

23. What were some negative features of free competition and what solutions were proposed for the problems it presented?

24. When did the most severe depression of the nineteenth century occur?

25. What types of natural monopolies existed at this period?

26. How would you explain what is meant by corporate amalgamation, and what two forms can it take?

27. What is a holding company?

28. How would you define a cartel?

29. What differing attitudes existed toward the formation of giant corporations and cartels?

30. What different roles did governments play in the economic life of Britain and the European states?

31. What is meant by economic integration and how would you summarize its progress during the nineteenth century?

32. What specific governmental measures were taken that promoted economic integration?

33. How would you characterize the morality and values of the nineteenth-century middle classes?

34. What class predominated in the political life of this period?

35. Why were the middle classes seen as natural leaders of society?
36. How would you describe the condition of the working class in industrial cities of this period?
37. How would you summarize the position of the aristocracies at this time?
38. How did many members of the upper classes adapt to new social and economic conditions?
39. In what ways were the lives of the peasantry affected by economic changes, and how were many peasants able to resist radical changes in their style of life?
40. By what means were country dwellers integrated into new national cultures?
41. What parts of Europe experienced the greatest population growth, and where did the population remain stable?
42. What were the causes of growth, where it occurred?
43. What factors were involved in the decline in the death rate?
44. What medical pioneers are mentioned in this chapter and how did their discoveries save lives?
45. How would you characterize the different types of migration within and between countries that occurred during the nineteenth century?
46. How would you describe life in the industrial cities, its advantages and disadvantages?
47. What was the general employment situation for women in this century?
48. What dilemma did working women face for the first time in the industrial era, and how did society attempt to resolve it?
49. Who was Florence Nightingale?
50. What factors were involved in the increased isolation of youth as a group during this time, and what was the result of this isolation?

Multiple-Choice Questions

1. During most of the nineteenth century,
   a. Britain failed to keep its earlier economic advantages
   b. business growth was retarded in Britain
   c. British industry was hampered by antibusiness prejudice and scarcity of financial support
   d. Britain maintained and expanded its economic predominance

2. All of the following are true of early European
   industrial development except that
   a. guild artisans still played an important role in
   production
   b. there was less demand, middle-class initiative, and
   capital investment than in Britain
   c. it failed to draw on British expertise
   d. it was slowed by an emphasis on quality handicraft
   production

3. German economic growth was characterized by
   a. heavy industry and government involvement
   b. small luxury businesses
   c. local textile industries
   d. emphasis on coal and steel production rather than
   railroads

4. The world leader in industrial production by 1900 was
   a. still Britain
   b. Japan
   c. Germany
   d. Russia

5. Large-scale industrial development in Latin America
   a. began about the same time as in the United States
   b. occurred in Brazil in the 1820s
   c. has not yet occurred
   d. took place in the twentieth century

6. New industrial power sources in the nineteenth century
   were
   a. new types of coal and steam
   b. developed in German laboratories
   c. electrical generators and internal combustion
   engines
   d. researched but not developed at that time

7. By the end of the nineteenth century, the basic
   structural material in demand was
   a. steel
   b. iron
   c. plastic
   d. synthetic fibers

8. All of the following were new chemical products
   developed in the nineteenth century except
   a. aniline dyes
   b. grain alcohol
   c. dynamite
   d. chemical fertilizers

9. The most significant developments in transportation during this period were
   a. gas-powered trolleys
   b. mass-produced automobiles
   c. clipper ships
   d. railroads and steamships

10. International and intercontinental communication was improved in the nineteenth century by
    a. extensive use of the telephone
    b. the telegraph
    c. radio broadcasts
    d. television

11. The profession which achieved new prominence and status during this period was
    a. farming
    b. coal mining
    c. engineering
    d. teaching

12. Free trade advocates argued for
    a. abolition of protective tariffs
    b. limits to competition
    c. more guild regulations
    d. mercantilism

13. The economic costs of free enterprise and the ravages of the business cycle led to
    a. more ruthless competition
    b. growth of monopolies
    c. a trend toward smaller businesses
    d. a return to mercantilism

14. Industrial combination in the nineteenth century was achieved through
    a. small-scale free enterprise
    b. economic integration
    c. government intervention
    d. corporations and cartels

15. All of the following were involved in European economic integration except
    a. customs unions
    b. a common European currency
    c. free trade
    d. international agreements

16.   The elite of the new middle-class society was mainly
      composed of
      a. civil servants
      b. professional people
      c. politicians
   ⌐d. successful and wealthy businessmen

17.   The working classes of this period
      a. shared in the affluence of the middle class
      b. were rarely seen in the cities
   ⌐c. were ruthlessly exploited in urban factories
      d. worked eight-hour days for little pay

18.   The nineteenth-century peasantry
      a. represented a small segment of the population
   ⌐b. had a negative image in the eyes of other classes
      c. was unaffected by the market economy
      d. was reduced to serfdom in most areas

19.   Population growth during this period
      a. occurred mostly in France
      b. was due entirely to a rise in birth rates
      c. stagnated due to disease and famine
   ⌐d. was mainly due to a gradual decline in death rates
      from disease and famine

20.   Migration in the nineteenth century
      a. occurred exclusively within national boundaries
      b. was limited to the move from countryside to city
   ⌐c. took place on a massive scale both within and
      between nations
      d. was a very small-scale phenomenon

21.   Women entering the work force in the nineteenth century
   ⌐a. faced the problem of separation of home from work
      for the first time
      b. found good pay and brisk competition for their
      skills
      c. were encouraged to abandon their homes and children
      for the workplace
      d. were excluded from the garment industry

22.   The isolation of youth was accomplished by all of the
      following except
      a. separation from family and native place
      b. universal schooling and conscription
      c. influence of peer pressure
   ⌐d. the transmission of traditional values to the young

Answer Key

Map Exercises

1.   On Map 23.1, page 705, locate the older centers of industrialization in Britain and on the continent. What new regions have become industrialized? What areas remain relatively untouched by industrialism at this period?

2.   On Map 23.2, page 707, where are the main industrial areas of the United States? Around what major cities are they located? What areas are in the position of supplying raw materials and food products rather than manufactured items? How far west has industrialism spread by 1860?

3.   On Map 23.3, page 709, note the areas of greatest railway building. Where were the earliest railroads? According to this map, has the world's longest railway line been started yet? Where will it be located? What reasons, other than economic, would some governments have for sponsoring the building of railways?

Essay Questions

1. The situation of the industrial working class is sometimes dismissed as "short-term misery, long-term gain"--a necessary stage in the development of modern society. Do you agree with this viewpoint after reading the chapter? Could the plight of the workers been relieved while still allowing for industrial progress, and if so, how? Do you think the urban poor generally regarded city life as an improvement over rural life, and if so, for what reasons? Develop an essay on one or more of these questions.

2. Discuss the contradictions in the positions of capitalists who on the one hand advocated free trade and laissez-faire, and on the other expected government to protect and assist them when they deemed it appropriate. What is the underlying assumption here as to the proper relationship between economic power and political authority?

3. Was nineteenth-century society unreasonable in wanting women to take care of their homes and children rather than leaving them for factory and office work? Employers often paid women less so that men could be paid enough to support families. Today, many employers conveniently assume that the wives of their male workers are also wage earners and no longer pay men enough to support families. Wives and mothers are thus forced to go out to work whether they want to or not. How do you view this issue, and can you think of a solution to this continuing dilemma?

4. Twentieth-century psychiatrists and psychologists have often held that the so-called generation gap and the revolt of young people against their parents are normal and somehow inherent in human nature. After reading the chapter, summarize the factors that tended to produce the subculture of youth only within the last century; are these factors still at work in our society, and do they have a similar effect today?

Chapter 24: An Age of Ideologies

<u>Outline</u>

A.   Characteristics of Ideology
     1. definition
        a. theory about society
        b. attempt to explain group behavior of humans
        c. variety of emphases
     2. new ideologies mainly programs for social action
        a. publications
        b. organization of parties and movements
        c. reform campaigns
        d. revolutions
     3. all values, history, human nature, seen in terms of
     the ideology
     4. the ideologue as "true believer"
        a. emotional commitment
        b. ideological leaders and writings evoke religious
     devotion
B.   Sources of Ideologies
     1. eighteenth-century Enlightenment ideas
        a. confidence in power of human reason
        b. belief in possibility of redesigning human
     society
     2. French Revolution and use of violence to attain
     ideological goal
     3. nineteenth-century problems and conflicts
        a. unprecedented technological, economic, social
     change
        b. class conflict
        c. conflicting ideologies arise from different
     milieus
        d. urbanization, decline of traditional communities
        e. undermining of religion
        f. other social changes
           1) spread of public education
           2) increase in printed material, newspapers
           3) voting rights in latter part of century
C.   Characteristics of Ideologues
     1. social activists among lower classes
     2. scholars, writers, politicians

3. appeal of ideological preachers to masses
    a. traditional views of social justice and **rights**
    b. traditional protest tactics
    c. new ideological convictions, class **consciousness,**
developed through struggle
4. means of influencing masses
    a. speeches and writings
    b. people organize own study groups

D.   Types of Ideology
    1. conservatism
        a. desire to preserve traditional beliefs and
existing social institutions
        b. Edmund Burke (1729-1797)
            1) critique of French Revolution
            2) insistence on wisdom of forbears and value of
time-tested institutions
            3) change should not be sudden, to avoid
disturbing and harming people
        c. aristocratic, clerical, peasant support for
conservatism
        d. changes in conservative ideology after 1850
            1) new response to Industrial Revolution
                a) oppose capitalist materialism
                b) resist militant workers' organizations and
socialism
                c) willingness to compromise to gain support
            2) supporters in late 1800s
                a) peasants
                b) country people arriving in cities, opposed
to liberal and socialist ideas
                c) lower middle-class business and
professional people
    2. nineteenth-century liberalism
        a. inspiration of Adam Smith and John Locke
        b. emphasis on political freedom and free enterprise
        c. belief in progress and human perfectibility
        d. liberation from past will lead to future golden
age
        e. narrower view of natural rights than in
twentieth-century liberalism
            1) oppose political limitations on human behavior
            2) support free trade and freedom from labor
unions
        f. middle-class support for liberalism
            1) government of the people understood as
government by bourgeois property owners
            2) ideas of Ricardo and Malthus used against
upper classes and against helping poor workers

g. changes in liberal ideas
  1) liberal propagandists take radical principles to logical conclusions
  2) liberals fearful of revolution compromise on democratic reforms
  3) liberal politicians compromise to obtain lower-class votes
  4) consequent evolution of democratic liberalism and socially concerned liberalism by end of century

3. nationalism
  a. traditional meaning of patriotism
  b. earlier loyalties to local communities and sovereigns rather than to nation-state
  c. change in nineteenth-century nationalism from earlier cultural commitment to ideology
    1) political in first half of century
    2) aggressively chauvinistic in latter half
    3) idea of one's own nation as superior to all others
  d. Johann Gottfried Herder (1744-1803)
    1) German Enlightenment figure
    2) first prophet of nationalism
      a) reaction to French influence in German states
      b) concerned with recovery of lost national culture and sense of national identity
      c) duty of Germans to develop national spirit
  e. political nationalism
    1) insistence that people sharing common national culture should have own political state
    2) influence of French revolutionary ideology
    3) spread of political nationalism
      a) culturally unified but politically separated German and Italian states
      b) peoples ruled by foreigners such as Slavs and Irish
    4) German student nationalist demonstrations
    5) Giuseppe Mazzini (1805-1872)
      a) influential nationalist
      b) goal of expelling Austrians, uniting Italy
      c) joins nationalist secret society, Carbonari
      d) founds Young Italy and other conspiratorial groups
      e) brief victory, then exile in England
      f) philosophy of history

     f. symbolism and chauvinistic nationalism
       1) creation of national flags, anthems,
   nationalistic expressions
       2) belief in abstract national qualities
         a) German Volksgeist
         b) qualities claimed by other nations
       3) idea of "national mission"
         a) British imperial responsibility
         b) French civilizing mission
         c) American "manifest destiny"
       4) more militant emphasis in late nineteenth-
   century nationalism
         a) adoption of new German anthem
         b) new French nationalist motto
         c) British jingoism
         d) admiration for national military leaders
         e) attraction of military victory for one's
   nation
4. utopian socialism
   a. ideological reaction to evils brought by
Industrial Revolution
   b. socialist solution: all means of production
should be owned by workers
   c. characteristics of utopian socialism
       1) vision of golden, peaceful future
       2) belief in human nature as cooperative and
   caring
       3) only necessary to eliminate competitive
economic institutions for humanity to flourish
   d. ideas of Charles Fourier (1772-1837)
       1) all classes should live and work together in
small communes
       2) factories should be abandoned in favor of
small-scale rural production
   e. other utopians
       1) Henri de Saint-Simon
       2) Robert Owen
         a) successful social welfare community at New
Lanark, near his mills
         b) failure of socialist commune in Indiana
       3) Etienne Cabet and <u>Voyage to Icaria</u>
5. Marxism
   a. collaboration of Karl Marx (1818-1883) and
Friedrich Engels (1820-1895)
   b. Marxist theory
       1) role of class conflict
       2) ultimate triumph of workers
       3) labor source of all value
       4) rejection of utopian socialist solutions
       5) economic determinism
       6) world revolution means of achieving utopia

6. social democracy
    a. late nineteenth-century economic and social changes
        1) labor unions legalized
        2) workers have right to organize and vote
        3) social reforms enacted
    b. many socialists abandon earlier radical strategies in favor of piecemeal change
    c. Social Democratic political parties formed in Europe
        1) German Socialist Workingmen's Party
        2) Fabian Society in Britain
        3) other socialist parties
        4) strategy of working within system without accepting free-market economics
7. utilitarianism
    a. connection with liberalism
    b. Jeremy Bentham (1748-1832)
        1) the happiness principle
        2) happiness of greatest number should be goal of all human institutions
    c. nineteenth-century followers apply principle
    d. challenge to both liberalism and conservatism
        1) exclusive emphasis on usefulness of institutions alienates conservatives
        2) idea of strong government role contrary to liberal views on limitation of government
    e. general goal, not Bentham's calculations or specific points, becomes part of reform mentality
8. anarchism and syndicalism
    a. opposition to all political authority
    b. advocate action by oppressed classes
    c. goal of stateless society dominated by workers
    d. syndicalists
        1) see trade union as vehicle for revolution
        2) general strike means for bringing down social order
        3) new society governed by conscience, coordinated by labor unions
    e. anarchists
        1) more committed to overthrow of all existing order
        2) sources of ideas
            a) Proudhon: "property is theft"
            b) Bakunin: advocate of mass uprising against all institutions

9. racism
    a. extension of nationalism
    b. theory
        1) primary importance of racial rather than national identity
        2) division of human race into categories
            a) skin color
            b) language group
            c) nationality
            d) elaboration of hereditary racial characteristics
        3) theorists
            a) Arthur Gobineau and the superiority of the white race
            b) Houston Stewart Chamberlain: "integral racism" and social Darwinism
    c. implications
        1) superiority of Western imperialists to non-Westerners
        2) fear of "yellow peril"
        3) antisemitism in Europe
        4) hostility to and mistreatment of African Americans in the United States
        5) Germans as the "master race"
10. feminism
    a. emergence around time of French Revolution
    b. gradually detached from other movements for social change
    c. relational feminism
        1) women's rights seen in context of society as a whole and woman's central role in family
        2) emphasizes role of "mother-educator"
        3) leads to espousal of other causes
    d. supporters of feminism
        1) John Stuart Mill
        2) Friedrich Engels

Read to Find Out

1. How would you define ideology? In what ways does it differ from earlier political philosophy?
2. What characterized the ideologues of the nineteenth century?
3. How would you summarize the sources of the new ideologies?

4. What is the relationship between ideology and religion?
5. In what ways did the new ideologues and the masses interact to produce nineteenth-century ideologies?
6. What were the main tenets of nineteenth-century conservatism?
7. How would you summarize the ideas of Edmund Burke?
8. Why did conservatives oppose the French Revolution?
9. How did conservatives think necessary changes should be implemented, and why did they take this position?
10. From what classes and segments of society did the early conservatives draw their support?
11. How did conservatism change after 1850?
12. In what ways did politicians such as Disraeli and Bismarck adapt their conservative politics to changed conditions?
13. What social groups supported late nineteenth-century conservativism and why?
14. What are the main premises of liberalism?
15. What writers were important in the early development of liberalism?
16. How did early liberal ideas differ from those of twentieth-century liberals?
17. Why did early liberals champion free trade and oppose labor unions?
18. From what classes did liberals draw their support and for what reasons?
19. Why did liberalism begin to move toward more radical leftist positions?
20. Why is nationalism a relatively new historical development? Where did the people of earlier ages see themselves as belonging?
21. What is cultural nationalism?
22. How did Herder express the main ideas of cultural nationalism?
23. How does political nationalism differ from cultural nationalism?
24. What were some of the reasons why political nationalism emerged when it did?
25. What was the Burschenschaften?
26. Who was Giuseppe Mazzini and what made him an influential nationalist?
27. What was Mazzini's plan for the Epoch of the Peoples and how did he envisage the role of the Italians?
28. What role was played by symbolism in the development of chauvinistic nationalism, and what are some examples of the symbols employed?
29. How did the emphasis of chauvinistic nationalism differ from earlier forms of nationalism?

30. What is the meaning of the term <u>utopian socialism</u>, and why was it so called?
31. What remedies did the utopians propose for the social ills of their time?
32. Who were some of the major utopian socialists and what were their projects?
33. Who was Karl Marx and who was his main supporter and collaborator?
34. What are the main tenets of Marxism, and in what ways did Marx differ from the utopian socialists?
35. How would you summarize the development of social democracy?
36. What were some examples of social democratic parties in the late nineteenth century?
37. What is meant by utilitarianism?
38. Who was Jeremy Bentham and what slogan sums up his ideas?
39. How did the utilitarians differ from both liberals and conservatives?
40. What are the similarities and differences between anarchism and syndicalism?
41. What was the role of Bakunin in the ideology of anarchism?
42. What were some of the categories into which racists divided the human race?
43. Who were Gobineau and Chamberlain, and what were their theories?
44. What were some consequences of the emergence of racist ideology?
45. What were some of the characteristics of relational feminism?
46. What famous writers championed women's rights and how did they view them?

Multiple-Choice Questions

1. Ideologies are mainly
   a. abstract political theories devoid of practical application
   — b. theories about society and programs for social action
   c. utopian programs that differ little among themselves
   d. a seventeenth-century development

2. All of the following were sources of the new ideologies except
    a. the teachings of orthodox Christianity
    b. Enlightenment ideas
    c. nineteenth-century conflicts
    d. the examples of the French and American revolutions

3. Masses of people responded to the nineteenth-century ideologues because of
    a. a misunderstanding of their programs
    b. the leadership of the upper classes
    c. a combination of traditional principles and activism and new convictions
    d. temporary enthusiasm for novelty

4. Early nineteenth-century conservatism embodied the view that
    a. change must never occur
    b. government should never interfere in the economy
    c. change should be sudden and radical
    d. existing institutions were generally worth preserving and change should be made gradually

5. Conservatism appealed to all of the following except
    a. aristocrats
    b. clergy
    c. followers of Bakunin
    d. peasants

6. After 1850, conservatives began to
    a. oppose the materialism and vulgarity of capitalism
    b. oppose the French Revolution
    c. espouse bourgeois capitalism
    d. reject all compromise with rival ideologies

7. Early nineteenth-century liberals believed in
    a. human irrationality
    b. government correction of economic abuses
    c. political freedom and free enterprise
    d. a golden age in the future

8. Middle-class liberals espoused
    a. radical democracy
    b. political domination of their own class
    c. cooperation with the aristocracy
    d. better wages and conditions for the workers

9.   Political nationalism
     a. aimed at founding cultural associations
     b. emphasized local loyalties
     c. demanded a united Europe
  ⎯ d. insisted that people sharing a common national
     culture should have their own political state

10. Giuseppe Mazzini
  ⎯ a. was one of the most influential nationalists of his
     time
     b. wrote revolutionary operas
     c. became president of united Italy
     d. had no utopian illusions

11. Nationalism in the late nineteenth century became
     a. less influential and more peaceful
  ⎯ b. more aggressive and militaristic
     c. absorbed in plans for one-world government
     d. unpopular in Europe

12. Utopian socialism
     a. was developed by Karl Marx
     b. held that human nature was prone to greed and
     aggression
  ⎯ c. believed in the elimination of competitive economic
     institutions so that people could live in natural
     harmony
     d. advocated the elimination of the exploiting classes
     by violent revolution

13. All of the following are Marxist ideas except
     a. labor is the source of all value
     b. class warfare will bring about socialism
     c. all institutions are economically determined
  ⎯ d. cooperative association is the means to build
     socialism

14. The social democrats of the late nineteenth century
     were
  ⎯ a. willing to work for gradual reform within the
     political system
     b. determined advocates of violent revolution
     c. generally to be found in isolated communes
     d. unwilling to compromise with capitalist society and
     politics

15. Utilitarians believed that
    a. government should not intervene to reform society
  - b. only institutions defined as useful to the happiness of the greatest number should be maintained
    c. it was important to preserve historic institutions and traditions
    d. human happiness was less important than the triumph of socialism

16. Both anarchism and syndicalism
    a. believed in a right to private property
    b. worked within the existing political system
  - c. saw government as a means of exploitation to be overthrown
    d. were two of the most popular ideologies of the nineteenth century

17. Racism in the nineteenth century
    a. produced positive and cooperative political programs
    b. existed only in Germany
    c. stressed the primary importance of one's cultural and religious identity
  - d. focused on the inferiority of races other than one's own

18. Relational feminism focused on
  - a. women's rights in the context of society and women's role in the family
    b. individual political equality
    c. access to easy divorce
    d. the establishment of day-care centers

Answer Key

1. b, 730-731
2. a, 731-732
3. c, 733
4. d, 734-735
5. d, 736
6. a, 736
7. c, 737-738
8. b, 739
9. d, 742-743
10. a, 742-743
11. b, 743-744
12. c, 745-746
13. d, 746-747
14. a, 747-748
15. b, 748
16. c, 749-750
17. d, 750-751

18. a, 752

Map Exercises

1. On Map 24.1, page 732, notice the growth of urban centers in the nineteenth century compared with the picture given by maps in earlier chapters. What areas show the greatest concentration of cities? What regions have the least urban development, and what reasons can you think of for regional differences in urbanization on the continent? How does England compare with Ireland in urbanization?

2. On Map 24.2, page 741, how many distinct nationalities do you see within this part of Europe? How practical does it seem for each nationality to have its own independent political state? How many different ethnic groups are included within the Austrian Empire? Within the borders of Hungary? How many different countries contain German populations?

Essay Questions

1. Which ideologies discussed in the chapter most resemble religions, with a canon of texts, charismatic preachers, and so forth? Which seem least like religions? Write an essay analyzing what seems to you the essential appeal of ideologies.

2. Analyze Edmund Burke's views on the French Revolution. Do you agree or disagree? Cite evidence for your opinion.

3. Argue the case for either conservatism or liberalism, in their nineteenth-century forms. Include a summary of the main principles of the position you are taking.

4. Did the liberal vision of the golden age that would occur when the creative potential of the people was liberated ever come to pass? How would liberals such as John Stuart Mill or John Locke view our society? Has more freedom meant a better society in which to live, and if so, how?

5. In what ways is nationalism still a force in the world today? Write a paragraph discussing nationalism in one modern country. Does it exist to any significant degree in the United States?

6. Does Bentham's utilitarianism sound reasonable to you? Investigate his ideas in more detail. How would he define happiness? What happens, in his system, to the minority who are not happy with utilitarian policies? What are the dangers involved in the government taking a major role in trying to make the majority happy? Argue the case for or against utilitarianism, citing as many examples as possible.

7.   Does anarchism, or the anarchist mentality, exist today? Have you read of any recent examples of persons or groups whose goal is the destruction of any and all authority? Give examples and analyze the appeal of anarchist ideas.

Chapter 25: Revolution and Reaction, 1815-1848

Outline

A. The Vienna Settlement
    1. the Congress of Vienna, 1814-1815
       a. purpose
       b. peace treaties
       c. delegates from all states involved in preceding
    wars
       d. leaders of great powers
          1) Prince Klemens von Metternich, Austria
          2) Viscount Castlereagh, Britain
          3) Emperor Alexander I, Russia
          4) King Frederick William III and Karl August von
          Hardenberg, Prussia
          5) Charles Maurice de Talleyrand, France
    2. the settlement
       a. differing judgments on it in nineteenth and
    twentieth centuries
       b. main object: prevent France from again imposing
    hegemony on Europe
       c. means
          1) France deprived of revolutionary and
          Napoleonic conquests, shrunk to 1790 size
          2) neighbors strengthened
             a) larger, stronger Austria
             b) expanded Prussia
             c) new Kingdom of Holland
             d) more unified Switzerland
             e) larger Kingdom of Piedmont
       d. other ambitions
          1) Russia and Congress Poland
          2) Prussian acquisitions in Saxony and
          Rhineland
          3) Austria
             a) nominal control over German
             Confederation
             b) power over most of Italy
          4) Britain: no European territorial demands
    3. the Restoration
       a. restore legitimate rulers
       b. reimpose stability of old social order
       c. Metternich's motives
          1) conservative principles
          2) awareness of vulnerability of Habsburg
          Empire to undermining by new ideologies
       d. religious revival and popularity of clergy
    with masses

4. international alliances
   a. the Holy Alliance
      1) organized by Czar Alexander I
      2) agreement by Christian monarchs to defend Restoration
   b. the Quadruple Alliance
      1) four great powers guarantee Vienna settlement
      2) later expanded to include France
      3) largely replaces Holy Alliance as vehicle for Congress political goals
         a) for Britain: only periodic consultations on international problems
         b) British reluctance to intervene actively on continent
         c) Metternich and Alexander ready to act to put down revolutionary outbreaks
         d) general agreement on responsibility of great powers to preserve peace and national independence
   c. doctrine of the Concert of Europe
      1) goes beyond old balance of power idea
      2) use of regular consultations and great power responsibility to maintain peace
5. results of Vienna settlement
   a. in general, worked
   b. France treated leniently, reintegrated into family of nations
   c. peace preserved among major nations for fifty years
   d. no major European war for a century
   e. but revolutionary ideology and dislocation of Industrial Revolution not easily suppressed

B.   First Wave of Nineteenth-Century Revolutions
1. concessions made to liberals by restored monarchs
2. immediate liberal criticism of Vienna settlement, revolutionary propaganda
3. disturbances of the first two decades of the nineteenth century
   a. Britain: "Peterloo Massacre," 1819
   b. German states
      1) militant student unions
      2) demands for united, liberal Germany
      3) murder of writer/secret agent
      4) the Carlsbad Decrees, 1819
   c. Iberian Peninsula, 1820; Naples and Piedmont, 1820, 1821
      1) radical opposition to restoration
      2) lack of some reform measures
      3) attacks on liberals

4) discontent of ill-paid soldiers leading revolts

5) some middle-class support for revolts

6) revolts crushed by Austria and France

d. disagreement among Congress powers

1) Britain ceases regular representation at international conferences after 1822

a) opposes intervention

b) George Canning and "splendid isolation"

2) Concert of Europe continues to function

e. Greek revolt against Turks, 1821

1) complications for European powers

a) several hope to profit from Ottoman collapse

b) issue of Greece as heart of Western civilization

c) Christians against Muslims

d) Turkish massacre of Greeks on Chios, death of Lord Byron

2) intervention of Britain, France, Russia on Greek side, 1820s

a) destruction of Turkish fleet, 1828

b) Bavarian prince as new king, 1832

3) victory for nationalism

f. the Decembrist Revolt in Russia, 1825

1) radicalization of army officers from exposure to French ideas during Napoleonic wars

2) secret societies and Jacobin-style plots

3) revolt after death of Alexander I

4) lack of support from masses

5) suppression of revolt

g. Latin America

1) Mexico

a) revolts of Father Miguel Hidalgo, 1810, and Father Morelos

b) seizure of power by Agustín de Iturbide, 1820, in reaction to liberal revolt in Spain

c) overthrown by republicans, 1824

2) South America

a) revolts triggered by Napoleonic takeover of Spain

b) Simón Bolívar and successful revolution in northern South America

c) José de San Martín in Chile and Peru

d) by 1825, most of Latin America has some form of republic

e) Monroe Doctrine, 1823, and British opposition discourage European intervention

C. Second Wave of Revolutions
1. causes
   a. worse socio-economic conditions
   b. political tensions
2. France
   a. policies of Louis XVIII and Charles X
   b. opposition
      1) ultra-royalist obstructionism
      2) bourgeois liberal demands
      3) workers' economic grievances
      4) revolutionary agitation of students
   c. unpopular measures taken by Charles X in July 1830
   d. revolt and expulsion of Charles
   e. Louis Philippe of Orléans
3. Britain
   a. domination of Tory Party
   b. some reforms in 1820s, 1830s
      1) lower tariffs
      2) some political rights for Catholics
      3) reforms in local government
   c. controversial measures
      1) creation of first British police force
      2) workhouses
   d. need for reforms in Parliament
      1) voting and office restrictions
      2) rotten boroughs
      3) no representation for new industrial cities
      4) Whig opposition
         a) Lord Grey
         b) Lord John Russell
         c) introduction of reform bill, 1831
   e. political and social turmoil, 1831-1832
      1) demonstrations in cities
      2) Whig majority passes bill in Commons
      3) King William IV forces House of Lords to accept
      4) mobs seize temporary control of Bristol
      5) passage of Reform Bill of 1832
         a) benefits middle classes most
         b) elimination of many rotten boroughs
         c) representation for some industrial cities
         d) increase in number of voters
4. other revolutions in 1830
   a. Belgium
      1) part of new Kingdom of Holland
      2) different from Dutch in language, culture, religion

3) liberal opposition, worker unrest, student agitation
4) overthrow of Dutch rule, July 1830
5) establishment of constitutional monarchy
b. north German states, 1830-1831
c. Poland, 1830
1) revolutionary sentiments of student clubs, military secret societies
2) lack of support from peasants
3) revolt suppressed, 1831
d. Italy
1) revolts in three Italian states
2) suppressed by Austria
D.   Politics and Ideology, 1830-1848
1. more liberal political structures
a. Britain
1) Whig domination of Parliament
2) Queen Victoria (r. 1837-1901)
b. France
1) Louis Philippe (r. 1830-1848)
2) liberals dominate political life
2. conservative regimes
a. Prussia
1) King Frederick William IV (r. 1840-1861)
2) conservative Christian principles
b. Russia
1) Czar Nicholas I (r. 1825-1855)
2) more rigid, though inefficient, autocracy
c. Austria
1) incompetence of Ferdinand I (r. 1835-1848)
2) Metternich and ministerial rule
3. western European ideologies
a. general liberal agreement on constitutional, representative government
b. oligarchical character of liberals in power
c. alliance of liberal opponents with more radical political elements
d. development of genuinely radical and revolutionary movements
1) Chartism in Britain
2) radical republicans in France
3) working-class movements influenced by socialism
4. eastern and central European ideologies
a. liberal agitation for goals already achieved in western Europe
b. liberal academic leaders stress constitutional forms and rule of law
c. little scope for liberal activity in Russia
d. radicals are prisoners, or exiles such as Marx, Bakunin, Mazzini

                e. working-class movements in some areas
                f. general focus of extremists on nationalism
                    1) German unification
                    2) Italian Risorgimento
                    3) Polish nationalists
                    4) Habsburg Empire
                        a) Hungarians
                        b) Czechs
                        c) other Slavic nationalists
        5. common economic and political grievances
            a. spread of radical ideologies
            b. economic problems
                1) potato blight of 1845
                2) effect of drought on grain harvest, 1846
                3) credit crisis, bankruptcies,
        unemployment, especially in France, 1847
            c. immediate cause of 1848 revolutions
                1) political, not economic
                2) resentment of governmental structures and
        policies
                3) indifference of bourgeoisie to public
        welfare
    E.   Third Wave of Revolutions
        1. France
            a. factors involved in outbreak of revolutions
        of 1848
                1) rising unemployment, agricultural crisis
                2) political demands for government reform
                3) government bans political opposition
        banquets
                4) workers demonstrate, some killed
                5) radicals, workers, secret societies start
        revolt
            b. course of the February revolution
                1) provisional government installed in City
        Hall
                    a) mixed opposition group
                    b) more radical workers force declaration
        of Second Republic, demand ministry of labor
                2) reforms of bourgeois provisional
        government
                    a) regulation of hours and wages
                    b) National Workshops
                3) radicals fail to gain power in new
        elections, invade assembly
                4) liberals close National Workshops
            c. course of the June revolution
                1) radicals mobilize workers
                2) bloody clash of lower classes with
        bourgeoisie and peasant allies
                3) defeat of workers

4) political power struggle after June Days
    a) moderate liberal-conservative alliance
    b) radical liberals attempt to rally support
    c) radicals discredited by opposing government's sending of troops to protect Rome and pope from Italian revolutionaries
5) rise to power of Louis Napoleon Bonaparte
    a) claims to be on side of people
    b) courts support of monarchist factions
    c) profits from influence of Napoleonic cult
6) new constitution, November 1848
    a) Second French Republic
    b) universal manhood suffrage
7) 75 percent of vote for Louis Napoleon in December
    a) coup d'état, 1851
    b) emperor of the French, 1852
    c) 90 percent of electorate ratifies both moves

2. Italy
  a. factors in outbreak of revolts
    1) Pope Pius IX (r. 1846-1878), implements reforms in papal states in 1846, encouraging unrest
    2) Metternich sends troops, increasing resentment
  b. course of revolutions
    1) revolt in Sicily, January 1848
      a) spreads to mainland
      b) king forced to grant parliament and constitution
      c) peasants seize land
    2) central Italy
      a) pope's reforms attract radicals to Rome
      b) papal attempt to reassert authority sets off revolt in November 1848
      c) pope flees; radicals proclaim Roman Republic
      d) three-man junta headed by Mazzini
    3) revolt in Venice
    4) Charles Albert of Piedmont (r. 1831-1859), self-appointed head of anti-Austrian movement
    5) Milan workers force withdrawal of Austrians
  c. reaction against revolutions, 1849
    1) in south, King Ferdinand rescinds constitution, suppresses parliament

2) King Charles Albert declares war on Austria and loses
   3) Austrian reprisals in Milan and Venice
   4) in central Italy, French expel Mazzini and followers, restore Pius IX
3. Germany
  a. factors involved
    1) surviving manorialism
    2) industrial dislocation
    3) potato famine
    4) example of February Days in France
  b. south German states
    1) peasants seize land, burn landlords' houses
    2) urban crowds demonstrate
    3) princes make concessions
  c. western Germany
    1) worker violence in Rhineland
    2) local politicians go to Berlin to ask for reforms
  d. Berlin
    1) Frederick William IV (r. 1840-1861)
      a) promises liberal measures and constitution in March 1848
      b) orders dispersal of crowd, asking withdrawal of garrison from capital
      c) uprising and deaths
      d) king withdraws soldiers, appoints liberal ministry, employs workers
    2) the Frankfurt Assembly, May 1848
      a) goal of liberal constitution
      b) made up of liberal nationalist intellectuals
      c) little popular support
    3) Prussian army back in Berlin in November
    4) king reasserts authority
4. Austrian Empire
  a. disaffected groups
    1) radical students
    2) liberal Czech and Hungarian nationalists
    3) unemployed workers
    4) Hungarian peasants
  b. course of the revolutions
    1) Vienna
      a) student demonstration, March 1848
      b) demands for constitution and dismissal of Metternich
      c) students fired on by troops, supported by workers
      d) Metternich goes into exile
      e) constitution promised

        2) Budapest
            a) liberal nationalist revolt
            b) role of journalist Lajos Kossuth
            c) republic declared with Kossuth as
        president
        3) Prague
            a) liberal nationalist revolt
            b) Bohemia given more democratic
        legislature
        4) other minorities
            a) some want independent states
            b) demands for autonomy within Empire
            c) sentiment for new Slav empire led by
        Russia
            d) Austria plays minorities off against
        each other
            e) Hungary imposes Magyarization
        5) reaction to revolutions
            a) Austrian troops recapture Prague
            b) Slavic revolt against Magyarization
            c) Austrian government asks for Russian
        troops to crush Magyars
            d) Vienna recaptured by Austrian troops
  F.   Outside the Revolutionary Orbit
    1. Russia
        a. quarrels within the intelligentsia
        1) westernizers
            a) position that Russia must modernize
            b) urge adoption of western European
        ideas and technology
        2) Slavophiles
            a) emphasize Russian Orthodox
        Christianity
            b) see traditional religion and way of
        life as expression of Slavic soul
        3) both groups criticize existing Russian
        society
            a) westernizers look to utopian socialist
        future
            b) Slavophiles want return to village
        commune and old style of Orthodoxy
        4) czarist reaction to revolutions of 1848
            a) arrest members of radical discussion
        groups
            b) members of Petrashevsky Circle sent to
        Siberia include Dostoyevsky
    2. Britain
        a. People's Charter of 1830
        1) proposals
            a) universal manhood suffrage
            b) annual elections

                    c) salaries for members of Parliament
                2) the Chartists
                    a) workers and labor leaders
                    b) middle-class radicals
                    c) popular orators
            b. Charter petition submitted with numerous
        signatures in 1839 and 1842
            c. resubmitted 1848
                1) radicals drill with weapons
                2) conspiracies and plots
                3) again rejected, conspiracies exposed
    G.   Patterns of Revolt
        1. early victories for rebels followed by
        repression
        2. reason for early successes
            a. weakness of governmental response to
        revolution
            b. effective action not taken
            c. inadequate police forces
            d. uncertainty of rulers
            e. brief alliances between radicals and
        moderates, lower and middle classes
        3. reasons for ultimate failure
            a. breakdown of rebel alliances, failure of
        unified action
            b. charge that excessive radical demands or mob
        actions disenchanted middle class
            c. charge that bourgeoisie too timid
        4. recovery of royal confidence in many nations
            a. successful military operations against
        rebels in 1849
            b. lack of rebel control of armies
            c. aristocratic officers and peasant soldiers
        unlikely to join urban radicals and ideologues
            d. most members of society not interested in
        revolution

Read to Find Out

    1.   What and when was the Congress of Vienna, and what
          were the major powers represented?
    2.   Who was Klemens von Metternich?
    3.   What is meant by the Vienna settlement?
    4.   How were national boundaries redrawn at the
          Congress?
    5.   What is meant by the Restoration?
    6.   What is meant by the Concert of Europe?
    7.   What was the great achievement of the Vienna
          settlement?
    8.   What were the causes of the revolutions that
          occurred around 1820, and where did they occur?

9. How were these revolutions dealt with by the Vienna powers?
10. Why was the situation in Greece exceptional? What factors were involved in the Greek revolt that did not exist in the other revolutions?
11. What were the causes of the Decembrist revolt and why is it significant?
12. How did the changing political situation in Spain during and after the Napoleonic era affect Latin America?
13. How would you summarize the stages of the Mexican revolt at this period?
14. Who was Simón Bolívar and what did he accomplish?
15. Who was José de San Martín and in what areas did he fight the Spanish?
16. What type of governments replaced Spanish colonial administration in Latin America?
17. What was the Monroe Doctrine?
18. What were the positions of the United States and Britain concerning the revolutionary states in Latin America?
19. What were the two categories of causes involved in the revolutions of 1830?
20. Where and why did revolution first occur in 1830?
21. Who came to power after the Revolution of 1830 in France?
22. How would you summarize the struggle over the Reform Bill of 1832 in Britain?
23. In what countries besides France did revolutions occur in 1830?
24. How did western European conservative regimes differ from those in eastern Europe during the period between 1830 and 1848?
25. What changes occurred in western European liberal ideologies during the 1830 to 1848 period?
26. How did liberalism take different forms in eastern and central Europe during this period?
27. What were some of the economic and political grievances that contributed to the revolutions of 1848?
29. Where did revolution first erupt in that year, and why?
30. How would you sum up the events of the February Days and the June Days?
31. Who came to power after the 1848 revolutions in France and what was his program?
32. Where did revolutions occur in Italy in 1848 and what issues were involved?
33. How did the Italian revolutions end?
34. Where in the German states did revolts occur in 1848?

35. How would you summarize the events of the revolution in Berlin?
36. What was the Frankfurt Assembly?
37. Where in the Austrian Empire did revolts occur, what course did they take, and what were their results?
38. What ideological dispute divided the Russian intelligentsia during this period?
39. What was the response of the czarist government to the threat of revolutionary activity in Russia?
40. How would you summarize the dispute over the People's Charter in Britain, the course it took, and the way it ended?
41. What characterized the response of governments to the revolutions of 1848?
42. Why did the revolutions ultimately fail?

Multiple-Choice Questions

1. The Vienna settlement involved
   a. plenary sessions of all powers at the Congress of Vienna
   b. private negotiations by only the leaders of the great powers
   c. an equal voice for smaller states
   d. nothing but balls and entertainments

2. The figure who dominated the proceedings of the Congress and its aftermath was
   a. Pope Pius IX
   b. Castlereagh
   c. Metternich
   d. Talleyrand

3. The territorial arrangements of the Vienna settlement involved all of the following except
   a. reduction of France to 1790 boundaries
   b. acquisition of Belgium by Holland
   c. Russian control of Congress Poland
   d. territory for Britain on the European continent

4. The Restoration refers to
   a. the general return of legitimate rulers, aristocrats, and clergy to their old positions and prestige
   b. only the restoration of a Bourbon king in France
   c. the return of Napoleon from St. Helena
   d. the replacement of Hanover rulers by Stuarts in England

5.   The principles of the Concert of Europe included
      all of the following except
      a. the responsibility of the great powers for
      peace in Europe
      b. noninterference in the affairs of other states
      c. regular consultations among the great powers
      d. each nation pursuing its own goals but
      contributing to the general harmony

6.   The Vienna settlement did all of the following
      except
      a. allow France to rejoin the ranks of the great
      powers
      b. prevent war among the great powers for half a
      century
      c. prevent a great European war until 1914
      d. permanently suppress revolutionary ideologies

7.   The Restoration establishment in the early
      nineteenth century
      a. was challenged and/or forced to compromise in
      many areas
      b. was as strong as in the eighteenth century
      c. was the same in all parts of Europe
      d. made no compromises with its enemies

8.   When the Greek revolt occurred, the great powers
      a. had no interest in weakening the Ottoman Empire
      b. eventually supported Greece
      c. were indifferent to the plight of the Greeks
      d. freed all of Greece and made it a democracy

9.   The Decembrist Revolt was significant
      a. for its success
      b. as a precedent for and symbol of later
      revolutions
      c. for the massive peasant support it received
      d. because hundreds of Decembrists were executed

10.   The Latin American revolutions
      a. were mostly failures
      b. were repressed by Spain and Portugal
      c. established republics in most of Latin America
      d. established monarchies in half the new states

11.   The 1830 revolution in France and the 1832 Reform
      Bill in Britain resulted in
      a. installing democracy in both countries
      b. considerable progress toward a welfare state
      c. a tightening of monarchical control
      d. more benefits for the liberal bourgeoisie than
      for the lower classes

12. The Revolution of 1848 in France did all of the following except
a. succeed in its more radical goals
b. unleash class warfare
c. bring a Bonaparte to power
d. alienate the support of French Catholics

13. The 1848 revolts in the Italian and German states
a. were supported by almost all Italians and Germans
b. aimed at a united Europe
c. resulted in division among revolutionaries, loss of popular support, and repression of the revolts
d. were successful everywhere except in the papal states

14. Liberal revolts in the Habsburg Empire were
a. all caused by the same problem
b. motivated by a variety of economic, political, and nationalist grievances
c. all inspired by Lajos Kossuth
d. suppressed by Austrian and Russian troops

15. Russia in 1848
a. experienced massive revolts in several regions
b. had no access to information from abroad or to western revolutionary theories
c. had a reactionary intellectual class that supported czarist policies 100 percent
d. had no revolution, but experienced continued intellectual ferment and critical discussion

16. Britain in 1848
a. experienced a crisis over Chartism
b. put down a massive revolt in Ireland
c. became involved in the suppression of revolt on the continent
d. was engaged in a war with the United States

17. All of the following are true of the Chartists except that
a. they demanded universal manhood suffrage
b. they collected numerous signatures for the People's Charter
c. the Charter was passed in 1848
d. their cause, conspiracies, and plots faded away after 1848

18. The early victories of the 1848 revolutionaries may be explained largely by
   a. their control of the military
   b. the indecisiveness and hesitation of governmental response to revolts
   c. the identity of interests among all revolutionaries
   d. the sympathy of governments with revolutionary aims

19. Subsequent failure of revolutionary movements was at least partially due to
   a. the breakdown of alliances forged among groups involved in the revolts
   b. mass execution of revolutionaries
   c. disagreements among revolutionaries over provisions of the new constitutions
   d. general loss of interest among all revolutionary groups

20. The basic reason for the ultimate failure of the revolutions seems to be
   a. military repression
   b. governmental inexperience on the part of the revolutionaries
   c. lower-class counterrevolutionary activity
   d. lack of support from most members of society

Answer Key

1. b, 757-759
2. c, 757-759
3. d, 760
4. a, 761
5. b, 761-762
6. d, 762
7. a, 763-765
8. b, 765-766
9. b, 766-767
10. c, 767-770
11. d, 770-774
12. a, 777-779
13. c, 779-782
14. b, 782-783
15. d, 783
16. a, 783-784
17. c, 783-784
18. b, 784
19. a, 784
20. d, 784

Map Exercises

1. On Map 25.1, page 758, locate the territorial measures taken by the Congress of Vienna mentioned in the chapter. How much more land was acquired by Prussia? What states does Prussia border in this map? Notice the size of Congress Poland. How much more land does Austria control? Note the borders of the German Confederation, the Kingdom of Holland, and the Kingdom of Piedmont.

2. Compare Map 25.2, page 764, with Map 25.1. What territorial changes have occurred? How large is Belgium compared with Holland? How much of Greece was liberated and how much still remains under Ottoman control? What areas did not experience revolutions in the 1820s and 1830s?

3. On Map 25.3, page 768, how many new Latin American republics are shown? What areas are still colonies? What is the status of Brazil? Trace the campaigns of Bolívar and San Martín as described in the chapter. Where was the Battle of Ayacucho?

4. Compare Map 25.4, page 778, with Map 25.2. Have there been any significant territorial changes? What countries did not experience revolutions in 1848? How many did? Locate the regions in which the following revolutionary motives predominated: a) unification of separate states into one nation; b) rights for ethnic minorities; c) desire for political and/or economic change within an established nation-state.

Essay Questions

1. Summarize the main characteristics of the Vienna Settlement, including territorial arrangements, general political goals, successes and failures.

2. Do research on the Decembrist revolt, from any point of view. You might like to read the article on the wives of the Decembrists in the June 1991 issue of <u>Smithsonian</u>. Analyze the manner in which the revolutionaries were treated by the Czar and compare it with the treatment of counterrevolutionists and dissidents by the Russian communists.

3. Write a biographical sketch of any ruler or revolutionary discussed in the chapter. Evaluate the reasonableness of his behavior and discuss reasons for his success or failure.

Chapter 26: Reshaping the Nations, 1848-1914

Outline

A. Political Change
    1. Britain
        a. rival political leaders
           1) Liberal party: William Ewart Gladstone (1809-1898)
           2) Conservative party: Benjamin Disraeli (1804-1881)
        b. role of both in governmental reform and political change
        c. reform measures
           1) Reform Bills of 1867, 1884
           2) Catholic emancipation
           3) municipal reform bills
           4) abolition of House of Lords' veto power, 1911
    2. France
        a. the Second Empire
           1) character and policies of Napoleon III
               a) social reforms
               b) rapid industrial and financial growth
               c) rebuilding of Paris
           2) military adventures
               a) Crimean War, 1854-1856
               b) support of Piedmont against Austria
               c) Franco-Prussian War, 1870
        b. the Third Republic
           1) Paris Commune, 1871
               a) Parisian revolutionary resistance both to Prussia and provisional French republic
               b) murder and destruction by Communards
               c) capture of Paris by French army
           2) characteristics of republican period
               a) continued political disagreement
               b) continued bourgeois liberal domination
               c) political scandals and corruption but general stability
    3. Austria
        a. reign of Emperor Francis Joseph (r. 1848-1916)
           1) Viennese culture
           2) industrial development
           3) growth of socialism
           4) foreign relations

        a) fear of Russian influence in Balkans
        b) loss of Italian hegemony in 1859
        c) loss of German predominance in 1866
    5) main problem: nationalities within the Empire
        a) demands for autonomy or independence
        b) government policies
b. the Dual Monarchy, 1867
    1) Francis Joseph both Austrian emperor and king of Hungary
    2) dissatisfaction of minorities not granted same status as Hungarians
    3) Balkan dilemmas
        a) emergence of new states from Ottoman control
        b) Russian pan-Slavism
4. Russia
  a. Crimean War (1854-1856)
    1) France, Britain, Turkey versus Russia
    2) causes
        a) ambitions of Napoleon III
        b) British fears of Russian expansionism
        c) Russian aggression against Turkey
    3) results
        a) demonstrates Western material superiority
        b) great cost and casualties
        c) Russian forbidden to maintain fleet in Black Sea
  b. Czar Alexander II (r. 1855-1881)
    1) sees need for reform
        a) military
        b) local government
        c) legal reforms
        d) freedom for serfs, 1861
    2) reforms encourage radicalism
        a) university students
        b) secret societies
        c) narodniki
    3) upper-class opposition to reforms
    4) narodniki terrorism and assassination, 1870s
    5) assassination of czar, 1881
  c. Alexander III (r. 1881-1894)
    1) reaction
    2) use of secret police
    3) Siberian labor camps
5. unification of Italy
  a. role of Piedmont
    1) political organization
    2) King Victor Emmanuel II
    3) Count Cavour

   4) French alliance against Austria
  b. Garibaldi
   1) guerrilla warfare career
   2) campaign in Sicily and southern Italy
   3) threatens goals of Piedmont
   4) agrees to recognize Victor Emmanuel as
  king of Italy
  c. expansion of new kingdom
   1) alliance with Prussia against Austria and
  acquisition of Venetia, 1866
   2) occupation of Rome during Franco-Prussian
  war
  d. political organization
   1) constitutional monarchy
   2) parliamentary domination of liberal
  oligarchy
  e. northern Italian industrialization
  f. southern Italy
   1) economically backward
   2) power of garrisons and landlords
   3) growth of Mafia
6. unification of Germany
  a. role of Prussia
   1) conservative, autocratic character
   2) economic prosperity
   3) military strength
  b. Otto von Bismarck (1815-1898)
   1) character and goals
   2) wars of 1860s
    a) Danish War of 1864
    b) Austro-Prussian War of 1866
   3) enlarged Prussia dominates new North
  German Confederation
   4) Franco-Prussian War, 1870-1871
    a) reason for French-Prussian
  disagreement
    b) the Ems Dispatch
    c) declaration of war
    d) Prussian victory
   5) results of war
    a) French to pay large indemnity
    b) French loss of Alsace-Lorraine
    c) other German states except Austria
  agree to join new German Empire under Prussia
    d) declaration of empire at Versailles,
  1871
   6) Bismarck's domestic policies
    a) dominates or ignores Reichstag
    b) Kulturkampf against Catholicism
    c) suppression of socialists
    d) pioneering social welfare measures

            7) foreign policy goals
                a) keep France diplomatically isolated
                b) keep Austria and Russia from going to
                war
    7. the United States
        a. nineteenth-century political conflicts
            1) issue of state's rights
            2) differing regional concepts of role of
            central government
            3) conflicting political ideals personified
            by presidents Jefferson and Jackson
            4) development of parties and evolution of
            two-party system
        b. campaigns for social reforms
            1) issues addressed
                a) institutional reforms
                b) hours of work
                c) temperance
                d) education
                e) women's rights
                f) abolition of slavery
            2) leading reformers
                a) Horace Mann
                b) Lucretia Mott and Elizabeth Stanton
                c) William Lloyd Garrison
                d) Frederick Douglass
        c. the Civil War, 1861-1865
            1) background of controversy over slavery
                a) Harriet Tubman and the underground
            railway
                b) John Brown and the raid on Harper's
            Ferry, 1859
            2) attempt of southern states to secede from
            Union
            3) relative advantages of North and South
            4) course of the war
            5) surrender of Robert E. Lee, 1865
        d. assassination of Abraham Lincoln
        e. the reconstruction period
            1) problems of freed slaves
            2) exploitation of South
            3) southern resentment and lack of
            development
            4) northeastern industrialization and
            prosperity
            5) the westward movement
        f. characteristics of the gilded age
        g. United States: leading agricultural and
    industrial power by end of century

8. Latin America
   a. new elite ruling class
   b. powerful urban middle classes
   c. abolition of slavery but poverty of lower classes
   d. prominent position of landowners and church
   e. economic situation
      1) dependence on export of raw materials and agricultural goods
      2) importation of manufactured goods, mostly from Britain
   f. conflicts
      1) between central and local authorities
      2) between urban liberals and rural conservatives
   g. the caudillos
      1) war leaders of private armies
      2) perpetuate violent revolutionary tradition
      3) often represent and advance interests of rural masses
      4) conflict between liberal political institutions and power of caudillo warlords

B. Social Change
   1. big government
      a. great growth of governmental functions and bureaucracy in late nineteenth century
      b. incompetence and inefficiency in early period
   2. reforms
      a. extension of suffrage
         1) ideology of democracy
         2) practical political motives
         3) continued middle-class political dominance but increased popular influence
      b. government intervention in economy
         1) humanitarian concern and fear of social upheaval
         2) emergence of problems requiring state action
      c. social measures
         1) regulation of working conditions
         2) public elementary education
            a) industrial economy requires more literate workers
            b) indoctrination in moral conduct and patriotism
            c) secularization of education
         3) higher education
            a) private and public secondary and technical schools
            b) more rigorous educational demands

c) reputation of German education and
research
3. the labor movement
a. historical background
b. early labor organizers sympathetic to
socialism
c. situation in late 1800s
1) legalization and great growth of unions
2) less political militancy, more focus on
practical issues within existing system
4. the women's movement
a. legal reforms
b. increased access to education
c. some women doctors and lawyers by 1900
d. association of radicalism with some women's
movements
e. demands for women's suffrage
1) tactics vary according to country
2) most militancy in Britain and United
States
3) limited gains by 1914
C. Unresolved Problems
1. international affairs
a. changing bases of foreign policy
1) introduction of ideological
considerations with French Revolution
2) increased influence of public opinion and
passions
3) sense of responsibility for peace on part
of foreign policy professionals
b. hopes for maintaining peace
1) influence of economic interdependence
2) international peace conferences
c. long periods of peace between 1815 and 1914
except for revolutions and colonial wars
2. military affairs
a. new wealth of industrial society supports
huge standing armies
b. Prussian military successes stimulate
preparedness in other nations
c. Prussian army demonstrates value of modern
technology
1) development of more effective weapons
2) vast increase in speed of deployment and
mobility
3) military planning becomes scientific
discipline
3. economic affairs
a. the depression of 1873-1895
1) controversial question
2) not universal or as severe as Great
Depression

        3) probable causes
            a) collapse of agricultural and raw
    materials prices
            b) severe business cycle declines in one
    country after another
            c) decline in some industries in some
    areas
        4) some classes continue to prosper
        5) severe effects on artisan class and urban
    poor
    b. unresolved issues at end of century
        1) business cycle ups and downs
        2) soft agricultural and raw material prices
        3) growth of unskilled, unemployed
    proletariat
4. the Jews
    a. rise and popularity of modern antisemitism
in late nineteenth century
    b. nineteenth-century Jewish history
        1) in western and central Europe
            a) professional, economic, political
    success
            b) assimilation of some, including
    conversion to Christianity
            c) Zionism of others
        2) in eastern Europe
            a) more restricted
            b) seen as hereditary enemies and
    exploiters
            c) persecution in Russia under Czar
    Alexander III
            d) migration of many to urban ghettos in
    western and central Europe
            e) differ from western Jews in language
    and customs
    c. variety of antisemitic sentiment
        1) conservatives see Jews as radicals and
    enemies of Christianity and traditional
    values
        2) liberals object to Jewish cultural
    identity
        3) socialists see Jews as capitalist
    exploiters
        4) racists add charge of biological
    inferiority
    d. examples of antisemitism
        1) Vienna: Mayor Lueger
        2) France: Dreyfus case
            a) Dreyfus accused of treason, later
    exonerated
            b) degree of antisemitism involved
    debatable

5. anarchists and other terrorists
   a. anarchism
      1) condemnation of all government
      2) practice of assassination
         a) four heads of state, 1894-1901
         b) bomb attacks
   b. other terrorism
      1) Fenians in Ireland
      2) narodniki in Russia
   c. political terrorism generally futile
      1) no positive results
      2) remains threat and dangerous problem for new century

Read to Find Out

1. How would you summarize the British political changes discussed in the chapter?
2. Who were Disraeli and Gladstone and what role did each play in changes and reforms?
3. What were the Reform Bills of 1867 and 1884?
4. What other major reforms had occurred in Britain by 1911?
5. What were the main domestic policies of Napoleon III?
6. What military adventures did he undertake and what were their results?
7. How did the Third French Republic come into being?
8. What was the Paris Commune?
9. How would you characterize the Third Republic from 1871 to 1914?
10. What were the main problems of the Austrian Empire and how did Francis Joseph and his ministers deal with them?
11. What was the Dual Monarchy?
12. What was the result of the Balkan Wars?
13. What was the Crimean War and how did it affect Russia?
14. Who was "the czar emancipator" and why is he so called?
15. What were the main reforms undertaken in Russia between 1855 and 1881?
16. Who were the narodniki?
17. What happened in 1881 to change Russian domestic policy from reform to reaction?
18. What state and what prime minister took the lead in the unification of Italy?
19. How would you sum up the course of Italian unification?
20. Who was Garibaldi and what was his role in Italian unification?

21. What state and what statesman played the leading role in unifying the German states?
22. By what means was Bismarck able to neutralize Austrian influence in Germany and promote Prussian hegemony?
23. What was the cause of the Franco-Prussian War and what were its results for France?
24. How did the war influence German unification and what was the climax of the unification movement?
25. How did Bismarck deal with domestic issues in the Second Empire?
26. How would you summarize the main economic, social, and political issues in United States history from 1800 to 1861?
27. What was the American System?
28. How did President Jefferson and President Jackson embody two different political mentalities?
29. What were some of the major reform movements in the United States during this period?
30. What were the relative advantages and disadvantages of the North and South during the Civil War?
31. What were some of the main postwar problems?
32. What was the general economic position of the United States at the end of the nineteenth century?
33. In what ways did the development of the Latin American states resemble that of the United States, and in what ways did it differ?
34. Who were the caudillos and how did they represent the interests of many Latin Americans?
35. How would you summarize the emergence of big government in the late nineteenth century?
36. What were some of the problems of large, centralized bureaucracies?
37. What social reforms were undertaken by governments in the late nineteenth and early twentieth centuries?
38. How did the labor movement evolve during this period?
39. What were some features of the women's movement at this time?
40. What areas of international tension remained at the turn of the century, and in what two ways did European states respond to them?
41. Why is the depression of 1873-1895 a controversial historical issue? What were the main features of the depression?
42. What were some results of economic dislocation by the end of the nineteenth century?
43. How would you describe the differences in the nineteenth-century history of the Jews in western

and central Europe, compared with those in eastern Europe?

44. Why did many Jews migrate westward at this time?

45. How did their presence in western and central European cities focus negative attention on them?

46. What were some reasons for nineteenth-century antisemitism among liberals and socialists?

47. What were some features of late nineteenth-century racism?

48. What were the tactics of the anarchists during this period? What did they hope to achieve by them?

49. What were examples of terrorism in Ireland and Russia?

Multiple-Choice Questions

1. The British Reform Bills of 1867 and 1884 provided for
   a. government workshops for the poor
   b. elimination of representation for rotten boroughs
   c. expansion of the suffrage
   d. universal public education

2. Other British reform measures provided for all of the following except
   a. women's suffrage
   b. Catholic emancipation
   c. city government reform
   d. abolition of House of Lords veto power

3. The policies of Napoleon III included
   a. glorious and successful military enterprises
   b. social reforms
   c. repudiation of the legislature and the suffrage
   d. lack of encouragement of industrial and financial growth

4. The Paris Commune of 1871
   a. was pro-Prussian
   b. established a parliamentary monarchy
   c. aimed only at local autonomy for Paris
   d. attempted to revive the radicalism of the French Revolution of 1789

5. The period of the Third Republic included all of the following except
   a. a religious revival
   b. a notable lack of political corruption
   c. bourgeois liberal dominance
   d. growth of labor unions

6. The main problem faced by the Austrian Empire was
   a. the radical nationalism of ethnic minorities
   b. fear of Russia
   c. lack of industrialization
   d. attacks by the Turks

7. The result of the Crimean War for Russia was
   a. victory over France, Britain, and Turkey
   b. increased influence over Christians in the Ottoman Empire
   c. loss of the right to keep a fleet in the Black Sea
   d. capture of Moscow by the Turks

8. Czar Alexander II was
   a. a reactionary autocrat
   b. interested in reform in theory but not in practice
   c. indifferent to reform
   d. called "the czar emancipator" because of his far-reaching reforms

9. In the reign of Alexander II the narodniki
   a. enthusiastically supported the czar's reforms
   b. opposed and finally assassinated the czar
   c. emigrated to Switzerland to follow Bakunin
   d. become more moderate in their demands

10. The unification of Italy was due primarily to
    a. the leadership of Piedmont and the strategy of Cavour
    b. the power of nationalism
    c. Garibaldi's redshirts
    d. Mazzini's revolutionary organization

11. German unification was brought about mainly through
    a. Austrian diplomacy
    b. universal German suffrage
    c. Bismarck's strategy and the power of Prussia
    d. general agreement of the great powers

12. The Franco-Prussian War involved all of the following except
    a. the victory of Napoleon III at Sedan
    b. the death of the French emperor
    c. loss of support for Prussia among the German states
    d. defeat of France and proclamation of the German Empire

13. Major features of United States history in the first half of the nineteenth century included
    a. acceptance of the American System by all regions of the country
    b. freeing of the slaves
    c. political, economic, and social conflict
    d. a large-scale revolution in 1848

14. The end of the Civil War saw
    a. a restoration of southern hegemony and prosperity
    b. industrial prosperity and profitable westward expansion
    c. economic decline throughout the country
    d. a great improvement in the condition of former slaves

15. In Latin America, the caudillos were generally all of the following except
    a. leaders of the urban proletariat
    b. revolutionaries
    c. spokesmen for the rural masses
    d. leaders of private armies

16. Governmental reforms at the end of the nineteenth century included all of the following except
    a. elimination of middle-class and upper-class dominance in politics
    b. improvement of working conditions
    c. public education
    d. women's suffrage

17. By the beginning of the twentieth century the labor movement
    a. had been effectively suppressed
    b. became increasingly alienated and oriented toward revolution
    c. was both more powerful and more willing to work within the existing social system
    d. had achieved little growth or popularity

18. Nineteenth-century international relations
    a. were impervious to the influence of ideology
    b. were characterized by both long-lasting peace and military buildup
    c. had so deteriorated that a general European war broke out in 1890
    d. involved a smaller number of great powers than in earlier periods

19. All of the following are true of the depression of 1873-1895 except that
    a. it was more severe than the Great Depression of the 1930s
    b. its nature and extent remain controversial
    c. not all segments of society were equally affected
    d. the lowest classes suffered most

20. A new feature of antisemitism in the nineteenth century was
    a. a view of Jews as enemies of Christianity
    b. economic resentment of Jewish bankers and financiers
    c. pseudoscientific racial analysis
    d. irritation at Jewish culture and customs

Answer Key

      1. c, 789-791
      2. a, 791
      3. b, 791-792
      4. d, 792-793
      5. b, 793
      6. a, 793
      7. c, 794
      8. d, 794
      9. b, 795-796
     10. a, 797-799
     11. c, 800-803
     12. d, 800-803
     13. c, 804-806
     14. b, 806-808
     15. a, 809
     16. d, 810-811
     17. c, 812
     18. b, 814-815
     19. a, 816-817
     20. c, 817

Map Exercises

1. On Map 26.1, page 799, locate the areas mentioned in the chapter section on Italian unification. How large is Piedmont? Where are Nice and Savoy, and why did they enter into Cavour's negotiations with Napoleon III? Where did Garibaldi begin his campaign and how far north did he get? Where is Lombardy and when was it acquired from Austria? Where is Venetia and when was it acquired? What areas remained outside united Italy at this time?

2. On Map 26.2, page 801, find Schleswig-Holstein. How was it involved in Bismarck's strategy, and in what year was it finally annexed by Prussia? What territories did Prussia gain in 1866? What were the boundaries of the North German Confederation? Where are Alsace and Lorraine and what was their fate after the Franco-Prussian War? What German-speaking areas lay outside the new German Empire?

3. On Map 26.3, page 807, note the relative size of North and South in the United States Civil War. How many states joined the South? Locate Fort Sumter. What incident occurred there to touch off the war? Where was the capital of the Confederacy? Where is Gettysburg and what is its significance?

Essay Questions

1. Summarize the progress of reform in Britain and the motives for which politicians often proposed reform measures.

2. One military adventure of Napoleon III not discussed in the chapter was the disastrous French expedition to Mexico in the 1860s to install a Habsburg prince and his wife, Maximilian and Carlotta, as rulers of the country. Write a short essay on this episode, focusing on the personality and tragic later life of Carlotta.

3. Read F. Meinecke's book, The German Catastrophe, mentioned in the chapter reading list, and summarize the points the author makes about "what went wrong" in the formation of the new German state.

4. Compare developments in the United States in the nineteenth century with those in any other major country. What are similarities and differences?

Chapter 27: Romanticism, Materialism, and Nonrationalism

Outline

A. Romanticism
   1. definition and cultural importance
   2. characteristics
     a. rebellion against Enlightenment artistic rules
     b. rejection of mathematical and scientific mentality
     c. opposition to narrow rationalism
     d. emphasis on originality, creativity, will
     e. emotions valued
       1) romantic love
       2) sensitivity to beauty
       3) melancholy
       4) longing for the infinite
   3. worldview
     a. types of people and places valued
     b. exoticism
     c. the supernatural
   4. literature
     a. late eighteenth through first half of nineteenth century
     b. influence of Rousseau
     c. romanticism in German literature
       1) Sturm und Drang movement
       2) Goethe
       3) Schiller
     d. English literature
       1) romantic poetry
         a) Wordsworth
         b) Coleridge
         c) Keats
         d) Shelley
         e) Byron
       2) novels
         a) Charlotte Brontë
         b) Emily Brontë
     e. French literature
       1) Victor Hugo
       2) Lamartine
       3) George Sand
       4) Alexandre Dumas
   5. art
     a. rejection of classical themes and techniques

        b. France
            1) Géricault
            2) Delacroix
        c. Britain
            1) Constable
            2) Turner
    6. music
        a. seen as the perfect art
        b. expansion of range of sound production
            1) development of modern symphony orchestra
            2) popularity of piano
            3) operas
            4) public concert halls
        c. composers
            1) Beethoven
            2) Liszt
            3) Chopin
            4) Schubert
            5) Verdi
            6) Rossini
            7) Wagner
    7. philosophy
        a. romantic characteristics
        b. religious thought: Kierkegaard
        c. Schopenhauer
            1) atheism
            2) all things driven by irrational will
        d. Hegel
            1) philosophical idealist
            2) concern with human consciousness and
history
            3) the dialectic of conflict and change
            4) a metaphysics of becoming, not being
B. Materialism
    1. philosophical materialism
        a. world composed only of matter
        b. no mind or spirit
        c. attack on Christianity
    2. factors in development of materialist mentality
        a. political disillusionment
        b. Industrial Revolution
        c. scientific discoveries
    3. reflects spread of industrialism
    4. effects on new ideologies
        a. nationalism more chauvinistic and aggressive
        b. socialism shifts from utopian to
"scientific," with emphasis on class war
        c. liberalism deals with concrete social
problems
        d. feminism and anarchism become more violent

5. science
   a. avenue for expression of materialism
   b. characteristics of science in second half of nineteenth century
      1) prestige, especially of biological sciences
      2) grim view of struggle and violence in nature replaces eighteenth-century vision of natural balance and harmony
      3) associated with nineteenth-century infatuation for progress
      4) connection of science with continuing success and development of industrial technology
   c. scientific breakthroughs
      1) modern atomic theory
      2) geology
      3) discovery of Neanderthal and Cro-Magnon remains
      4) biology
         a) cellular composition of animal tissue
         b) germ theory of disease
         c) Darwin's theory of evolution: "survival of the fittest"
6. social Darwinism
   a. attempt to explain human society in terms of Darwinian biology
   b. T.H. Huxley and Herbert Spencer
      1) Spencer's view of all human social institutions as products of evolution
      2) built-in natural progress, leading to better, more complex, future
   c. later social Darwinist ideas
      1) trends in big business explained in terms of survival of fittest
      2) war healthy struggle for survival, result shows evolutionary superiority of victorious nation
      3) imperialism justified as fittest humans triumphing over less fit
   d. philosophical significance of Darwinian denial of human uniqueness
7. positivism
   a. scientific method only source of truth
   b. Auguste Comte (1790-1857)
      1) religion and philosophy merely primitive attempts to understand world
      2) only modern "positive" approach can bring real understanding

c. atheist theories
   1) Ludwig Feuerbach's view of deities as human inventions
   2) Ernest Renan's rejection of divinity of Christ
   3) David Strauss's view of Christianity as myth
   4) Ludwig Büchner's <u>Force and Matter</u>: universe spiritually meaningless
d. more affirmative aspects of positivism
   1) Comte's "religion of humanity"
    a) elaborate attempt at encouraging humanity to worship itself as substitute for revealed religion
    b) permeates ideologies that exalt human nature, rights, nationality
   2) positivist theory of knowledge
    a) capable of answering basic questions about mechanics of things
    b) closes mind to other sources of truth
8. materialist influences in the arts
a. realism in literature
   1) beginnings in early nineteenth century
   2) England
    a) Jane Austen (1775-1817)
    b) Charles Dickens (1812-1879)
   3) France: Balzac
b. naturalism
   1) later nineteenth century
   2) Emile Zola
    a) fictional analysis in terms of genetic factors interacting with environment
    b) range of novels
c. Russian realist novelists
   1) Leo Tolstoy
   2) Ivan Turgenev
   3) Fyodor Dostoyevsky
d. realism in drama: Henrik Ibsen
e. realism in art
   1) Gustave Courbet and followers
   2) characteristics
    a) rejection of classicism and romanticism
    b) clinical portrayals of people devoid of noble qualities
f. impressionism
   a) painters
    1) Monet
    2) Manet
    3) Degas

                4) Morisot
                5) Renoir
                6) Cassatt
            b) characteristics
                1) represent scenes and people accurately
                2) capture play of light on objects
                3) utilize new optical theories
    C.   Nonrationalism
    1. new cultural characteristics of last decades of
    nineteenth century
        a. renewed rejection of reason
        b. reaction against materialism
            1) rejection of liberal secularism,
            resurgence of religious commitment
            2) increasing racism
            3) revival of romantic emotionalism in the
            arts
                a) Rostand's <u>Cyrano de Bergerac</u>
                b) Puccini's <u>La Bohème</u>
            4) rejection of positivism by intellectuals,
                new emphasis on primacy of emotional and
                irrational factors
    2. continued survival of materialism
        a. continued prestige of science and technology
            1) discovery of X-rays by Roentgen
            2) discover of radium by the Curies
            3) Henry Ford's automobile
            4) first motion picture camera developed by
            the Lumière brothers
        b. materialist thinkers
            1) Freud
            2) Nietzsche
    3. perverse and violent quality of late
    nineteenth-century society and culture
    4. theories of Sigmund Freud, (1856-1939)
        a. primacy of nonrational urges and energies
    over mind, reason, will
        b. centrality of sex drive
        c. process of repression into unconscious mind,
    producing neurotic or psychotic symptoms
        d. application of theories to institutions,
    religions, civilization
        e. technique of psychoanalysis
    5. Friedrich Nietzsche (1844-1900)
        a. attacks on God and Christianity
        b. hypocrisy of modern society
        c. characteristics of "slave morality"
        d. only hope: supermen with will to power
        e. influence

6. other nonrational theories
    a. Georges Sorel (1847-1922)
        1) preaches value of myth of general strike
        2) value of force and violence
    b. Henri Bergson (1859-1940)
        1) rejection of Enlightenment rationalism
        2) theory of vitalism
        3) importance of intuition, not reason
    c. Helena Petrovna Blavatsky (1831-1891)
        1) founder of Theosophical Society
        2) claims supernatural powers
        3) stimulates interest in spiritualism and psychic phenomena
7. the fin-de-siècle mood
    a. rejection of traditional values
    b. affirmation of decadence
        1) artificiality and eccentricity
        2) sensuousness and mysticism
    c. perversion and cruelty
    d. art
        1) Vincent Van Gogh
        2) Paul Gauguin
        3) Henri de Toulouse-Lautrec
        4) Aubrey Beardsley
        5) Viennese Secession group
    e. literature
        1) characteristics
            a) sex, violence, hallucination
            b) emphasis on the perverse and decadent
        2) poetry
            a) Baudelaire
            b) Rimbaud
        3) drama: Oscar Wilde
        4) symbolism
            a) characteristics
            b) plays of Schnitzler admired by Freud
            c) Maeterlinck's <u>Pelléas and Mélisande</u>

<u>Read to Find Out</u>

1. What are the main characteristics of romanticism?
2. What did the romantics object to in the ideas of their predecessors?
3. What emotions were especially valued by the romantics?
4. What are some examples of works expressing the romantic worldview?
5. Who were some major exponents of romanticism in literature?

6.   How did the lives of the romantics often reflect their romantic ideals?
7.   What were the main features of romanticism in painting, and who were its main exponents?
8.   How did romantic music differ from classical in style and presentation?
9.   Who were some of the major romantic composers?
10. How can such disparate thinkers as Kierkegaard, Schopenhauer, and Hegel all be described as romantics?
11. How would you define philosophical materialism?
12. What features of nineteenth century life contributed to the spread of materialism?
13. In what way did the scientific vision of this period differ from that of the Enlightenment?
14. What were some of the scientific breakthroughs that occurred in various fields at this time?
15. What were the main points of Darwin's theory of evolution?
16. What is meant by social Darwinism, and to what aspects of society was it applied?
17. What is positivism and who was its main exponent?
18. Who were other atheist thinkers of this period?
19. What did Comte mean by the "religion of humanity," and how did it affect nineteenth-century ideologies?
20. In what way was the postivist theory of knowledge limited by its method and its ability to answer only one type of question?
21. What characterized realism in literature and who were some important realistic novelists?
22. How does naturalism differ from realism and who was its main exponent?
23. Who were the great figures of Russian literature in the nineteenth century?
24. What were some distinctive features of realist painters, and what was their attitude toward their subjects?
25. How would you sum up the aims and approaches of impressionist artists?
26. How would you describe the nonrationalism of the late nineteenth century?
27. In what ways was materialism rejected and in what ways was it still strong during this period?
28. How would you summarize the main points of Freud's theories?
29. What were the main objects of Nietzsche's scorn and bitter attacks in his books? What one hope did he see for human society?
30. What were the main ideas of Georges Sorel?

31. Who was Henri Bergson and what was vitalism?
32. Why did Helena Blavatsky found the Theosophical Society, and to what widespread popular interests did her activities appeal?
33. What were some of the features of fin-de-siècle art and literature?
34. Who were major figures of this period in art and literature?
35. What was symbolism and who were two symbolist dramatists?

Multiple-Choice Questions

1. Romanticism involved all of the following except
   a. a rejection of Enlightenment rationalism
   b. emphasis on the emotions
   c. admiration of creative originality
   d. respect and esteem for science

2. The romantic worldview was characterized in part by
   a. an interest in exotic people and places, and in supernatural phenomena
   b. artistic nihilism
   c. naturalism
   d. a systematic, analytical approach

3. Romantic writers
   a. never practiced what they preached
   b. often lived adventurous, passionate, or otherwise romantic personal lives
   c. invented positivism
   d. drew up strict rules for the composition of romantic literature

4. Romantic music
   a. changed in form, but maintained the size of the eighteenth-century orchestra
   b. rejected the use of percussion instruments
   c. was performed for much larger audiences in concert halls and outdoors
   d. appealed only to the elite

5. What the philosophers of the romantic age had in common was
   a. the same religious faith
   b. atheism
   c. concern with emotion, change, longings
   d. an admiration for Aristotle

6. Philosophical materialism included all of the following except
   a. a new interest in theology
   b. an admiration for science and technology
   c. an influence on the new ideologies
   d. the idea that mind and spirit do not exist

7. The theories of Darwin as applied by others included
   a. the reaffirmation of creationism
   b. the application of the idea of survival of the fittest to business, war, and imperialism
   c. a denial of the possibility of human progress
   d. the equality of all peoples

8. Positivists held that
   a. truth can be attained only through the study of the natural world with scientific methods
   b. certitude results from the study of philosophy
   c. some truths can be learned only through divine revelation
   d. human beings, created by God, are composed of matter and spirit

9. Naturalism is
   a. the romantic idealization of nature
   b. the experimental science promoted by the positivists
   c. the original back to nature movement
   d. a literary analysis of fictional characters in terms of genetics and environment

10. Realism in art involved all of the following except
    a. a rejection of classicism and romanticism
    b. painting scenes of ordinary life
    c. excluding charm, nobility, or larger significance from the subjects of their pictures
    d. impersonal objectivity

11. The nonrationalism of the late nineteenth century included
    a. a rejection of positivism
    b. a rejection of romantic emotionalism
    c. a repudiation of the emotional factors in society
    d. complete irrationality

12.   Freud's theories explained psychic disorders as
      a. diabolic possession
      b. the result of nonrational forces operating
      below the level of consciousness
      c. insufficient development of rational faculties
      d. the results of civilization

13.   Nietzsche held all of the following positions
      except that
      a. his middle-class contemporaries were governed
      by a slave morality
      b. there is no God
      c. modern society is profoundly hypocritical
      d. salvation lies in the equality and brotherhood
      of all persons

14.   At the end of the century, reactions against
      positivism and materialism took all of the
      following forms except
      a. praise of force and violence
      b. search for intuitive contact with the infinite
      c. a return to rationalism
      d. an interest in spiritualism and the occult

15.   The fin-de-siècle mentality involved
      a. a return to traditional values
      b. an affirmation of decadence
      c. a rejection of cynicism and worldliness
      d. a more rational approach to art

Answer Key

     1. d, 823-825
     2. a, 825-826
     3. b, 826-829
     4. c, 830-831
     5. c, 831
     6. a, 831-832
     7. b, 833-834
     8. a, 835
     9. d, 836
    10. c, 837-838
    11. a, 838-839
    12. b, 839
    13. d, 839-840
    14. c, 840-841
    15. b, 841-842

Essay Questions

1. Write an essay summarizing the different facets of romanticism. Define the term, and then discuss the various manifestations of the romantic mentality in the arts. Include a description of the romantic worldview.

2. Write a short biography of one of the great composers of the romantic period; can this musician's life, as well as music, be described as romantic?

3. Describe the changes in musical performance during the nineteenth century and the types of music that became popular.

4. Discuss the meaning of materialism and its various manifestations and influences.

5. Several recent works, such as Philip Johnson's <u>Darwin on Trial</u>, have pointed out the lack of substantiation for Darwin's theories. Look into some of these critiques, perhaps starting with the video entitled <u>Evolution: Fact or Belief?</u> which also discusses the geological findings mentioned in the chapter.

6. Discuss the ramifications of social Darwinism. Can you think of possible applications of Darwinian theory not covered in the chapter?

7. Summarize the theories of Sigmund Freud and look into some of the new thinking being done on his ideas and methods. A negative view of the value of his work occurs in Paul Johnson's <u>Modern Times</u> (1983). Other recent criticism has focused on the manner in which Freud developed his theories (through self-analysis, which he forbade others to practice), and on the possible psychic harm done by consciously recalling dreams.

8. Are there any similarities between the fin-de-siècle mood of the late nineteenth century and that of the late twentieth century? Compare the cultural and social attitudes and mentalities of both periods.

Chapter 28: Zenith of Empire

Outline

A. The Nature of the New Imperialism
  1. chronology
    a. relatively slow pace through most of nineteenth century
    b. rapid Western expansion, c.1870-1914
  2. forms taken by new imperialism
    a. colonization
    b. protectorate
    c. sphere of influence
    d. economic imperialism
    e. cultural imperialism
  3. causes
    a. economic consequences of Industrial Revolution
      1) increased demand for natural resources and cheap labor
      2) need for colonial markets
    b. political and military motives
    c. humanitarian motives
      1) religious conversion
      2) opposition to barbarous institutions such as slavery
    d. psychological motives
      1) sense of Western superiority
      2) aggressive instincts
      3) desire for adventure
  4. reasons for success
    a. Western self-confidence
    b. superior organization and efficiency
    c. technology
B. The New Imperialism in Asia
  1. features of the Asian continent
    a. four times the size of Europe
    b. twice the population
    c. great age of Asian civilizations
    d. geographical and cultural diversity
  2. predominance of spheres of influence as method of imperialist control
  3. the Middle East
    a. decline of Ottoman Empire
    b. the Eastern Question
      1) interests of great powers in the area
        a) Russia
        b) Austria

        c) France
        d) Britain
        e) German Empire
        f) Italy
      2) British and Russian rivalry in Iran and
      Afghanistan
      3) European struggles to control, but maintain
    existence of, Ottoman regime
4. British India
   a. geographical features
   b. historical background of British presence
      1) the East India Company
        a) brings some benefits and reforms to India
        b) main interest: high profits, political
    stability
      2) the Indian Mutiny, 1857
      3) India taken over by British government in
    second half of nineteenth century
        a) advantages and disadvantages of British
    rule for India
        b) large Indian army gives Britain land force
    equal to that of France or Germany
5. Southeast Asia
   a. geography
   b. European presence in earlier centuries
   c. French in Indochina
   c. British in Burma and Malay Peninsula
   d. Siam alone remains independent
   e. Pacific islands by imperial powers in second half
of nineteenth century
6. China
   a. geography
   b. historical background
   c. weakness of Manchu rulers
   d. blows to China's isolationism
      1) Opium War, 1839-1842
      2) attack by Britain and France, 1860
      3) Taiping Rebellion
      4) Boxer Rebellion, 1900
   e. results
      1) extraterritoriality for Westerners
      2) "treaty ports" opened to Western merchants
      3) foreign powers acquire Chinese territory
7. Japan
   a. different reaction to Western challenge than that
of China
      1) avoids being colonized
      2) acquires Western skills
      3) embarks on its own imperialist expansion
   b. historical and political background
   c. Commodore Perry and the "opening" of Japan, 1853

        d. the Meiji Restoration, 1868
            1) westernization and modernization of Japan
            2) military power and wars
                a) war with China, 1895
                b) Russo-Japanese War, 1905
            3) territorial gains
C.   The Scramble for Africa
    1. interior of continent little known by Europeans
    until nineteenth century
    2. geographical and cultural variety
    3. pattern of Western penetration
        a. interest aroused by explorers and missionaries
        b. treaties between Europeans and Africans
        c. dispatching of troops to reaffirm terms of
    treaties
        d. imperial governors take over
    4. Great Britain
        a. African territories controlled
            1) Egypt
            2) the Sudan
            3) Kenya and other black colonies
            4) South Africa
                a) "Great Trek" of Dutch settlers, 1835-1843
                b) Boer War, 1899-1902
            5) West Africa
                a) Nigeria
                b) Gold Coast
        b. general policy of indirect rule
    5. France
        a. North Africa
            1) Algeria, 1820s and 1830s
                a) many French settlers
                b) source of grain
            2) Tunisia
            3) Morocco
        b. French West Africa
        c. French Equatorial Africa
        d. Madagascar
        e. character of French rule
            1) more authoritarian than British
            2) goal of assimilation of peoples into larger
        French cultural community
                a) produces African elite more imbued with
        French than with African culture
                b) spreads Western ideologies
    6. other imperialist countries in Africa
        a. Portugal
        b. Belgium
        c. Germany
        d. Italy
    7. Ethiopia remains independent

D.   Internal Imperialism
       1. definition and main areas involved
          a. geographical similarities
          b. domination by populations of European origin
          c. negative views of these populations
          d. indigenous non-Western peoples at earlier stage
of development
       2. conditions for conquest
          a. motives for migration
          b. economic factors
          c. technological means
       3. Russian expansion eastward into the steppes
       4. the United States and the westward movement
       5. Australian migration to interior of Australia
E.   Consequences of the New Imperialism
       1. Western global predominance by 1914
          a. characteristics
          b. short period of duration
       2. effects on West
          a. large scale of European investment and trade with
imperial territories
          b. but larger investment in independent nations
outside empires, within Western world
          c. European emigrants generally settle outside
imperial territories
          d. colonial populations contribute to labor force
and military
          e. colonies add to political status, but overseas
bases actually of little use in wartime
          f. high costs of maintaining colonies, not such huge
profits for mother countries as hoped
       3. non-Western world
          a. imperialism oppression
             1) Belgian Congo
             2) Cherokees in United States
             3) Aborigines in Australia
          b. imposition of Western ways
          c. loss of resources, destruction of native industry
          d. urbanization undermines traditional life
          e. adoption by many non-Westerners of Western
languages, culture, religion
          f. benefits of European opposition to barbarous
practices and slavery
          g. benefits of railroads, science, technology
          h. influence of Western ideologies

1. When did the new imperialism flourish?
2. How would you define new imperialism?
3. What were some motives for the resurgence of Western expansion during the period discussed in this chapter?
4. Why was the new imperialism so successful?
5. What is the difference between a colony, a protectorate, and a sphere of influence?
6. What is meant by economic or cultural imperialism?
7. How would you summarize the causes involved in the new imperialism?
8. What was the main advantage possessed by the Western powers in the development and expansion of their hegemony?
9. How would you describe the geographical and cultural features of Asia before the advent of the new imperialist powers?
10. What is meant by the Eastern Question, and what countries were particularly involved in it?
11. What European countries were chiefly involved in the Middle East?
12. How would you summarize the history of British involvement in India?
13. What two imperialist countries controlled South Asia and Southeast Asia?
14. What was the only Southeast Asian state to remain independent?
15. What happened to the Pacific islands at this period?
16. How was war instrumental in destroying the isolation of China?
17. What was the Boxer Rebellion?
18. What is meant by extraterritoriality and treaty ports?
19. How would you summarize the history of Japan through the nineteenth century?
20. How was Japan opened up to Western influences?
21. What were the results of the Japanese war with China, and the Russo-Japanese War?
22. How would you describe the geographical and ethnic features of Africa before the period of the new imperialism?
23. What was the pattern of Western penetration into Africa?
24. What were the characteristics of Britain's indirect rule in Africa?
25. How did France's colonial administration and goals differ from Great Britain's?
26. What other European countries acquired African colonies, and in what parts of the continent?
27. What was the only independent African nation remaining by the twentieth century?

28. What is meant by internal imperialism, and in what countries was it taking place during the period covered in this chapter?

29. What facilitated the migration of Russian peasants and American settlers in the second half of the nineteenth century?

30. How were the non-Western inhabitants of Russia, the United States, and Australia affected by internal imperialism?

31. What were the main aspects of Western global predominance in 1914?

32. What were the main effects of the new imperialism on the Western imperial powers?

33. What were some negative effects on the peoples of the Western empires?

34. What were some benefits brought to non-Western peoples by the imperialists?

35. What Western ideologies affected colonial peoples, and in what ways?

36. What was probably the greatest consequence of the new imperialism?

Multiple-Choice Questions

1. The process of Western overseas expansion
   a. accelerated until 1800 and then entered a permanent decline
   b. was especially rapid in the last third of the nineteenth century
   c. was most rapid after 1945
   d. did not involve the United States

2. Imperial control of foreign territories tended to be
   a. the same everywhere
   b. under the control of the League of Nations
   c. equally beneficial to all parties concerned
   d. one of three main types

3. Motives for the new imperialism included all of the following except
   a. religious and humanitarian concerns
   b. economic considerations
   c. the need to defend Europe against the aggression of more advanced African and Asian societies
   d. political and military aims

4. The success of the new imperialism was due primarily to
   a. Western political, economic, and technological superiority
   b. the eagerness of non-Westerners for Western culture
   c. mass migration of Westerners to the new colonies
   d. a unified cooperative effort by all the European powers

5. In the Middle East,
   a. only Great Britain had any influence
   b. several of the European great powers competed for control
   c. a six-nation international commission administered protectorates
   d. France was the leading power from Egypt to Afghanistan

6. During the second half of the nineteenth century, India
   a. was generally ignored by the imperial powers
   b. was run by the East India Company
   c. became united and independent
   d. came under direct control of the British government

7. In Southeast Asia,
   a. Siam was taken over by Great Britain
   b. Portugal remained dominant
   c. France was not involved
   d. only Siam remained independent

8. Nineteenth-century China experienced all of the following except
   a. a golden age
   b. the end of her isolation
   c. wars and loss of territory
   d. ineffective rule

9. Extraterritoriality and treaty ports were
   a. legal agreements between France and Britain
   b. rights granted by the East India Company to native Indians
   c. features of the "unequal treaties" China was forced to accept
   d. concessions by the United States to Hawaiians

10. One effect of the new imperialism on Japan was
    a. the permanent collapse of the country
    b. the defeat of Japan by Russia
    c. westernization of the country
    d. a weakening of the military

11. All of the following are true of Western imperialism in Africa except that
   a. Britain practiced indirect imperialism
   b. British colonies were governed directly, as provinces of Britain
   c. Belgium and Germany set up colonies in Africa
   d. Portugal and Italy were involved in Africa

12. By the early twentieth century,
   a. only Ethiopia retained its independence
   b. most African states had gained their independence
   c. only central Africa remained uncontrolled by Western powers
   d. all African nations were under Western control

13. The countries most affected by internal imperialism had all of the following in common except
   a. their large size and the great extent of undeveloped land
   b. domination by European-descended populations
   c. condescending and negative European views of them
   d. lack of non-Western inhabitants

14. In Russia, the United States, and Australia, internal imperialism was mainly stimulated by
   a. the missionary impulse
   b. a desire for gold, land, and industrial development
   c. the intention of exterminating the native population
   d. the request of the aboriginal inhabitants

15. The original inhabitants of Russia, the United States, and Australia
   a. successfully defended themselves against internal imperialism
   b. survived in diminished numbers but were unable to preserve their cultures
   c. were eliminated
   d. maintained large populations and thriving cultures

16. All of the following are true of the economic activities of the imperial powers in the nineteenth century except that
   a. trade and investment took place exclusively within their empires
   b. more trade and investment were carried on outside the empires
   c. the greatest flow of goods and capital was within the Atlantic community of nations
   d. the colonies did provide some degree of profit to the ruling countries

17. Negative effects of imperialism on native peoples in the nineteenth century included
a. the reintroduction of slavery by the Europeans
b. extermination camps for Indians and Aborigines
c. some physical brutality, resource depletion, undermining of traditional life by industrialism
d. the exclusion of native peoples from contact with Western education and thought

18. Benefits of imperial rule during the nineteenth century included all of the following except
a. suppression of cruel customs and institutions such as the slave trade
b. the setting up of independent self-governing states
c. the benefits of Western science and technology
d. the spread of Western languages and consequent access to Western culture, trade, ideas

Answer Key

1. b, 848-849
2. d, 849
3. c, 850-853
4. a, 853-854
5. b, 855-856
6. d, 856-857
7. d, 856-857
8. a, 858-859
9. c, 858-859
10. c, 860
11. b, 862-865
12. a, 865
13. d, 865
14. b, 866-867
15. b, 867-868
16. a, 869-870
17. c, 871-873
18. b, 873

Map Exercises

1. On Map 28.1, page 855, locate the areas controlled by the new imperialist powers mentioned in the text. What was the extent of British control of India and the surrounding area? Where was the Khyber Pass and why was it important? What is the extent of the Ottoman Empire on this map, and how does its size compare with that shown on the maps in Chapters 19 and 25? Where is Indochina and into what states is it divided today? Where are Burma, the Malay peninsula, and Singapore? What imperial power controlled

them? Where is Siam, what is its modern name, and what was its historical significance in the new imperialist period? What does the map show about the Western presence in China? Where are Manchuria and Korea, and what country fought Russia for influence in these areas?

2.   On Map 28.2, page 861, how many European states are represented as claiming parts of Africa? Into what parts is South Africa divided? Which European country has claimed the most territory on this map? Which areas of Africa discussed in the chapter contained gold, diamonds, and important natural resources? What ancient African state remained independent of imperial control at this time, and what European power did it defeat?

3.   On Map 28.3, page 866, trace the progress of the American westward movement. What were the major routes for pioneers traveling west? What incentive did many Americans have for moving west in the 1860s? Where was the transcontinental railroad line? Where did the Cherokee "trail of tears" begin and end?

4.   On Map 28.4, page 870, compare the overseas investments of the main imperial powers mentioned in the chapter. Which nation accounted for the greatest share of investment? Compare the areas in which the investments were made. Which benefited most? Least?

5.   On Map 28.5, page 871, what European countries show the largest numbers of emigrants? To what areas did they move? Where did most of the Irish go? From information given in earlier chapters, what reasons would you give for the movements of so many people from their native lands?

Essay Questions

1.   What were the main differences between the old imperialism and the new imperialism? Develop an essay comparing the goals and methods of sixteenth-century and seventeenth-century colonialism with those of nineteenth-century imperialism.

2.   Summarize the motives of the new imperialists and the reasons for their success. What elements do you think were most crucial in ensuring the victories of the Europeans throughout the world?

3.   What political weaknesses were the Western imperialists able to exploit in the Asian and African countries they took over? How do you account for the ability of one Asian state and one African country to resist imperial conquest and remain independent?

4.   Discuss the factors that motivated Japan to become an aggressive imperialist state. How did elements of traditional Japanese culture play a role in the new political orientation of the country?

5.   Investigate the history of Ethiopia and write a report on its political, social, and cultural structure in the nineteenth century.

6.   When the Americans reached California, both the Indians and the descendants of the Spanish colonizers who had lived there for generations suffered. You might like to read Gertrude Atherton's novel Ramona for a fictional treatment of this episode in American history. The True Story of "Ramona": Its Facts and Fictions, Inspiration and Purpose by Carlyle Davis and William Alderson, published in 1914, is an old-fashioned but interesting analysis that contains additional eyewitness accounts.

7.   The Cherokees, who were sent on the infamous Trail of Tears because Americans wanted their land, were a civilized tribe who published a newspaper in their own language and argued their case before the Supreme Court. Read about this famous case and the arguments presented on each side for an insight into the mentality of Jacksonian America and its internal imperialism.

8.   Is opposition to polygamy by the Western imperialists an example of ethnocentric prejudice or humanitarianism? Develop an argument for one side or the other of this question.

Chapter 29: A Century Begins in War and Revolution

<u>Outline</u>

I.   World War I
     A. The Early Twentieth Century
        1. economic progress and problems
        2. class structures
           a. continued frictions
           b. the new white-collar workers
           c. increase in size and militancy of industrial
              proletariat
        3. politics
           a. central and eastern European autocracy
              1) Germany
              2) Austria-Hungary
              3) Russia
           b. western European regimes
              1) anticlerical laws in France
              2) liberal reforms in Britain
           c. political ideologies
              1) German chauvinistic nationalism
                 a) great material progress of Germany after
                    unification
                 b) military supremacy
                 c) cultural and militaristic nationalism
                 d) racism
                 e) imperialism
                 f) ambition for international leadership
              2) Russian revolutionary socialism
                 a) problems of peasantry
                 b) economic reforms create expanding
                    industrial proletariat
                 c) liberal demands
                 d) revolutionary socialist underground and
                    its factions
                 e) Lenin and his program
                 f) failure of Revolution of 1905
                 g) limited reforms granted by czar
              3) United States progressive movements
                 a) problems caused by rapid technological
                    and business growth
                 b) writings of the muckrakers
                 c) Populism among farmers and miners
                 d) Progressivism and wide-ranging reforms

        e) presidents Theodore Roosevelt and
     Woodrow Wilson
        f) crusading mentality
B. Causes of the First World War
   1. economic competition between Germany and Britain
   2. imperial rivalries
      a. conflicts between Germany and Great Britain
      b. French competition with Germany in Africa
   3. militarism
   4. national rivalries
      a. French desire for revenge for defeat of 1870
      b. Balkan nationalism
      c. Russian pan-Slavism
   5. influence of public opinion in favor of war
   6. international alliances
      a. Central Powers: Austria-Hungary, Germany,
   Italy
         1) background of Bismarck's diplomatic
   alliances against France
         2) Bismarck's attempt to avoid involvement in
   war between Austria and Russia through alliances
   with both powers
         3) Emperor William II's dismissal of Bismarck
   and nonrenewal of Russian alliance
      b. Triple Entente: Great Britain, France, Russia
         1) French-Russian agreement of 1894
         2) British agreements with France and Russia
   settling imperial differences
   7. crises leading to war
      a. the Moroccan crises of 1905 and 1911
      b. the Bosnian crisis of 1908
      c. the Balkan Wars of 1912-1913
      d. assassination of Archduke Francis Ferdinand,
   June 28, 1914
         1) Gavrilo Princip and Union or Death
         2) political ambitions of Serbia
         3) the assassination
         4) Austria's ultimatum to Serbia
            a) Serbia partially rejects, prepares for
         war
            b) "blank check" to Austria from Germany
   8. the declarations of war
      a. Austrian declaration of war on Serbia, July
   28, 1914
      b. Russian mobilization
      c. German declaration of war on Russia
      d. French announcement of support for Russia
      e. German declaration of war on France, August
   3, 1914

  f. German violation of Belgian neutrality leads
to British declaration of war on Germany, August 4
   g. other countries eventually involved
    1) Ottoman Turkey on side of Central Powers
    2) Italy, Japan, United States on side of
  Allies
  9. motives of combatants
   a. territorial and financial motives
   b. claims of idealistic motives
    1) Austria punishing terrorism
    2) God on side of Germany
    3) Allied war to save civilization
    4) Wilson's Fourteen Points
C. Campaigns and Battles
  1. the western front
   a. the first German offensive
    1) the Schlieffen Plan, August 1914
    2) shelling of Paris
   b. first Allied response
    1) Belgium
    2) the Marne, September 1914
  2. Verdun and the Somme, 1916
  3. the eastern front
  4. other areas
   a. Italy joins Allies, 1915
   b. Turkey joins Central Powers, 1915
    1) closes Straits to Allies
    2) Gallipoli, 1915
  5. the war at sea
   a. Jutland, 1916
   b. blockade used by both sides
   c. submarine warfare
  6. new military technology
   a. submarines
   b. tanks and airplanes
   c. poison gas
  7. trench warfare
  8. the home front
   a. total mobilization of national resources
   b. increase of government control over economy
and lives of citizens
   c. women in war industries and other jobs
  9. 1917
   a. troop mutinies and desertions
   b. Bolshevik Revolution and withdrawal
   of Russia from war
   c. entry of United States into the war
  10. failure of final German offensives
  11. armistice, November 11, 1918

II. The Russian Revolution
     A. Revolutionary Organizations
        1. Social Revolutionary party
        2. Social Democratic party
           a. Mensheviks
           b. Bolsheviks
     B. Leaders
        1. Lenin (1870-1924)
        2. Leon Trotsky (1879-1940)
        3. Joseph Stalin (1879-1953)
     C. Politics and Society
        1. different groups and allegiances among working
     classes
        2. differences among peasantry
        3. increased alienation of liberals and middle
     classes from radicals and lower classes
      D. 1917
           1. disruption caused by World War I
           2. Alexandra and Rasputin
           3. February Revolution
              a. abdication of czar
              b. Kerensky regime
              c. continued military failures
           4. October Revolution
              a. domestic crises
              b. Bolshevik agitation
              c. role of Lenin
              d. fall of Kerensky government
           5. problems of Bolshevik regime
              a. maintaining power
              b. civil war
              c. rebellion of national minorities
              d. foreign intervention
              e. policies of Lenin
                 1) nationalization of industry
                 2) formation of Red Army by Trotsky
                 3) use of autocratic political methods
                 4) repression and the secret police
III. Consequences of World War I
     A. Changes in Political Map of Europe
        1. fall of Romanovs, Hohenzollerns, Habsburgs,
           Ottomans
        2. peace treaties create countries, alter
           borders
     B. Negative Results of War
        1. enormous casualties
        2. psychological disruption
        3. physical destruction
        4. influenza epidemic of 1918-1919
        5. continuation of strife and revolution in many
     parts of world

C. The Peace Settlement
   1. delegates to peace conference
      a. Clemenceau of France
      b. Lloyd George of Britain
      c. Woodrow Wilson of the United States
   2. complexity of national interests and claims
           3. harsh treatment of Germany by
  Versailles Treaty
      a. return of Alsace-Lorraine, temporary cession
  of Saar to France
      b. loss of other territory
      c. German disarmament
      d. admission of war guilt
      e. excessive reparation
   4. treatment of Austria
   5. other provisions
      a. transfer of colonies
      b. mandates and protectorates
      c. the League of Nations

Read to Find Out

1. How would you characterize Western society on the eve of World War I?
2. What was the political situation in each of the major Western powers?
3. What new ideologies were emerging and becoming more militant at this time?
4. What were the causes of the First World War?
5. What role did imperial rivalries play in producing international tensions on the eve of the war?
6. How did nationalism play a major role in the outbreak of the war?
7. What countries were allied on either side at the start of the war?
8. What international crises led up to the outbreak of war?
9. What incident began the war?
10. What was Germany's strategy in the early stages of the war?
11. What were some of the major battles and campaigns of 1914-1916?
12. How would you describe the progress of the war on the eastern front?
13. What other regions became battlegrounds in 1915?
14. What is the meaning of the statement that World War I was "a war of position rather than a war of movement"?

15. What advances in military technology made warfare more deadly during this conflict?
16. What social, political, and economic changes took place on the home front due to the war?
17. In what ways was the year 1917 a turning point in the world war and in world history?
18. Why did the United States enter the war?
19. How would you describe the last stages of the war in 1918?
20. When was the armistice signed?
21. Which revolutionary organizations were active in Russia in 1917?
22. Who were the most prominent figures in the Bolshevik party?
23. What conditions favored rebellion in Russia?
24. What were some reasons for the fall of the monarchy in Russia?
25. Who was Rasputin and what role did he play in the coming of the Revolution?
26. What effect did World War I have on the course of the Revolution?
27. How did Lenin get Russia out of World War I?
28. What foreign nations became involved in the Russian Revolution?
29. Who was Leon Trotsky?
30. How could you summarize the revolutionary career and policies of Lenin?
31. What empires had fallen by the end of World War I, and what were some of the consequences of their fall?
32. What was the political situation of Russia after the war?
33. How would you describe the human suffering caused by the war and its aftermath?
34. Where did conflicts and revolutions break out at the end of the war?
35. Who were the major figures at the Paris peace conference and what were the goals of each?
36. How would you characterize the manner in which Germany was treated by the Treaty of Versailles, and what attitudes did the treaty terms reflect?
37. How was Austria-Hungary affected by the peace settlement?
38. What was the League of Nations?
39. How did the United States react to the prospect of international involvement after the war?

Multiple-Choice Questions

1. German nationalism in the early twentieth century involved all of the following except
   a. resentment against the military, economic, and political weakness of Germany
   b. pride in German unity and achievement
   c. militarism
   d. racism

2. Sergei Witte and Pyotor Stolypin were
   a. Russian literary figures
   b. leaders of the Social Democrats at the time of the 1905 revolution in Russia
   c. radical Bolsheviks
   d. effective, progressive ministers of Nicholas II

3. All of the following were contributory causes of World War I except
   a. chauvinism
   b. economic competition
   c. the arms race
   d. Bolshevism

4. Colonial rivalries that helped to increase international tensions included
   a. German-Russian conflicts in Africa
   b. United States ambitions in Turkey
   c. British and French conflicts with Germany
   d. Serbian hostility to Russia

5. A powerful new factor pushing various nations toward war was
   a. populism
   b. public opinion
   c. feminism
   d. spiritualism

6. The secret treaties and diplomatic alliances of the early twentieth century were
   a. powerful factors in preserving the peace
   b. of little real significance
   c. causes of the war
   d. effective in limiting wars to local conflicts

7. The main motive for the assassination of Archduke Francis Ferdinand and his wife was
   a. a desire to start World War I
   b. Serbian nationalism
   c. the unpopularity of Sophie
   d. French anti-Habsburg intrigue

8.	All of the following are true of World War I except
a. it was a war of movement
b. trench warfare was one of its important features
c. it saw the first use of devastating modern weapons
d. it was the first total war

9.	The United States entered the war largely because of
a. the Bolshevik Revolution
b. Caporetto
c. sympathy for the Serbs
d. submarine warfare

10.	The main cause for the fall of the Russian monarchy in 1917 was
a. Lenin
b. Rasputin
c. World War I
d. inflation

11.	The main accomplishment of the Bolsheviks was
a. seizing power in October 1917
b. maintaining their power over Russia
c. making peace with Germany
d. establishing a just social order in Russia

12.	All of the following were consequences of the war except
a. a great number of casualties
b. the strengthening of the Austrian Empire
c. economic dislocation
d. harsh treatment of Germany

13.	The three main figures of the Paris peace conference
a. differed both in personality and goals
b. were all military men
c. were all idealists
d. differed in temperament but shared the same practical political outlook

14.	The German colonies
a. declared independence
b. increased in size and number
c. were taken over by the Allies
d. came under Ottoman control

15.   The League of Nations embodied the hopes for a peaceful
        international order of
        a. V.I. Lenin
        b. Kaiser William II
        c. Georges Clemenceau
        d. Woodrow Wilson

Answer Key

1. a, 883
2. d, 884-885
3. d, 887-888
4. c, 887
5. b, 888
6. c, 888-889
7. b, 890
8. d, 891-895
9. d, 895
10. c, 900
11. b, 901-902
12. b, 904-907
13. a, 905
14. c, 908
15. d, 908

Map Exercises

1.   On Map 29.1, page 886, locate the battle sites and campaigns
mentioned in the text. What is meant by the eastern and western
fronts? What was the Schlieffen Plan followed by the German army
and what was the route taken by the army into France? How did
this route bring Britain into the war? Where are the Marne and
the Somme? What is Verdun and what happened there? What is the
significance of Tannenberg and Caporetto? Where did the newly
arrived American troops fight in 1918?

2.   On Map 29.2, page 897, locate St. Petersburg. Why did the
Russian Revolution begin there? Where is Georgia, and what major
revolutionary leader came from that area? Where is Moscow and
what episode of the October Revolution occurred there? How much
territory did Lenin give the Germans at Brest-Litovsk in return
for peace? In what areas did minority nationalities revolt
against the communists? Where are Archangel and the Crimea, what
foreign troops were sent there, and why?

3.   Compare Map 29.3, page 904, with the map of Europe in 1815
in Chapter 25, and the maps in Chapter 26. What main differences
do you find in the former Hohenzollern, Habsburg, Romanov, and

Ottoman empires? How have the sizes of Austria, Hungary, and Turkey changed dramatically? What new states appear on this map that were not on previous maps? What states have greatly enlarged their territory? What is the status of the Baltic states, Finland, Ukraine? Where is the "Polish corridor"?

Essay Questions

1. What role does Serbia play in the Balkans today, and how have its ambitions changed since 1914?

2. Some recent historical work has focused on the achievements of Stolypin, chief minister of Nicholas II, which included (but were not limited to) the distribution of land to the peasants. Some historians see the terrorist assassination of Stolypin as a major blow to the czarist regime, and imagine that Russian history would have been very different had he survived and continued his reforms.
Look up information on Stolypin and write an essay on his policies.

3. Reread the last paragraph chapter section on Progressivism in the United States, and consider the implications of considering foreign policy as a form of crusade. What are the implications of this mentality? What consequences could it have? Discuss this point in an essay.

4. The famous Humphrey Bogart-Katherine Hepburn film The African Queen is set in colonial Africa during the German-British conflicts discussed in this chapter. See the film with this background in mind and decide how well it seems to recreate the historical period.

5. The attempt by the British to capture or destroy the great German warship the Königsberg, trapped in an African delta, resulted in the longest standoff in naval history. Investigate the story of this legendary naval duel or one of the other famous incidents of World War I in the colonies.

6. Much historical debate has recently centered on the fate of the Russian royal family, especially with the revival of royalist feeling among some Russians. Persistent rumors of the survival of one or more family members seem to be supported by the discovery and analysis of the remains of some, but not all, of the children. You might want to look into this historical detective work.

7. Write an essay comparing the characters of Louis XVI and Nicholas II, and their reactions when faced with revolution.

8. Compare the Peace of Paris with the Vienna settlement of 1815. What are similarities and differences in the approach of the great powers to the redrawing of the map of Europe? How did the treatment of Germany in 1919 compare with the terms imposed on France in 1815?

Chapter 30: Dictators and Depression

Outline

   A.   The Western Economy
      1. the problem of overproduction
      2. economic dislocations
         a. continued decline of old industries, including
      agriculture
         b. continued growth of newer industries
      3. central position of United States in world economy
      4. role of U.S. loans in European economy
         a. help Germany pay reparations to Allies
         b. U.S. insistence on Allies paying debts to United
      States
      5. the Great Depression
         a. theory of cyclical depressions
         b. role of stock market collapse of 1929
         c. saturated U.S. demand leads to domestic economic
      collapse
         d. spread of Depression throughout world
            1) effects
            2) contributing factors to severity of Depression
      6. reactions to Depression
         a. economic nationalism
            1) protective tariffs
            2) welfare payments
            3) abandonment of gold standards
         b. two basic strategies for coping with effects of
           depression
            1) western European capitalist countries
               a) cut labor bill
               b) minimum unemployment payments to keep
      national debt low
            2) authoritarian regimes, and United States under
      Roosevelt
               a) subsidize public works programs to employ
      workers, stimulate demand, encourage business
               b) partially successful in Germany and USSR
   B.   Between the Wars
      1. the Jazz Age in the United States
         a. "the business of America is business"
            1) general economic boom
            2) technological advances
         b. unimpressive political situation
         c. militant prejudice and racism

                1) Ku Klux Klan
                2) Immigration Act to keep out Catholics, Jews
            d. hedonistic culture
            e. President Franklin Roosevelt, 1933-1945
                1) early political career
                2) marriage to Eleanor Roosevelt
            f. the New Deal
                1) the "New Deal coalition"
                2) measures enacted
    2. Britain
        a. economic problems
            1) losses due to war
            2) general strike of 1926
            3) effects of Great Depression
        b. political situation
            1) dominance of Conservative party
            2) emergence of Labor party as major rival
            3) continued conservative economic policies, but
        some economic and political changes
        c. the Empire
            1) restructured as British Commonwealth
            2) Ireland
                a) the Easter Rebellion, 1916
                b) uprising in 1920
                c) the Irish Free State
    3. France
        a. greater suffering from war than Britain
        b. more rapid economic recovery
            1) reparation payments from Germany
            2) use of Saar coalfields
            3) massive immigration aids recovery
            4) increased foreign trade
            5) increase in big business
            6) large number of small businesses aid recovery
        from Depression
        c. politics
            1) dominance of the Right
            2) fear of Germany
                a) occupation of Ruhr (1923) to obtain
        reparations
                b) the Maginot line
            3) fragmentation of the Left over Bolshevism
    4. other Western states
        a. more developed states preserve economic and
    political stability
            1) Scandinavian countries
            2) Netherlands and Belgium
            3) Switzerland
            4) British Commonwealth countries

         b. newly formed and less developed states
economically and politically less stable
                1) southern Europe
                2) new eastern European states
                3) new Austrian and German regimes
                4) relative stability of Czechoslovakia
C.   The New Dictators
1. distinctions between dictatorship and
totalitarianism
2. nature of totalitarianism
         a. various theories explaining it
         b. factors involved
                1) charismatic leaders
                2) rise of mass politics
                3) role of modern communications technology
                4) ideologies
3. Italy
         a. career of Benito Mussolini
         b. chaotic Italian political situation
         c. Mussolini asked to form government
         d. establishment of Fascist state
                1) one-party system
                2) control of economy
                3) social and cultural dominance of party
4. Germany
         a. structure of postwar regime
         b. problems of Weimar Republic
                1) demoralization of defeat in World War I
                2) political extremism
                3) economic crises
         c. rise of Adolf Hitler (1889-1945)
                1) early career
                      a) cultural and ideological influences
                      b) oratorical talent
                      c) doctrines preached
                      d) organization of National Socialist Workers
          (Nazi Party)
                2) political crisis of early 1930s
                      a) President von Hindenburg persuaded to rule
                       by decree
                      b) Hitler becomes chancellor, 1933
                      c) basis of support
                3) policies of the Nazi regime
                      a) elimination of political rivals
                      b) goal of founding a Third Reich
                      c) rapid economic recovery
                      d) rearmament

            4) Nazi government figures
                a) Hermann Goering
                b) Josef Goebbels
                c) Heinrich Himmler
            5) totalitarian control of political,
        social, cultural, religious life
            6) elimination of undesirables, especially
                Jews
                a) Nuremberg Laws of 1935
                b) Kristallnacht, 1938
                c) ghettos and camps, 1940s
                d) killing of the mentally handicapped
    5. the Soviet Union
        a. New Economic Policy of the 1920s
            1) Lenin's compromise with capitalism to allow
        postwar recovery
            2) agriculture not fully collectivized
        b. power struggle after death of Lenin, 1924
            1) Leon Trotsky and the "world revolution"
            2) Joseph Stalin and "revolution in one country"
            3) Stalin's organizational ability and control of
        Communist party machine
        c. dictatorship of Stalin
            1) motives for change in government policies
            2) achievement of state socialism and
                totalitarianism
                a) the Five-Year Plans
                b) government-controlled industrialization
                c) collectivization of agricultural and
        elimination of kulaks in labor camps
                d) deliberate starvation of farmers
            3) purges and elimination of perceived enemies
                a) elimination of rival party members
                b) the secret police and show trials
                c) the Gulag Archipelago
            4) expansion of bureaucracy and complete
        control of Russian society by party
            5) persecution of religion
    6. other European dictatorships or authoritarian states
        a. authoritarian regimes in southern, central, and
        eastern Europe
            1) not totalitarian states
            2) contributing factors in emergence of
        dictatorships
                a) economic underdevelopment
                b) appeal of authoritarian regimes to more
        traditional societies

          c) economic and political problems of new
states
   b. Austria
     1) problems of Austrian Republic
     2) enthusiasm for Anschluss
     3) Austrian Nazi party
     4) Chancellor Engelbert Dolfuss (1892-1934)
       a) suppresses Nazis and quells worker unrest
       b) murdered by Nazis
     5) Chancellor Kurt von Schuschnigg (1897-1977)
and renewed defeat of Nazis
   c. Poland
     1) serious problems of new postwar state
     2) autocratic rule of Marshal Josef Pilsudski
beginning in 1926
   d. Yugoslavia
     1) ethnic tensions
     2) King Alexander suspends democratic
institutions
     3) assassination of king, 1934
   e. Bulgaria and rule of King Boris III (r. 1918-
1943)
   f. Romania
     1) pro-Nazi sentiment
     2) royal rule until 1940
   g. Portugal
     1) instability and violence of republican regime
     2) restoration of order under Antonio Salazar
       a) economic reforms
       b) one-party dictatorship
   h. Spain
     1) nominal constitutional monarchy, actually
ruled by dictator Primo de Rivera from 1923 to
1930
     2) revolutionary and nationalist agitation and
other conflicts
     3) dictatorship of General Francisco Franco
following civil war
7. Latin America
   a. effects of Great Depression
   b. revolutions in most countries resulting in
dictatorships
   c. Argentina
     1) military coup, 1930
     2) economic reform and prosperity
   d. Brazil
     1) Getulio Vargas
     2) centralization and economic progress

        e. the Somoza family in Central America
    8. Japan
        a. character of political regime
        b. historical background
        c. political instability
            1) alliance of rival groups through 1920s
            2) increasing influence of nationalistic
    militarists in 1930s
                a) appeal to peasant grievances and
    traditional loyalties
                b) support of big business
                c) political assassinations in 1932 and 1936
D.   Society in the Interwar Period
    1. new features of middle-class life in the consumer
society
        a. defined more by consumption than production
        b. influence of the automobile
        c. new electric appliances
        d. mass media and the entertainment industry
    2. the working classes
        a. attempts to increase productivity
            1) new machinery puts laborers out of work
            2) programs to make people work harder
                a) scientific management studies in United
    States and western Europe
                b) Stakhanovite programs in Soviet Union
        b. problems of farm workers
            1) general agricultural depression in 1920s and
    1930s
            2) United States farmers
                a) exploitation by railroads, banks, marketing
    firms
                b) loss of jobs to new farm machinery
            3) European peasants
                a) lack of capital and knowledge of new
    technology
                b) low productivity, bitterness at changes
            4) Soviet Union
                a) collectivization produces famine, greatly
    reduces productivity
                b) former grain-exporting nation depends on
    foreign imports for rest of century
        c. mass culture
            1) increasingly undermines traditional town and
                neighborhood life
            2) radio and films reshape values
            3) consumer products foster homogenization of
    society

3. women in the interwar society
   a. fewer children and labor-saving appliances encourage jobs outside the home
   b. types of jobs taken by women
   c. decline in jobs during interwar period
      1) loss of war industries jobs with return of troops
      2) unemployment caused by Depression
   d. changes in lifestyle
      1) dress and hair styles
      2) sports and social activities
   e. features of women's lives in totalitarian states
      1) Fascist Italy
      2) Nazi Germany
      3) Soviet Union
4. effects of mass education
   a. progressive education for citizenship in United States
   b. nursery schools and kindergartens
   c. great growth in university population
   d. isolation of young people from other age groups
      1) youth culture based on mass media
      2) adulation of entertainers and other celebrities
      3) greater affluence of young consumers
5. conflict of generations
   a. revolt of younger generation first analyzed in 1920s and 1930s
   b. the "lost generation"
   c. bitterness at World War I leads to rejection of Western civilization
   d. social behavior of rebellious youth
   e. renewed political activism in 1930s

Read to Find Out

1. What were some features of the 1920s and 1930s in the West?
2. How did overproduction become a major problem during this period?
3. What effects did the end of World War I have on the economy?
4. Why was the economic strength of the United States so important to the postwar Western economy?
5. How would you describe the cycle formed by U.S. loans to Germany, German reparations payments, and Allied repayments of loans to the United States?
6. How have economic historians attempted to explain the Great Depression?

7. What event began the Depression?
8. What were some of the causes of the Crash of '29?
9. How would you state the essential cause of the Great Depression?
10. How would you summarize the effects of the Depression on the world economy and on people's lives?
11. What is meant by economic nationalism?
12. What two basic strategies were used by governments to deal with the economic collapse?
13. What finally ended the Great Depression in the capitalist democracies?
14. What is meant by the term the Jazz Age?
15. How would you describe the mood of American society in the 1920s?
16. How did President Franklin Delano Roosevelt attempt to deal with the Depression?
17. What role did Eleanor Roosevelt play in American politics?
18. What was the New Deal?
19. How would you summarize domestic conditions in Great Britain during the Great Depression?
20. What developments occurred in British politics?
21. What changes took place in the British Empire?
22. How did the Depression affect France, and how did the French economy differ from that of the United States?
23. What characterized French politics during this period?
24. What was the main preoccupation of French foreign policy?
25. What was the Maginot Line?
26. How would you sum up political and economic conditions in the smaller European nations and the British Commonwealth states?
27. What is totalitarianism?
28. What factors helped maintain totalitarian rulers in power?
29. What kind of mentality fosters a commitment to totalitarianism?
30. Who was Mussolini and how did he begin his political career?
31. How was he able to obtain power in Italy?
32. How was Italian society organized under Mussolini?
33. How did the German defeat in World War I contribute to the rise of authoritarianism?
34. How would you describe Germany under the Weimar Republic?
35. Who were the Spartacists?
36. What role did economic instability play in the failure of the Republic?
37. What was Hitler's background and early career?
38. From what social groups did Hitler draw his support?
39. How did he achieve power in Germany and how did he deal with his political rivals?

40. What were some of the elements of Nazi organization?
41. What tangible benefits did Hitler's regime produce for German citizens?
42. What were the Gestapo and the SS?
43. What elements of racism were present in Nazi propaganda?
44. Why did Hitler target the Jews for extermination?
45. How and why did Lenin's NEP allow for the limited survival of private property?
46. What men were involved in the struggle for power after Lenin's death?
47. What qualities did Stalin possess that facilitated his rise to power?
48. What were the Five-Year Plans?
49. What was Stalin's agricultural policy and how was it implemented?
50. Who were the kulaks and how did Stalin deal with them?
51. What were purge trials?
52. What is meant by the Gulag Archipelago? What sort of people, and about how many, were sent there?
53. What economic, social, and religious policies did the communists enforce on the Russians?
54. What other European countries developed authoritarian regimes in the 1930s?
55. What conditions favored the emergence of such regimes?
56. How would you describe the political situation in Austria at this time?
57. Who was Marshall Pilsudski?
58. What was the political situation in the Balkan states?
59. What happened in the Iberian peninsula to bring dictators to power during this period?
60. Who were Antonio Salazar and Primo de Rivera?
61. What types of regimes developed in Latin America, and what conditions favored them?
62. Who was Getulio Vargas?
63. Who was Somoza?
64. How was the authoritarian government of Japan in the 1930s different from those of Germany and the Soviet Union?
65. How did the Japanese military come to have so much political power?
66. What were some of the technological innovations of the period between the wars?
67. How did automobile production increase during this period?
68. What developments revolutionized communications and entertainment?
69. What exacerbated class conflict and social agitation during the 1920s and 1930s?
70. In what ways was a one-culture society emerging at this time?

71. What was the status of Western women during the 1920s and 1930s? How did their situation differ in the authoritarian states?
72. What is meant by the conflict of generations and how many reasons can you find for its development in the 1920s and 1930s?

Multiple-Choice Questions

1. All of the following statements are true of the 1920s and 1930s except
   a. they were decades of political change
   b. technological innovations multiplied
   c. popular culture was frivolous and resolutely modern
   d. prosperity was built on unshakable foundations

2. A major problem of the postwar world economy was
   a. overproduction and a saturated market
   b. underproduction and unsatisfied demand
   c. U.S. cancellation of war loans made to the Allies
   d. German payment of huge reparations bill ahead of schedule

3. Both the Crash of '29 and the Great Depression
   a. had multiple causes
   b. were primarily due to a plot by international financiers
   c. occurred for one reason
   d. remained unexplained

4. The most successful strategy used to deal with the effects of the Great Depression, mostly used in the authoritarian states, was
   a. lowering tariffs
   b. cutting the labor bill
   c. subsidizing massive public works
   d. abandoning the gold standard and reducing the national debt

5. The United States in the 1920s experienced
   a. one of the great ages of democracy
   b. a series of great political leaders
   c. shallow culture, economic boom, growth of ideologies and prejudice
   d. a general mood of anxiety, pessimism, Puritanism

6. The anti-depression measures of Franklin Roosevelt did
    all of the following except
    a. provide work for many of the unemployed
    b. begin American involvement in welfare-state policies
    c. instill confidence in the American public
    d. stop the Depression

7. Within the British Empire, Great Britain was able to
    a. destroy the independence movement in Ireland
    b. set up a commonwealth system
    c. keep the loyalty of India
    d. remove Protestant settlers from northern Ireland

8. France in the 1920s and 1930s
    a. suffered more than other countries from the
    Depression
    b. had the most modern military technology in Europe
    c. experienced a time of political discord and military
    conservatism
    d. was no longer concerned with reparations or the
    threat of another war with Germany

9. One characteristic of twentieth-century authoritarian
    regimes was that they were generally
    a. imposed by terror rather than elections
    b. put into power by foreign occupation
    c. popular with their people
    d. unpopular and short lived

10. The new totalitarianism included all of the following
    features except
    a. a goal of total control over society
    b. a multiparty system and decentralization
    c. expansion of bureaucratic control
    d. total ideological commitment

11. The first state in western Europe to employ many of the
    features of totalitarian control was
    a. Nazi Germany
    b. Italy
    c. Spain
    d. Poland

12. All of the following contributed to popular German
    support for Hitler except
    a. the backing of communist labor unions

b. autocratic historical traditions
c. economic problems caused by the Depression
d. political instability and governmental inertia

13. Nazi ideology called for the extinction of
a. chauvinism
b. non-Prussians
c. class enemies
d. certain "non-Aryan" ethnic groups

14. Stalin's major goal was
a. merely a continuation of earlier Russian autocratic traditions
b. a new type of benevolent dictatorship
c. massive transformation of the Russian economy into totalitarian state socialism
d. to promote agricultural changes while neglecting industrialization

15. Stalin's achievements included all of the following except
a. establishing a multiparty republic
b. collectivizing Russian agriculture
c. increasing industrialization
d. establishing a totalitarian state

16. Repression and execution under Stalin were aimed at
a. only non-Aryans
b. atheists
c. Stakhanovites
d. "class enemies" of communism and individuals and groups who opposed Stalin

17. Authoritarian regimes came to power in the interwar years
a. in Scandinavia
b. in many southern and eastern European countries
c. everywhere in Europe
d. only in Germany, Italy, and Russia

18. Most of the eastern European countries that developed authoritarian regimes were
a. newly independent
b. economically affluent
c. immune to ideological currents
d. technologically advanced

19. Many Latin American governments of the 1930s
    a. brought economic disaster to their countries
    b. were highly successful liberal democracies
    c. achieved economic progress and political stability
    d. were Marxist

20. The rise of Japanese militarism was
    a. the work of one talented leader
    b. popular with the Japanese people
    c. successfully opposed by the emperor
    d. favored by the communists

21. Technological progress and new inventions
    a. affected all areas of life
    b. had little effect on popular culture
    c. did not affect agriculture
    d. did not extend to transportation until the 1940s

22. Women in the 1920s and 1930s
    a. became much more militant about women's political
    rights
    b. increasingly sought jobs outside the home but
    experienced loss of jobs after the war and during the
    Depression
    c. generally rejected the role of housewife
    d. behaved with more decorum and dignity than
    previously

23. The new youth culture of this period involved all of
    the following except
    a. the shaping of the minds and values of the young by
    mass media
    b. segregation of youth from the rest of society
    c. rejection of Western civilization and morality
    d. a rediscovery of parents as role models and a new
    appreciation for traditional values

Answer Key

1. d, 912-918
2. a, 913-915
3. a, 914-917
4. c, 917
5. c, 917
6. d, 919-920

7. b, 921-922

```
 8. c, 922
 9. c, 923-924
10. b, 923-924
11. b, 924-925
12. a, 925-928
13. d, 929
14. c, 931-932
15. a, 931-933
16. d, 932-933
17. b, 933-934
18. a, 933-934
19. c, 935
20. b, 935
21. a, 937-938
22. b, 938-940
23. d, 940-941
```

Map Exercises

1.   On Map 30.1, page 916, locate the major western European countries discussed in the chapter. Which was hardest hit by the Great Depression? Were any countries unaffected? Which country suffered more, economically, in the postwar period--Britain or France? What factors account for the difference? Locate the totalitarian states discussed in the chapter; what measures did they take to reverse the effects of the Depression, and how successful were they?

2.   On Map 30.2, page 921, trace the progress and effects of the Great Depression in the United States. Where did it begin? What areas were affected first? What agricultural areas were most affected and what were some of the consequences?

3.   On Map 30.3, page 936, locate the major Western democracies mentioned in the chapter. What were their main political and economic problems in the 1920s and 1930s? Where is the Ruhr and why did the French occupy it in 1923?
Locate the first totalitarian state in western Europe. Who was its leader? Notice the borders of the Weimar Republic, which will change after 1939. When did Hitler come to power in Germany? What states in eastern and southern Europe were ruled by authoritarian regimes in the 1920s and 1930s, and what were the reasons for this? What type of government emerged in each of the new states created after World War I?

Essay Questions

1. A major difficulty in coping with problems caused by the Great Depression was that many of the elements that brought on the Crash were new in history and no one had much experience in dealing with them. How depression proof is the world economy today? Look into the measures that most countries have taken to guard against stock market failure and excessive speculation, and consider how well they are currently working.

2. How did Northern Ireland come to be inhabited by Anglo-Protestants although it is one of the most historic areas of ancient Ireland? Look up the history of the English presence in Ireland and the policies of such British rulers as Elizabeth I, Cromwell, and William I.

3. Given the apparent preference of people in many countries for stable, economically progressive, authoritarian regimes, would you conclude that political democracy may not be suitable for all countries at all times, or is democracy a kind of absolute that is by definition the only desirable form of government? Should the United States insist on the democratization of all governments, and if so on what grounds?

4. Some recent historians have argued that if Germany had been allowed to keep the Hohenzollern dynasty or some other monarchical regime after the war, Hitler would not have been able to develop mass popularity and support. What do you think of this thesis? What are some arguments for and against it?

5. Several recent books have focused on the early extermination programs in Germany. In The German Euthanasia Program, excerpted from his larger work, A Sign for Cain, Dr. Fredric Wertham discusses the large-scale murder (called euthanasia) of undesirable people by German psychiatrists independently of any authorization by Hitler. This development was apparently an outgrowth of the European and American eugenics/euthanasia movement of the 1920s. Now that euthanasia is again a timely topic, you might like to look into its early twentieth-century background. How might acceptance of these psychiatric killings have disposed Germans to accept Hitler's mass murders?

6. Although both Nazism and Bolshevism were defined by their leaders as forms of "socialism," they are often treated as opposite extremes of "left" and "right." What do these terms mean, and how relevant are they to a comparison of communism and Nazism? Is it possible to determine which of these ideologies was morally worse? Does the fact that Soviet communism claimed the lives of many times the number of Hitler's victims reflect a more depraved system, a longer time in which the system could operate, both, or neither?

7. It is sometimes still argued that Stalin's reign of terror

reflects his personal cruelty and paranoia and does not discredit true communist principles. Read Leon Trotsky's famous "Terrorism and Communism: A Reply to Karl Kautsky" and see how many points you can find to which Stalin could appeal for justification of his mass executions.

8. Stalin's deliberate starvation of millions of Ukrainian peasants has been documented in Robert Conquest's recent book, <u>Harvest of Sorrow</u>. An intriguing question is how so many people were systematically exterminated without the world taking much notice. You might like to explore the extraordinary career of Pulitzer Prize-winning <u>New York Times</u> Russian correspondent Walter Duranty, the subject of a recent biography, who knew of the killings but lied about them in his newspaper column. Duranty was not the only Western observer to suppress the truth in this manner, while the few reporters who wrote accurate stories were disregarded. Why would anyone lie about such an atrocity? Is deliberately false reporting still possible today? Why or why not?

9. Is all progress necessarily good? Why or why not? Do you agree or disagree with the morals and mentality of the Jazz Age? Are mass media figures appropriate role models for young people? Is a homogeneous one-culture society necessarily a good thing? Why or why not?

Chapter 31: World War II

<u>Outline</u>

    A.   Causes of the Second World War
        1. the revisionist nations
           a. dissatisfaction with territorial losses
              on part of Germany, Soviet Union, and other
              states
           b. desire for "revisionism"
        2. failure of attempts to secure international peace
           a. Locarno treaties, 1925
           b. Kellogg-Briand Pact, 1928
           c. disarmament measures
           d. antiwar sentiment
        3. the Great Depression
           a. factor in rise of Hitler
           b. Western powers weakened and demoralized
        4. ideological causes
           a. nationalism in Europe and Japan
           b. antipathy of liberals for authoritarianism
           c. American isolationism
           d. revolutionary Marxist ideology and policies of
Soviet Union
    B.   International Crises Preceding War
        1. Japanese attacks on China
           a. Manchuria, 1931
           b. invasion of China, 1937
           c. division between Chinese Nationalists and
Communists
        2. Italian designs on Ethiopia
           a. Italian invasion, 1935
           b. Mussolini's motives
           c. ineffective international protests and sanctions
        3. Spanish Civil War, 1936-1939
           a. background of political anarchy
           b. Nationalist revolt under General Franco
           c. foreign intervention
           d. victory of General Franco
        4. German aggression
           a. German rearmament
           b. remilitarization of Rhineland, 1936
           c. Hitler's designs on German-speaking areas
               outside Germany
              1) Hitler's strategy in Austria
              2) Anschluss, March 1938

       d. the Axis alliances of 1936 and 1937
       e. Hitler's designs on non-German countries
          1) Sudetenland, 1938
          2) Munich conference, September 1938
          3) rest of Czechoslovakia, March 1939
          4) Nazi-Soviet Pact, August 1939
          5) Poland, September 1, 1939
             a) Germans invade from west
             b) Russians invade from east

C.   Axis Victories
    1. rapid military pace of World War II
    2. German victories
       a. rapid, mechanized, offensive warfare
       b. German campaign in Poland
       c. the phony war: Allied action limited to naval
engagements and border raids
    3. Soviet Union takes over much of eastern Europe
    4. Germany occupies, or controls through satellite
regimes, other eastern European and Balkan areas
    5. German Blitzkrieg in western Europe, 1940
       a. Scandinavia
       b. Low Countries
       c. France
          1) failure of Maginot Line
          2) Dunkirk
       d. Britain
          1) Winston Churchill, prime minister
          2) the Battle of Britain
          3) United States aid to Great Britain
    6. Axis mistakes in 1941
       a. Hitler's invasion of Russia
       b. Japanese attack on Pearl Harbor, bringing
United States into war
       c. Japanese conquests in the Pacific and Southeast
Asia

D.   Allied Victories
    1. the Grand Alliance
       a. the Atlantic Charter
       b. Allied war strategies
    2. great American production of war materials
    3. turning points of the war, 1942
       a. British victory at El Alamein
       b. Stalingrad (July 1942-February 1943)
       c. Guadalcanal
    4. counteroffensives of 1943
       a. Russia
       b. North Africa
       c. campaigns in Italy and Italian surrender
    5. final campaigns in Europe
       a. eastern and southern Europe

            b. D Day, 1944
        6. war in Asia and the Pacific
            a. U.S. naval victories in the Pacific
            b. recapture of Philippines, 1945
            c. British victories in Burma and Malaya
            d. fierce struggle for Pacific Islands between
United States and Japan
        7. end of the war, 1945
            a. May 8, V-E Day: surrender of Germany
            b. fall of Japan
                1) aerial bombardments
                2) atomic bombs on Hiroshima and Nagasaki
                3) September 2, V-J Day: surrender of Japan
    E.   Consequences of World War II
        1. the demands of total war for both sides
            a) increase in governmental political control
            b) governmental regulation of economic life
            c) increase in number of women in armed
        services and war industries
            d) civilian populations become military targets
        2. casualties and ruin
        3. Western fear and control of possible enemy aliens
            a. British internment of Germans
            b. U.S. internment of Japanese
        4. resistance movements in countries occupied by Axis
        powers
            a. underground activities
            b. attempts to kill Hitler
            c. killing of Mussolini
            d. reprisals
                1) execution of members of the White Rose
                2) execution of five thousand after attempt to
            assassinate Hitler
                3) brutalization of civilians by Japanese
                4) treatment of Germans by Allied troops
        5. Hitler's genocide
            a. early actions against Jews
            b. murder of Jews, Gypsies, Slavs in the course of
        military campaigns in eastern Europe
            c. establishment of death camps
            d. inadequate attempts to explain how it could have
        happened

Read to Find Out

    1. What were the main causes of World War II?
    2. What crises led up to the outbreak of the war?
    3. How did Japanese militarism and nationalism develop
    during the prewar period?
    4. What were the territorial ambitions of Italy and what
    aggressive steps did it take prior to the war?
    5. What were the causes of the Spanish Civil War?

6. Why did the war in Spain become an international cause?
7. What steps did Hitler take in the late 1930s that led to the outbreak of war in Europe?
8. What was the Munich agreement and what did the Western powers hope to achieve by signing it?
9. What event triggered the start of the war?
10. In what ways was World War II more of a global war than World War I?
11. What nations were allied on either side at the start of the war?
12. What was the blitzkrieg?
13. What was the Phony War?
14. How would you summarize goals and strategy in the early part of the war?
15. What was the Battle of Britain?
16. Why did Hitler invade Russia?
17. What was the result of Germany's campaigns on the eastern front?
18. What did Japan hope to gain by entering the war?
19. What were the initial results of the first Japanese offensives?
20. In what two periods can the war years be divided, and what is the theme of each period?
21. What was the Grand Alliance and who were the Big Three?
22. Where did the first major Allied victories take place?
23. Who was the Desert Fox?
24. Why are the battles of Stalingrad and El Alamein considered turning points in the war?
25. How did the war in the Pacific develop and what were some of the major battles?
26. What were the final stages of the war in Europe?
27. What happened to Hitler?
28. What United States action hastened the end of the war in the Pacific?
29. In what ways was World War II a total war?
30. What were some of the major consequences of the war?

Multiple-Choice Questions

1.   All of the following were causes of World War II except
     a. the Great Depression
     b. the Versailles Treaty
     c. nationalism and other ideologies
     d. persecution of virtuous nations by evil nations

2. The Japanese invasion of China in 1937 resulted in
   a. an immediate U.S. embargo on shipments of war materials to Japan
   b. the death of Chiang Kai-shek
   c. no effective foreign action against Japan
   d. the British declaration of war on Japan

3. The Italian invasion of Ethiopia
   a. came at the invitation of Haile Selassie
   b. was followed by an embargo on oil shipments to Italy
   c. caused little international protest
   d. began World War II

4. The Spanish Civil War was a step toward the outbreak of World War II because
   a. the Republic won
   b. totalitarian intervention on both sides polarized public opinion
   c. famous writers took part in it
   d. Spain joined the Axis powers

5. Hitler's main territorial objectives lay in
   a. central and eastern Europe
   b. France
   c. Scandinavia
   d. Great Britain

6. The German act of aggression that led to the declarations of war which began World War II was
   a. the Anschluss
   b. the invasion of Poland
   c. annexation of the Sudetenland
   d. militarization of the Rhineland

7. In the course of World War II, the newly independent eastern European countries found themselves
   a. strengthened and maintained by the Western powers
   b. united in a new Austrian empire
   c. eliminated from the map of Europe
   d. conquered by either Nazi Germany or the Soviet Union

8. Unlike World War I, World War II
   a. involved extremely rapid-moving campaigns over large areas
   b. included a German invasion of France
   c. had eastern and western fronts in Europe
   d. was a war of position and trench warfare

9. One of Hitler's greatest mistakes of the war was
    a. invading England
    b. the Anschluss
    c. occupying Denmark
    d. invading Russia

10. Japan's greatest mistake was
    a. its alliance with Germany
    b. the invasion of China
    c. cutting off the Burma Road
    d. attacking Pearl Harbor

11. The Grand Alliance was
    a. the code name for the invasion of Sicily
    b. a military coalition of Roosevelt, Churchill, and Stalin
    c. the alliance between France and Britain
    d. the alliance between Hitler and Stalin

12. Two major turning points of the war were the battles of
    a. Paris and Leningrad
    b. the Marco Polo Bridge and Moscow
    c. El Alamein and Stalingrad
    d. Stalingrad and Prague

13. The first of the Axis powers to be invaded by the Allies was
    a. Italy
    b. Japan
    c. Germany
    d. Turkey

14. The D-Day invasion by the Allies
    a. was foiled by Rommel
    b. began in Normandy and proceeded through Belgium to the Rhine
    c. required a massive evacuation from Dunkirk after the failure of the Allied offensive
    d. occurred in Sicily

15. The surrender of both Germany and Japan
    a. occurred because of land invasion by Allied armies
    b. took place in 1945
    c. happened because of the suicides of Hitler and Emperor Hirohito
    d. occurred because the Allies accepted German and Japanese peace conditions

16. One of the economic effects of World War II was
a. a worsening of the Depression
b. in increase in government control
c. exclusion of women from the work force
d. the triumph of laissez-faire capitalism

17. One of the features of World War II, as compared
with earlier wars, was
a. increased targeting of civilians
b. decreased casualty rate
c. its limitation to Eurasian territories
d. military concentration on land instead of
aerial strategy

18. The democracies dealt with the possibility of
enemy subversion within their countries by all of
the following means except
a. internment of resident aliens
b. censorship
c. civil rights guarantees even for suspected
enemy sympathizers
d. propaganda

19. Resistance movements in Europe included all of the
following except
a. underground opposition groups in Axis-occupied
territory
b. German officers who killed Hitler
c. anti-Nazi Catholic students
d. Italian partisans who killed Mussolini

20. Hitler's "final solution" was
a. limited to making life in Germany unbearable
for Jews so that they would leave
b. the confinement of Jews to ghettos
c. aimed at total extermination of European Jews,
along with Gypsies, Slavs, and other groups
d. mostly an anti-Jewish propaganda campaign, with
little implementation

Answer Key

1. d, 945-948
2. c, 950-51
3. c, 951-952
4. b, 952
5. a, 952-953
6. b, 954-955
7. d, 955-956
8. a, 955

```
 9. d, 958
10. d, 958
11. b, 959
12. c, 961
13. a, 962
14. b, 963-964
15. b, 966
16. b, 967-968
17. a, 968
18. c, 969
19. b, 969
20. c, 969-970
```

Map Exercises

1. On Map 31.1, page 949, locate the major German conquests and campaigns mentioned in the chapter. What neighboring country had Hitler already occupied by 1939? Where is the Sudetenland and what is its importance? Where is Danzig, and why did Hitler want both that city and the "Polish corridor"? What route did the German armies take into France? How much of France remained free of direct German occupation? What was the route taken by the German armies into Russia, and where were major battles fought? What eastern European countries had been occupied by Germany by 1942?

2. On Map 31.2, page 951, trace the Japanese conquests discussed in the chapter. Where is Manchuria and when was it occupied by Japan? When was China invaded, and how much of it was occupied by Japanese armies? Where is Peking (Beijing)? Where is the Yangtze River and what is the importance of the area around it? What southeast Asian territories fell to Japan in the early years of the war?

3. On Map 31.3, chart the counteroffensives of the Allies in the last three years of the war. Where is Sicily and why was it crucial to the strategy of the Allies? Where did the German armies suffer reversals in the Soviet Union during this period? Where did the D-Day invasion take place? Where was the Battle of the Bulge?

4. On Map 31.4, page 965, find the sites of the important battles mentioned in the chapter. Where is Hawaii? Where was the Battle of Guadalcanal? Where are the Philippines? Where are Leyte Gulf, Iwo Jima, and Okinawa? Where is the Coral Sea and where is Midway Island? Why were the battles in these areas significant?

Essay Questions

1. Many questions about the Spanish Civil War are still debated among historians, as they were among the intellectual foreign volunteers who survived the war. Compare some recent contrasting evaluations of the war and of the long rule of General Franco. You might start with the relevant sections in Paul Johnson's recent book, <u>Modern Times</u>.

2. There are revisionist studies of Vichy France, most of them so far available only in French, arguing that Marshal Pétain not only saved most of France from German occupation but that most of the Jews in Vichy territory (including refugees) survived the war. By contrast, very few Jews (less than percent) in German-occupied lands survived. Vichy has also been called one of Hitler's greatest blunders because it blocked German access to the French Mediterranean coast and deprived it of the French fleet, which Pétain ordered scuttled so it would not fall into German hands. For an eyewitness account by a British journalist of events in Vichy France, consult the books of Sisley Huddleston, especially <u>France: The Tragic Years</u> (1955).

3. The revelation, after thirty-five years of secrecy, of the intelligence operation known as Ultra which cracked the German code and provided the Allies with advance knowledge of enemy tactics, has been the subject of several books. Not only has Ultra necessitated the rewriting of part of the history of World War II, but it has raised questions about the morality of allowing the German bombing of Coventry, for example, to avoid revealing Allied knowledge of the cipher. Look into the issues of how much Ultra contributed to the Allied victories at El Alamein and Midway, and how much destruction of Allied targets was involved in keeping the secret.

4. If it took thirty-five years for historians to learn about Ultra, how certain can we be of having all the "facts" about more recent historical events? Are all historical judgments uncertain, or is twentieth-century history particularly complex? What important collections of documents, for example, still elude historians of World War II and in what areas is our knowledge reasonably complete?

5. Two recurrent issues concerning United States involvement in World War II are the question of the American government's advance knowledge of Pearl Harbor, and the debate as to why Western troops were apparently held back deliberately so that the Russians could reach Berlin first, thereby beginning their nearly fifty years of domination of

east Germany and eastern Europe. What is the current historical thinking on these points?

6. The firebombing of Dresden was one of the great Allied atrocities of the war. There have also been accusations of Allied, especially American, mistreatment even starvation of German prisoners of war made in the controversial work, Other Losses by James Bacque (1989). Look into the question of how well Bacque's accusations are founded.

7. What became of Raoul Wallenberg, the Swedish diplomat in Budapest who saved thousands of Hungarian Jews from the Nazis, only to be arrested by the Red Army? Several books have attempted to trace the story of Wallenberg, whose survival in Soviet prison camps has been persistently rumored, even in recent years. Look up the most recent work on this tragic historical mystery.

8. According to Pinchas Lapide, Israeli consul in Italy, "The Catholic Church saved more Jewish lives during the war than all the other churches, religious institutions, and rescue organizations put together. Its record stands in startling contrast to the achievements of the International Red Cross and the Western Democracies." For an only slightly fictionalized version of the activities of one cleric stationed at the Vatican during the war, see the film The Scarlet and the Black, with Gregory Peck. What does the film show about the problems encountered by other diplomats in openly opposing anti-Jewish persecution?

9. In recent years several books, articles, and even a historical journal have argued that the Holocaust never took place. This argument is analyzed in a recent book by Deborah E. Lipstadt, Denying the Holocaust (1993). Look into the amount of solid historical evidence that exists for the reality of the Holocaust. On what grounds could such evidence be rejected?

Chapter 32: Cold War

<u>Outline</u>

    A.   Conflict in the Postwar World
1. historical background of suspicion and antagonism between United States and USSR
   a. American capitalist ideology and Enlightenment idealism
   b. Russian traditional mentality and Marxist ideology
2. conflicting postwar plans for the world
   a. United States encouragement of democracy and economic recovery
   b. Soviet desire for communist buffer zone in eastern Europe, appropriation of eastern European resources
3. theories of causes for cold war
   a. communist ideology
   b. traditional Russian interest
   c. American economic aggression
4. the peace settlement
   a. lack of common goals of Allies
   b. separate treaties signed in 1940s, 1950s
5. territorial arrangements
   a. Italy loses territory gained under Mussolini and predecessors
      1) Albania
      2) Ethiopia
      3) Libya
      4) Somaliland
   b. Japan loses Korea, Taiwan, islands
   c. Austria separated from Germany, divided into zones
   d. division of Germany
      1) first divided into four zones
      2) zones of Western powers become West Germany
      3) Soviet zone becomes East Germany
   e. Polish borders
   f. Stalin rejects right of eastern Europeans to choose their governments, imposes Soviet regimes
6. lack of agreement among Big Three after Potsdam, 1945

B.   Soviet Gains and Influence
    1. acquisitions from Stalin's alliance with Hitler
        a. Baltic states
        b. parts of Finland, Poland, Romania
    2. acquisitions from alliance with Roosevelt and
    Churchill
        a. domination of eastern Europe from Poland and East
    Germany to Balkans
        b. Russian puppet state in north Korea, influence in
    China
    3. the eastern European satellites
        a. process of imposing communist rule
        b. elimination of opposition
        c. state control of economy, collectivization of
    agriculture
        d. ineffective Western objections
    4. Soviet setbacks in Europe
        a. Marshall Plan stimulates western European economy
        b. popularity, then decline of communism among
    Western voters, especially French and Italian
        c. Truman Doctrine, 1947
        d. Yugoslavia
            1) resistance to Soviet pressure
            2) successful diplomacy of Tito
        e. Germany
            1) Soviet blockade of Berlin, 1948
            2) Berlin airlift mounted by United States
            3) integration of West Berlin into Federal
        Republic
    5. China
        a. decades-long revolution
        b. Western ideological influence
        c. leaders
            1) Sun Yat-sen
            2) Chiang Kai-shek
            3) Mao Zedong
        d. struggle between Chiang's Nationalists and Mao's
        communists
            1) early Nationalist victories
            2) the Long March
        e. regime of Chiang Kai-shek
            1) war with Japan
            2) wartime truce with communists
            3) support of United States
        f. triumph of Mao Zedong
            1) Chinese territory liberated by Soviet
            Union and turned over to Mao
            2) United States pressure on Chiang
            3) withdrawal of Chiang to Taiwan
            4) treaty with Soviet Union; Soviet aid and
        influence

6. southeast Asia
   a. many organizers and leaders of colonial revolts
      are communists
   b. Soviet defense of revolutionary movements
   c. Vietnam
      1) Ho Chi Minh
      2) defeat of French at Dien Bien Phu, 1954
      3) communist regime in North Vietnam, 1954
   d. other southeast Asian regions
   e. the Korean War
      1) background of North and South Korea
         a) Soviets in north
         b) Americans in south
      2) invasion of South Korea by North, 1950
         a) U.S. and UN "police action"
         b) Chinese intervention
         c) truce, 1953
C. Organized Opposition
   1. ideological and military organizations
      a. Soviet Cominform, 1947
      b. U.S. bases and military alliances
      c. North Atlantic Treaty Organization, 1949
      d. Warsaw Pact, 1955
   2. rival economic organizations
      a. European Common Market in western Europe
      b. COMECON in eastern Europe
D. Crises in the 1950s and 1960s
   1. Hungary, 1956
      a. October revolution
      b. Imre Nagy
      c. massive Soviet repression
   2. disturbances in Poland, 1956
   3. the Suez crisis, 1956
   4. Latin America
      a. Guatemala
         1) leftist President Arbenz
         2) U.S. intervention and overthrow of Arbenz
      b. Cuba
         1) pro-Soviet regime of Fidel Castro
         2) Bay of Pigs
   5. major confrontations between Kennedy and Khrushchev
      a. Berlin Wall, 1961
      b. Cuban missile crisis, 1962
E. Crises in the 1960s and 1970s
   1. main political leaders
      a. Soviet Union: Leonid Brezhnev
      b. United States: four presidents, Johnson and Nixon
most important

2. Czechoslovakia
   a. the Prague Spring, 1968
   b. causes
   c. Dubçek regime
   d. Soviet military occupation
3. Chile
   a. Communist ruler Salvador Allende
   b. U.S. opposition
   c. economic chaos and overthrow of Allende, 1973
   d. General Pinochet president, 1973-1990
4. Vietnam
   a. U.S. support for Diem regime in South Vietnam
   b. Soviet support for Ho Chi Minh in north
   c. North Vietnamese and Soviet support for
      guerrilla warfare against South Vietnamese
      government
   d. U.S. military intervention
   e. U.S. withdrawal, 1973
      5) North Vietnamese conquest of South Vietnam
      (1975) and other parts of Indochina
5. Afghanistan
   a. revolt against Soviet-supported communist
   regime of Nur Mohammed Taraki
   b. Russian military intervention
   c. inability to crush rebels
   d. Soviet withdrawal (1989) and overthrow of pro-
   Soviet government
F. The 1980s
1. Presidents Reagan and Bush, and their policies
2. Soviet rulers Brezhnev, Andropov, Chernenko,
Gorbachev, and their policies
3. areas of Soviet involvement
   a. Afghanistan
   b. Angola
   c. Poland
4. areas of U.S. involvement
   a. Grenada
   b. El Salvador
   c. Nicaragua
5. breakup of old alliances
   a. loosening of Soviet hegemony over eastern bloc
   b. French defection from NATO
      1) de Gaulle's resentment of American and British
      prominence in NATO
      2) forges alliances with West Germany, negotiates
      independently with Soviet Union and China
      3) withdraws France from NATO

      c. split between Soviet Union and China, 1960
        1) background of Russian-Chinese friction
        2) Chinese anger at Khrushchev's attack on
Stalinism
        3) lack of sufficient Soviet technical and
economic aid to China
        4) consequences of end of alliance
            a) half-finished Soviet projects abandoned in
China
            b) China becomes chief rival to Soviet
leadership of world communist parties, influence
in Third World
            c) Chinese-Albanian alliance
            d) Soviet patronage of North Korea and North
Vietnam
            e) Chinese rapprochement with United States
6. movement toward ensuring international peace
    a. Khrushchev and peaceful coexistence
    b. Brezhnev and détente
    c. SALT treaty
    d. Reagan-Bush policies
      1) Reagan's military buildup
      2) summit meetings with Soviet leaders
      3) visit to Soviet Union
      4) nuclear weapon removal treaty
7. end of Cold War, 1989-1991
    a. pro-Soviet governments overthrown in eastern
Europe
    b. Soviet Union disintegrates
    c. communism seemingly no longer major force in
Western world
    d. causes for collapse
      1) economic problems
      2) popular opposition to oppressive political
system
      3) role of Gorbachev
    e. course of the "revolutions of 1989"
      1) Hungary
      2) Poland and Solidarity
      3) East Germany
         a) fall of the Berlin Wall
         b) reunification with West Germany
      4) Czechoslovakia
      5) collapse of Warsaw Pact; retreat of Soviet
troops for first time since World War II
      6) Soviet Union
         a) Gorbachev's reforms bring economic crisis
         b) political and nationalist opposition within
USSR
         c) overthrow of Gorbachev, replaced by Yeltsin
         d) dissolution of Soviet Union

f. theories about end of Cold War
   1) roles of individual statesmen
      a) Gorbachev's reforms and consent to freedom of satellites
      b) Reagan's military buildup seen as forcing Gorbachev to recognize inadequacy of Soviet economy
      c) Bush's encouragement of Gorbachev
      d) West German Chancellor Helmut Kohl's diplomatic achievements in getting Soviets out of East Germany, reunification of country
   2) larger forces involved
      a) basic weakness of communist economy
      b) revival of nationalism
g. costs of Cold War
   1) money and lives
   2) domestic problems on both sides
   3) disillusionment, ideological disorientation
   4) potential of chaos and instability of Soviet Union and eastern bloc for future conflict

Read to Find Out

1. What is meant by the cold war?
2. How would you summarize the historical background of U.S. relations with Russia, and how would you describe the political outlook of each country at the beginning of the cold war?
3. What conflicting plans did the two superpowers have for the postwar world?
4. How would you describe the three main American theories of the causes for the cold war? What was the official interpretation?
5. What is meant by the policy of containment?
6. What is meant by the Iron Curtain?
7. What were the main points of the peace settlement after World War II?
8. What territorial changes were made immediately after the war?
9. How was Germany divided after the war?
10. How did the borders of Poland change?
11. What caused the Grand Alliance to fall apart?
12. What was the role of the Soviet Union in eastern Europe?
13. What territorial gains did the Soviet Union make as a result of World War II?
14. How would you describe the process by which communist regimes were imposed on the eastern European satellite states?
15. What stimulated the European economy recovery after the war?

16. Why were communist parties popular in some Western countries in the postwar period, and how were they defeated?
17. What measures did the United States take as a result of Soviet activities after the war?
18. What was the Truman Doctrine?
19. How did the Allies respond to Soviet attempts to blockade Berlin?
20. How did Soviet actions in the Far East cause new tensions with the West?
21. How would you describe the Chinese Communist Revolution?
22. How did Chiang Kai-shek manage to unify China, and how did he attempt to deal with his communist opponents?
23. What were the tactics of Mao Zedong?
24. How did the rival parties cooperate during World War II?
25. What was the political situation in China at the end of the war?
26. Where did conflict between the Western powers and the Soviet Union first emerge in Southeast Asia during the postwar period?
27. How would you summarize the conflicts in Vietnam and Korea in the 1940s and 1950s?
28. What was the Cominform?
29. What is NATO and why was it formed?
30. What were the European Economic Community and Comecon?
31. How did the Hungarian Revolution of 1956 originate and what were some of its results?
32. What occurred in Poland in 1956?
33. What crisis took place in Egypt in 1956?
34. How did the United States intervene in Latin American affairs during this period?
35. How did Fidel Castro come to power in Cuba?
36. What was the Bay of Pigs operation?
37. When and why was the Berlin Wall built?
38. What was the Cuban missile crisis and how was it resolved?
39. What was the Prague Spring?
40. How did the Soviet Union deal with developments in Czechoslovakia in 1968?
41. To what degree did the United States intervene in Chile?
42. How did the United States become involved in Vietnam and what were the results of American intervention?
43. Why did the Soviet Union invade Afghanistan and what was the result of the ensuing war?
44. In what African country did Soviet troops intervene?
45. What was the policy of President Reagan in Central America?
46. Who were the Sandinistas, and how did their struggle for power end?

47. What independent policies did Charles de Gaulle pursue, and what were his reasons for doing so?
48. What caused the rift between China and the Soviet Union?
49. What is meant by peaceful coexistence, and who proposed it?
50. What is the meaning of détente?
51. What steps were taken to reduce superpower tensions in the 1970s and 1980s?
52. Who is Mikhail Gorbachev and what was his role in the dramatic changes in eastern Europe and Russia in the 1980s?
53. What happened to the Soviet satellite states at this time?
54. When and how did Germany come to be reunited?
55. Who is Helmut Kohl?
56. What were the respective domestic and foreign problems of the United States and the Soviet Union in the early 1990s?

Multiple-Choice Questions

1. After World War II the world entered an era of
    a. international peace and cooperation
    b. European imperialism
    c. world government
    d. cold war

2. American-Soviet antagonism stemmed largely from
    a. bitterness at earlier Russian-American wars
    b. conflicting ideologies
    c. anti-Slav racism among Americans
    d. American envy at Soviet economic success

3. American policy toward the Soviet Union during the cold war period may be described as
    a. détente
    b. peaceful coexistence
    c. containment
    d. a crusade to destroy all communist regimes

4. World War II peace settlements
    a. reflected the breakdown of the Grand Alliance
    b. resulted from an international conference like the Congress of Vienna
    c. showed that the Allies remained politically united
    d. resulted in a peace treaty with Germany

5. What was significant about Allied treatment of Germany
    was that
    a. it amounted to a repetition of the Versailles
    settlement
    b. Germany came under Soviet control
    c. Germany was divided into Allied-controlled zones
    d. the United States treated Germany as a colony

6. The boundaries of Poland were changed so that
    a. Poland would not include any German population
    b. Poland would effectively cease to exist
    c. the Soviet Union could keep Polish territory
    d. Poland would be a free country

7. As a result of World War II, the Soviet Union
    a. acquired a huge empire in eastern Europe
    b. lost much of its territory
    c. entered a period of economic boom
    d. suffered little destruction

8. European economic recovery was
    a. immediate and spectacular
    b. never achieved
    c. hampered by a second Great Depression
    d. greatly stimulated by the Marshall Plan

9. In Berlin, the Soviet Union attempted
    a. to build a wall around the whole city
    b. an airlift
    c. to withdraw from East Berlin
    d. a blockade

10. Sun Yat-sen was famous for having been
    a. the second president of the Chinese republic
    b. the assassin of Ci Xi
    c. the first leader of the Chinese revolutionary
    movement
    d. untouched by Western influence

11. The tide turned against Chiang Kai-shek, in his duel
    with Mao Zedong, when
    a. U.S. support for Chiang began to weaken
    b. the Soviet Union invaded Taiwan
    c. Chiang lost Taiwan
    d. he had Mao assassinated

12.   In both Korea and Vietnam, the main source of conflict
      was
      a. Japanese aggression
      b. national division into communist north and non-
      communist south
      c. American desire for an Asian empire
      d. French colonialism

13.   In the 1950s, a revolt that triggered massive Soviet
      intervention and repression occurred in
      a. each of the Soviet satellites
      b. Albania
      c. Hungary
      d. the Baltic states

14.   Fidel Castro's Cuba
      a. revolted against its communist dictatorship
      b. defeated a CIA-trained expeditionary force
      c. was successfully invaded by the United States
      d. became an ally of the United States

15.   One of the most dangerous superpower confrontations was
      a. the Cuban missile crisis
      b. the Sandinista war
      c. the Afghan rebellion
      d. the creation of East Germany

16.   The "Prague spring" refers to
      a. the great drought of 1968
      b. a cultural flowering of Czech literature
      c. an economic leap forward
      d. the unsuccessful liberalization program attempted by
      Alexander Dubçek

17.   The results of American withdrawal from Vietnam
      included all of the following except
      a. the annexation of South Vietnam by communist North
      Vietnam
      b. communist Vietnamese domination of Laos
      c. the survival of Cambodia as a noncommunist state
      d. peace in Indochina

18.   The Soviet attempt to control Afghanistan resulted in
      a. division of the country into North and South
      Afghanistan
      b. withdrawal of Soviet troops and overthrow of the
      pro-Soviet regime
      c. an overwhelming Afghan vote for the communist
      government
      d. the final victory of the Moscow-sponsored government

19.   The most serious split in the communist bloc was
       a. the loss of Albania
       b. the defection of Tito
       c. Cuba's objections to Soviet policy
       d. the rupture of the Soviet-Chinese alliance

20.   The arms race led to
       a. clear superiority for the United States
       b. attempts to negotiate disarmament
       c. nuclear war
       d. rejection of all attempts to limit weaponry

21.   One of the most dramatic results of the "Revolutions of
       1989" was
       a. Soviet invasion of Romania
       b. renewed German-Russian hostility
       c. the reunification of Germany
       d. an unprecedented bloodbath

Answer Key

    1. d, 975
    2. b, 977-978
    3. c, 979
    4. a, 982
    5. c, 982
    6. c, 982
    7. a, 982-985
    8. d, 985
    9. d, 985
   10. c, 986
   11. a, 986
   12. b, 987
   13. c, 989-990
   14. b, 990-991
   15. a, 992
   16. d, 992
   17. c, 994
   18. b, 994
   19. d, 997
   20. b, 997-998
   21. c, 998-999

Map Exercises

1. Compare Map 32.1, page 981, with maps of the same area in
previous chapters. How have the borders of Poland changed from
their post-World War I status? Why were these changes made? How

have the borders of Germany changed, and how is the country divided on this map? What is the furthest point of western penetration of the Red Army into Europe at the time World War II ended? What is the status of Austria on this map? Has the status of Ukraine, the Baltic states, and Finland changed from the period immediately following World War I? What countries were first helped by the Truman Doctrine and for what reason?

2. On Map 32.2, page 988, locate the countries mentioned in the chapter as forming part of the Western or Soviet alliances. What countries made up the Warsaw Pact? Which states belonged to NATO? What nations are shown as nonaligned, and what reasons can you think of for their neutrality? What major NATO member later withdrew from this organization, and why?

3. On Map 32.3, find the southeast Asian countries where hostilities first began between Western powers and communist revolutionaries in the cold war period. Where were French troops engaged, and what was the result? Where did American troops fight in Asia in the 1950s? Where is Taiwan, who controlled it in the late 1940s, and how did this situation come about? Where is Malaya and what struggle occurred there? Where is Afghanistan, and what geographical reasons can you see for the desire of the Soviet Union to control this area? Where is Iran, and why would the Soviet Union want to maintain a presence there? Where are Laos and Cambodia, and what happened to them when American troops withdrew from Vietnam?

Essay Questions

1. Develop an essay supporting one of the interpretations of the cold war discussed on pages 979-982. Survey the historical literature presenting the various viewpoints; are the American revisionists mentioned in the chapter Marxist historians, and if so, how might their ideology affect their interpretations?

2. When Roosevelt gave diplomatic recognition to the Soviet Union, Stalin was in the process of exterminating millions more of his own people than Hitler was to do, including the deliberate starving of millions of Ukrainians in the 1930s. Do you agree with Roosevelt's action? What do you think motivated it? Should the United States have been willing to cooperate more closely with the Soviet Union in the prewar period?

3. How does the Allies' acquiescence in Stalin's takeover of eastern Europe differ from their appeasement of Hitler at Munich? Write an essay taking any point of view on this question; substantiate your argument with examples.

4. Were the Soviet missiles taken out of Cuba ever put back? Is there any current danger of a Cuban missile attack on the United

States or any Latin American countries? Look up the most recent discussions of the military situation in Cuba.

5.   Find information for a comparison between the Taiwanese regime and that of mainland China. Which government do you think has governed its people better, and why? With the hindsight thus acquired, decide which side, if any, the United States should have supported in the Chinese civil war. Give reasons for your choice.

Chapter 33: An Age of Affluence and Uncertainty

Outline

I. The West in the Postwar Period

    A.   Postwar Integration
        1. increased global integration
            a. the idea of European unity
                1) economic measures
                2) political measures
            b. Western expansion
                1) new states included in Western family of nations
                2) some states westernized, but not Western countries
            c. United Nations
                1) purpose
                2) organization
                3) various activities
                4) early dominance of United States
    B.   The United States
        1. liberal postwar presidencies in the United States
            a. Truman years, 1945-1953
                1) the Fair Deal
                2) continued New Deal policies
             b. Eisenhower years, 1952-1961
                1) first Republican president since Depression
                2) progressive Republican administration
            c. the 1960s: John F. Kennedy, 1961-1963
                1) first Catholic president
                2) the New Frontier
                3) assassination
            d. the 1960s: Lyndon B. Johnson, 1963-1969
                1) more New Deal-style programs
                2) the Great Society
                3) strained economy, antiwar movement
        2. political and social issues
            a. anticommunism
                1) Senator Joseph McCarthy
                2) attempt to eliminate domestic communist influence in American institutions

b. expansion of welfare state
      1) extension of social security
      2) food stamps
      3) aid for mothers and dependent children
      4) aid for education
   c. rights for African Americans
      1) integration of army under Truman
      2) Supreme Court outlaws segregated education
      3) civil rights legislation
   d. revival of women's movement
   e. the civil rights movement
      1) Martin Luther King, Jr. (1929-1968)
      2) tactics and results
   f. the "new left" of the 1960s
      1) political activism of youth
      2) support for President Johnson's "war on
   poverty"
      3) antiwar movement
   g. postwar prosperity and Democratic coalition end
3. conservative presidencies
   a. Richard Nixon, 1968-1974
      1) political pragmatism
      2) foreign policy
         a) ends Vietnam War
         b) improves U.S. relations with USSR and
            China
      3) domestic problems
         a) illegal means used in struggle with antiwar
   movement
         b) Watergate crisis
         c) resignation of president
   b. Gerald Ford, 1974-1977, and Jimmy Carter, 1977-
   1981
   c. Ronald Reagan, 1981-1989
      1) rebirth of conservatism
      2) popularity of president
      3) cutback of liberal programs
      4) conservative social activism
      5) military buildup
      6) economic growth continues longer than under
   any other president
   d. George Bush, 1989-1993
      1) recession succeeds boom
      2) huge national debt
      3) social tensions and problems
4. election of Democrat Bill Clinton, 1992
   a. renewed liberal activism
   b. continuing national debt and budget problems

C. Western Europe
  1. Germany
    a. postwar political and economic evolution of
Federal Republic
        1) first stage: 1949-1964
            a) Konrad Adenauer, chancellor
            b) reasons for spectacular economic recovery
        2) second stage: 1960s
            a) growing confidence in government
            b) youth movement
            c) assault on right-wing periodical press
        3) third stage: from 1970s
            a) chancellors Willy Brandt and Helmut Schmidt
            b) relations with East Germany and Soviet bloc
            c) economic decline
            d) radical terrorist groups
    b. return to power of conservative Christian
       Democrats, 1982
        1) Helmut Kohl, chancellor
        2) economic and foreign policy
        3) reunification of Germany
            a) opening of Berlin Wall, 1989
            b) reunification, 1990
  2. France
    a. second most prosperous European power
    b. immediate postwar governments unstable
    c. unsuccessful colonial wars in Indochina and
       Algeria
    d. revival in 1960s and 1970s
        1) Charles de Gaulle and successors
        2) Fifth Republic
        3) foreign policy of de Gaulle
    e. 1968 student uprising in Paris, retirement of de
       Gaulle
    f. Socialists in power from 1981
        1) President François Mitterand
            a) nationalization of industry, increased
welfare benefits
            b) economic problems cause reversal of
policies, more conservative orientation
  3. Britain
    a. Labor prime minister Clement Atlee, 1945-1951
        1) nationalization of industry
        2) socialized medicine and other welfare measures
    b. postwar problems
        1) loss of empire
        2) economic decline, class antagonisms
        3) racial tensions caused by flood of immigrants

c. Conservative prime minister Margaret Thatcher, 1979-1990
    1) reversal of socialist measures in favor of "enterprise culture"
    2) Falkland Islands war popular with voters
    3) foreign policy
4. other Western European states
    a. prosperity and stability in northern countries
        1) Scandinavia, Finland, Iceland
        2) Benelux countries
        3) Switzerland and Austria
    b. economic progress in southern countries
        1) Italy
        2) Greece
        3) Spain and Portugal
5. the leading Commonwealth nations
    a. generally more prosperous than Britain
    b. Canada
        1) one of leading capitalist states
        2) economic dependence on United States
        3) problem of Quebec separatism
    c. Australia
        1) high standard of living
        2) increasing economic and political interests in Asia
        3) easing of immigration restrictions on Asians

II. Postwar Eastern Europe

A. The Soviet Bloc
    1. postwar Soviet political history
        a. Nikita Khrushchev, 1956-1964
            1) de-Stalinization
                a) secret speech, 1956
                b) "the thaw"
            2) inability to solve agricultural problems
            3) crushing of Hungarian Revolution, 1956
            4) Cuban missile crisis, 1962
            5) forced resignation, 1964
        b. Leonid Brezhnev, 1964-1982
            1) return to old political system
            2) little economic progress
            3) arms buildup
            4) intervention in Afghanistan (1979)
    2. the Soviet satellites
        a. common characteristics
            1) agricultural regions
            2) mostly new nations
            3) nationalism and minority problems
        b. differing relations with Soviet Union

1) secession of Yugoslavia and Albania from Soviet bloc
2) other six countries
    a) less commitment to communism with each new generation of rulers
    b) increasing political and economic autonomy
    c) increasing resentment of communist restrictions at end of 1980s
3. accession of Mikhail Gorbachev, 1985
  a. background and personality
  b. <u>glasnost</u> and <u>perestroika</u>
  c. results of new policies
    1) some economic changes
    2) political reorganization
4. the revolutions of 1989
  a. demands of demonstrators all over eastern Europe
  b. opening of borders, fall of puppet regimes
  c. probable motive of Gorbachev for nonintervention
  d. new eastern European political leaders
4. collapse of Soviet Union
  a. political factions and rivalries
  b. nationalist demands for autonomy of republics
  c. rivals of Gorbachev
    1) Boris Yeltsin
    2) the communist establishment and KGB
    3) attempted coup of 1991
  d. resignation of Gorbachev, 1991
  e. Boris Yeltsin, president of Russian Republic
    1) economic problems
    2) lack of massive foreign aid
    3) uncertain future of country

III. The Postwar Economy

  A. The United States and Western Europe
1. great economic upturn as result of war
  a. new foreign markets formerly controlled by Europeans
  b. benefits of Marshall Plan for United States
2. reconstruction of global economy
  a. World Bank
  b. International Monetary Fund
  c. General Agreement on Tariffs and Trade
3. result: biggest economic expansion in Western history
  a. great economic demand
  b. increased government regulation of economy

           c. increased international economic cooperation
              1) European Coal and Steel Community
              2) European Atomic Energy Community
              3) joint international commercial ventures
              4) European Economic Community
              5) regular meetings of leaders of major
           capitalist countries to coordinate economy
        4. economic downturn
           a. causes of century's second worst depression
              1) sated postwar demand
              2) competition from Asian countries
              3) decline in Western production leads to
           unemployment, lower demand
              4) the oil crisis of 1973, accelerating
           inflation
              5) result: <u>stagflation</u>
           b. political consequences
              1) frequent return to conservative policies
           to deal with economic problems
              2) various measures taken by different
           countries
              3) lack of social and economic collapse that
           had occurred in 1930s
           c. uncertain future of European economy and
        economic integration
   B.   Eastern Europe
        1. Soviet postwar economic policy for eastern bloc
           a. direct looting and exploitation of
        satellites
           b. integration of satellites' economies with
        that of Soviet Union
        2. results for eastern Europe
           a. slower economic growth than that of western
        Europe
           b. economic stability, employment, welfare
        services
           c. unproductive agriculture, lack of consumer
        goods
           d. lack of incentive to produce or innovate
   C.   Postwar Technology
        1. importance of scientific and technological
        growth
        2. range of innovative products, techniques,
        weaponry
        3. space technology and exploration
        4. problems caused by technological progress
           a. deaths and injuries from automobile
        accidents
           b. depletion of natural resources and pollution
           c. examples of <u>Challenger</u> and Chernobyl
        disasters

IV. Postwar Western Society

  A. Population Growth
     1. higher birth rates and lower death rates
     2. new waves of migration
        a. political refugees
           1) German immigrants to West Germany after war
           2) Cuban and Vietnamese immigrants to United States
        b. economically motivated migrants
           1) from Third World countries to Europe and United States in search of work
           2) from less prosperous southern Europe to western Europe
        c. consequences
           1) ill treatment of migrants
           2) racist antagonism
           3) change in population mix of Western countries
           4) contributions of some groups of migrants
  B. Urban Development
     1. rebuilding of cities in Europe
     2. move to suburbs in United States and parts of Europe, decay of inner cities
     3. some urban renewal and attempts to bring affluent taxpayers back to cities
  C. The Welfare State
     1. Britain and Scandinavia
     2. conflicting views
        a. conservatives oppose increased taxation to pay for increasing social services
        b. socialists and liberals demand welfare services even in periods of depression
     3. education
        a. general expansion of educational opportunities
        b. variations among states
        c. educational fads in United States
           1) progressive education
           2) "open schools"
           3) "back to basics"
           4) "multiculturalism"
     4. increase in technological education, and use of technology in teaching
     5. class structures
        a. changes in the middle classes
           1) rise of middle-class managerial elite
           2) increase in government bureaucrats
        b. changes in blue-collar work
           1) greater increase in service industries than in manufacturing
           2) rise in working-class living standards

         c. the unemployed
              1) partially result of decline of jobs in
         industry
              2) difficulty of undereducated poor in finding
         and holding jobs
              3) occasional eruptions of rioting and
         violence
         d. generally less class conflict in West than
         previously; some resentment of new class of former
         communists in eastern Europe
         e. status of women
              1) more women working outside home
                   a) many because of financial necessity
                   b) many because of desire for careers
              2) examples of women in politics
              3) problems combining work and home
              responsibilities
              4) radical women's movement in 1960s and
         1970s
                   a) militant women writers
                   b) various demands
         f. the youth subculture
              1) increase in growth of subculture mentality
         after 1945
              2) fashions and entertainment
              3) radical political activism in 1960s
              4) characteristics of the counterculture
   D.   Post-Cold War Discontents
         1. political dissatisfaction with leaders in most
         major countries
         2. lack of western European enthusiasm for
         European union
         3. eastern European disillusionment with new
         leaders, free-market economics, dislocation
         4. economic problems of United States, Germany,
         Japan
         5. resurgence of aggressive nationalism
              a. Yugoslavia
              b. Czechoslovakia
              c. resentment of immigrants in western Europe

<u>Read to Find Out</u>

1. What were some features of twentieth-century political
expansion and integration?
2. What is the United Nations and how is it organized?
3. What is meant by the <u>Third World</u>?
4. How would you summarize American political history in the
second half of the twentieth century?
5. Who was Senator Joseph McCarthy?

6. What were the main achievements of the Kennedy and Johnson administrations?
7. What course did the civil rights movement in the United States take?
8. How would you summarize the presidency of Richard Nixon?
9. How did the policies of President Reagan differ from those of his immediate predecessors?
10. How do you account for Reagan's great popularity and landslide reelection?
11. How would you describe the presidency of George Bush?
12. What was the postwar history of Germany to 1990?
13. How does the postwar history of France compare with that of Great Britain?
14. Who was Margaret Thatcher and what were some of her achievements?
15. How did the condition of the smaller northern European states differ from the southern European countries?
16. What were the leading nations of the Commonwealth and how would you describe their postwar circumstances?
17. What were some features of the regime of Nikita Khrushchev?
18. In what ways was the Soviet "Thaw" temporary?
19. How would you describe the Brezhnev era?
20. Which two Soviet satellites had defected from the Soviet bloc by the 1960s, and what was the position of the others in the 1970s and 1980s?
21. What is meant by the Gorbachev Revolution?
22. How would you describe the revolutions of 1989?
23. What were the demands of some of the Soviet republics?
24. What led to the fall of Gorbachev, and who succeeded him?
25. How had World War II contributed to U.S. economic growth?
26. How did the Marshall Plan foster economic growth in both Europe and America?
27. What institutions were set up to promote the reconstruction of the global economy?
28. How was the postwar Western economy regulated?
29. What were some of the causes of the economic downturn of the 1970s and 1980s?
30. What were the economic effects of the 1970s rise in oil prices?
31. How did Western governments react to the new inflation and economic stagnation?
32. What factors accounted for the much slower growth in the economies of the eastern European states during the postwar period?
33. How did communist economic policies provide stability and full employment, while at the same time causing serious weaknesses in the economy?
34. What are some examples of twentieth-century technological innovations?

35. Who were Yuri Gagarin and Neil Armstrong and what is their significance?
36. How did migration play an important role in population changes in the late twentieth century?
37. What were some problems encountered by the migrants?
38. In what ways did middle-class occupations develop and change during this period?
39. How would you describe the condition of the working classes in the West during the postwar era?
40. What political causes did the subculture of youth espouse in the 1960s?
41. How did general political discontent manifest itself in the 1990s?
42. What sort of economic difficulties did most countries face at this time?
43. What are the possible dangers of resurgent nationalism in today's world?

Multiple-Choice Questions

1. The postwar West was characterized by
   a. slow economic growth rates
   b. an oversupply of oil
   c. integration and economic growth
   d. underdevelopment due to socialism

2. The presidency of Harry Truman was a period of
   a. Republican political power
   b. détente
   c. fewer social welfare programs
   d. continuing New Deal measures

3. U.S. domestic issues in the 1960s included
   a. McCarthyism
   b. civil rights
   c. beginning of social security
   d. the Watergate scandal

4. Following the presidential popularity and economic boom of the Reagan years, the presidency of George Bush was marked by
   a. greater prosperity
   b. a new Cold War
   c. recession and social problems
   d. budget surplus

5. Germany in the postwar years went from
   a. Nazism to Stalinism
   b. ruin and division to reunification and prosperity
   c. four-part division to permanent two-part division
   d. a first-rate European power to third-rate status

6. France in the postwar period experienced all of the following except
   a. impoverishment and loss of international political prestige
   b. loss of its colonial empire
   c. political instability
   d. a student rebellion

7. Margaret Thatcher was
   a. able to solve Britain's economic problems
   b. unwilling to deal with Gorbachev
   c. victorious in the war over the Falklands
   d. a major supporter of the Common Market

8. Postwar Canada
   a. became a socialist nation
   b. traded most heavily with Japan
   c. had no problems with its French-speaking minority
   d. became one of the seven leading capitalist nations

9. Between the death of Stalin and the rise of Gorbachev, the Soviet Union
   a. solved its agricultural problems
   b. renounced repression of revolt in the satellites
   c. dismantled the KGB
   d. experienced some liberalization along with increasing economic decline

10. Gorbachev's attempts to reform the Soviet system led to
    a. resounding success
    b. economic recovery
    c. satellite revolt and Soviet disintegration
    d. increased presence of the Red Army in Europe

11. Western European recovery after the war was largely due to
    a. massive U.S. assistance
    b. Soviet loans
    c. the adoption of socialism by most countries
    d. the natural operation of the business cycle

12. The economic decline of the 1970s and 1980s was due to all of the following except
a. a saturated market
b. lack of the stimulus of foreign competition
c. a large jump in oil prices
d. the exporting of Western manufacturing jobs to Asian countries

13. The postwar economic history of eastern Europe
a. closely resembled that of western Europe
b. included a major postwar boom
c. began with the looting and exploitation of the eastern European countries by the Soviet Union
d. featured more dramatic ups and downs than Western economic history of the same period

14. The development of twentieth-century science and technology has
a. proved to be an unmixed blessing
b. solved the problem of pollution
c. not been used to make warfare more deadly
d. posed unprecedented dangers to human life

15. Late twentieth-century migrants to European countries and the United States have experienced all of the following except
a. low pay and poor living conditions
b. a welcoming attitude from residents of the host countries
c. racist attacks
d. lack of success in their new homes

16. Class conflict in the capitalist countries during this period
a. was generally in decline
b. was on the rise in most states
c. became much more violent
d. spread from cities to rural areas

17. Groups that became radicalized during the 1960s included
a. women and young people
b. industrial workers
c. farmers
d. government bureaucrats

<u>Answer Key</u>

    1. c, 1004-1005
    2. d, 1007
    3. b, 1009
    4. c, 1010
    5. b, 1011
    6. a, 1012-1013
    7. c, 1013-1014
    8. d, 1015
    9. d, 1017-1018
   10. c, 1018-1021
   11. a, 1023
   12. b, 1025
   13. c, 1026
   14. d, 1027
   15. b, 1029
   16. a, 1030-1031
   17. a, 1031-1032

<u>Map Exercises</u>

1.   On Map 33.1, page 1016, trace the stages in German
reunification. In what zone was Berlin immediately after the war?
What was the capital of the Federal Republic of Germany? Where
did revolts first occur in the Soviet bloc after the war? Where
did a major revolt break out in 1956? What countries shown on the
map received aid under the Marshall Plan? What two groups of
northern European countries formed economic unions during this
period?

2.   On Map 33.2, page 1020, locate all the countries that had
revolutions in 1989. What country was the last to overthrow its
dictator, and what was his name? In what countries did the
revolutions start?

3.   On Map 33.3, page 1022, trace the collapse of the Soviet
Union as described in the chapter. How large is the Russian
Republic? How many former Soviet republics declared their
independence? Which is the largest of them? What territory in the
Baltics does Russia still claim, according to the map?

<u>Essay Questions</u>

1.   The period following World War II saw the extraordinarily
rapid reconstruction and development of Germany and Japan, due to
the help of the United States. The spectacular economic growth of
both those countries inspired Leonard Wibberley's comic novel <u>The</u>

<u>Mouse That Roared</u>, about the efforts of a small bankrupt country to attain prosperity by going to war with the United States and losing. You might enjoy reading this entertaining book or seeing the film version.

2.   Senator McCarthy's personality and tactics may have left much to be desired, but communists such as Alger Hiss, Harry Dexter White, and Frederick Vanderbilt Field did influence U.S. State Department policies, especially concerning China. (Hiss accompanied President Roosevelt to the Yalta conference.) The extent of their influence is still debated. Look into the current thinking on both sides of this issue.

3.   There is still a bitter debate in France over the purge of political opponents undertaken by members of the resistance after the war, apparently without any effective opposition by de Gaulle. Estimates of summary executions run as high as 100,000. See if you can find information about this remarkably little-known episode in postwar history.

4.   Some of the most advanced welfare states such as Sweden have been turning to increased privatization because of serious economic problems. Can any economy really sustain the burden of "cradle to grave" security for all citizens, or is such a goal unrealistic no matter how the economy is organized? Is it a good thing for citizens to be cared for by the state to that extent? Give reasons for your opinions.

5.   Does "equal pay for equal work" always serve the common good of society? Should a married woman working primarily for self-fulfillment be paid the same wage as the father of a large family, or should he receive more so that his children's mother will not have to leave them to seek work?

Chapter 34: A Revolution in Western Culture

<u>Outline</u>

   A.   The Revolution in Literature
      1. literary modernism
         a. characteristic features
         b. social criticism
         c. influence of some nineteenth-century
     attitudes
         d. examples of modernist writers
           1) Germany: Thomas Mann
           2) France: Marcel Proust
           3) Britain: D.H. Lawrence
           4) United States: Hemingway, Faulkner, Eugene
     O'Neill, Arthur Miller
           5) Soviet Union: Anna Akhmatova, Boris Pasternak
         e. three typical representatives of modernism in
          fiction
           1) Virginia Woolf (1882-1941)
             a) character of work
             b) stream of consciousness technique
           2) Franz Kafka (1883-1924)
             a) life and influences on his work
             b) features of his stories
           3) James Joyce (1812-1941)
             a) life
             b) style and complexity of work
             c) use of "dream language"
        f. modernist drama
           1) Bertold Brecht (1898-1956)
             a) emphasis on social issues
             b) method of presentation
           2) Eugene O'Neill (1888-1953)
             a) best-known American playwright
             b) variety of experimental work
           3) Luigi Pirandello (1867-1936)
             a) abandonment of traditional theatrical
     conventions
             b) exploration of relations between theater
     and world outside theater
           4) other dramatic experimentation
             a) sources of dramatist's ideas
             b) methods of staging
             c) work of Jerzy Grotowsky and Peter Brook

        g. poetry
           1) clearest expression of modernist spirit
           2) lack of popularity of modernist poetry
           3) characteristics
           4) examples
               a) William Butler Yeats (1865-1939)
               b) Anna Akhmatova
               c) T.S. Eliot (1888-1965)
2. dadaism and surrealism
    a. rejection of bourgeois values, traditional artistic practices
    b. appeal to nonrational forces
    c. characteristics of dadaist mentality
    d. André Breton (1896-1966)
        1) leader of surrealist movement
        2) surrealist ideas and approach derived from dadaists and theories of Freud
    e. Salvador Dali, 1904-1989, and surrealist painting
    f. surrealist film
3. socialist realism and magical realism
    a. Russia
        1) brief period of relative artistic freedom in 1920s
        2) examples of artists and writers
        3) control of art and literature by Communist party in 1930s
           a) rejection of modernism
           b) demands for socialist realism
           c) features and examples
           d) works of Mikhail Sholokov
    b. Latin America
        1) features of literary trend beginning in 1960s
        2) magical realism
        3) literary figures
           a) Jorge Luis Borges (1899-1986)
           b) Gabriel García Márquez
4. more recent literary trends
    a. late modernism
        1) American "beat" writers
        2) Britain's "angry young men"
        3) Yevtushenko and Solzhenitsyn attack communist system in Soviet Union
        4) theater of the absurd: Samuel Beckett's atheism
    b. postmodernism
        1) characteristics
        2) rejection of distinctions between good and bad art

            3) view of world as meaningless
            4) depression, drugs, alcohol kill off several
         postmodernists
            5) examples of postmodernist writers
            6) the postmodernist dilemma
   B.   Modernism in the Other Arts
         1. painting
            a. characteristics
               1) revolt against Renaissance traditions
               2) concentration on pure form
            b. examples
               1) Paul Gauguin (1848-1903)
                  a) life
                  b) characteristics of paintings
               2) Georgia O'Keeffe (1887-1986)
                  a) life
                  b) manner of painting
               3) Pablo Picasso (1881-1973)
                  a) skilled naturalist painter
                  b) rejection of naturalism, invention of
         cubism
               4) Piet Mondrian (1872-1944)
                  a) abstract, nonrepresentational art
                  b) characteristics of neoplasticism
               5) Jackson Pollock (1912-1956)
                  a) abstract expressionism
                  b) characteristics
            c. other developments
               1) color field painting
               2) minimalism
         2. sculpture
            a. styles
            b. early modernist representatives
               1) Alberto Giacometti (1901-1966)
               2) Henry Moore (1898-1986)
               3) Constantin Brancusi (1876-1957)
               4) Alexander Calder (1898-1976)
            c. late twentieth-century sculptors
               1) David Smith (1906-1965)
               2) Louise Nevelson (1900-1988)
         3. architecture
            1) new building materials and styles
            2) functionalism
               a) Frank Lloyd Wright (1867-1959)
               b) Mies Van der Rohe (1886-1969)
            3) the skyscraper
            4) postmodern architecture
               a) rejection of earlier modernist ideas such as
         functionalism
               b) draws on past and present styles

4. modern music and dance
   a. first half of twentieth century
      1) Arnold Schönberg, 1874-1951, and the twelve-tone scale
      2) Igor Stravinsky (1882-1971)
      3) Anton Webern (1883-1945)
      4) Béla Bartók (1881-1945)
      5) John Cage, 1912-1992, and indeterminism
   b. second half of the century
      1) electronic compositions
      2) jazz
         a) origins
         b) popularity in first half of century, continued development in second half
         c) Louis Armstrong (1900-1971)
         d) Edward "Duke" Ellington (1899-1974)
      3) rock and roll
         a) characteristics
         b) performers
   c. dance
      1) emphasis on self-expression rather than traditional patterns
      2) Martha Graham (1894-1991)
5. film
   a. technical development of motion pictures
   b. primacy of Hollywood in film making
      1) types of films
      2) early stars
         a) Rudolph Valentino
         b) Marlene Dietrich
         c) Charlie Chaplin
   c. directors
      1) D.W. Griffith (1875-1948)
         a) techniques
         b) <u>Birth of a Nation</u>
      2) Sergei Eisenstein (1898-1948)
         a) influence of communist mentality on subject matter of his films
         b) technique of montage
      3) Roberto Rossellini (1906-1977)
      4) Alain Robbe-Grillet and French new wave cinema
      5) Ingmar Bergman and Akiro Kurosawa
      6) late twentieth-century American directors and their films
   d. popularity of films and television
C.   The Twentieth-Century Scientific Revolution
1. twentieth-century research calls into question basic scientific assumptions
   a. qualities of matter
   b. Marie Curie's work on radiation

           c. Albert Einstein (1879-1955)
              1) theory of relativity
              2) new definition of gravity
              3) relationship between matter and energy
        2. developments in various sciences
           a. astronomy
              1) better instruments and techniques
              2) George Gamov and the big bang theory
           b. biology and related fields
              1) discovery of DNA
              2) study of animals in their native habitat
              3) study of human behavior as biologically rather
           than culturally conditioned or determined
           c. psychology
              1) Sigmund Freud
                 a) controversial figure
                 b) theory of two primary drives: life instinct
           and death instinct
              2) Carl Jung (1875-1961)
                 a) methods of study
                 b) theories of human archetypes and racial
           memory
              3) Ivan Pavlov (1849-1936)
                 a) the conditioned reflex
                 b) behaviorist theory of conditioned reflex
              as determining human behavior
                 c) work and theories of John Watson and B.F.
           Skinner on human conditioning
              4) study of brain and body chemistry to determine
           causes of psychological imbalance, development of
           new drugs to restore balance
        3. new paradigms
           a. features of new scientific worldview
           b. Heisenberg's principle of
        indeterminacy
           c. Thomas Kuhn and theory of paradigms
   D.   Religion and Philosophy
        1. continued advance of secularism and attacks on
        Scriptures
        2. survival of religion
           a. social activism of many Christians
           b. insistence on primacy of spiritual message by
        others
              1) "born-again" theology
              2) neo-orthodoxy
                 a) Carl Barth
                 b) Reinhold and Richard Niebuhr
                 c) philosophical critique of modern rejection
           of God and modern goal of earthly perfection

                c. other religious thinkers
                    1) Protestant Paul Tillich
                    2) Catholic Gabriel Marcel
                    3) Jewish Martin Buber
            3. schools of philosophy
                a. logical positivism
                b. William James's pragmatism
                    1) emphasis on usefulness of concepts
                    2) truth is the "cash value" of an idea
                c. John Dewey's instrumentalism
                d. existentialism
                    1) roots and premises
                    2) radical atheist materialism
                    3) exponents
                        a) Jean-Paul Sartre (1905-1980)
                        b) Martin Heidegger (1889-1976)
                    4) meaninglessness and anguish of life
                    5) value must be invented and imposed on life by
                human consciousness
                e. structuralism
                    1) basic approach
                    2) Lévi-Strauss and application of structuralism
                to anthropology
                    3) contradiction of some principles of
                existentialism
                f. Michel Foucault's poststructuralism
                    1) analysis of society and culture in terms of
                "discourse," and its use as a means of social
                control
                    2) no such thing as truth
                g. Jacques Derrida's deconstruction
                    1) rejection of search for author's intention in
                writing a literary text
                    2) disassembly of text to discover true meaning,
                whether intended by author or not

Read to Find Out

    1. What are some general characteristics of Western culture
    in the twentieth century?
    2. What is modernism?
    3. In what ways was twentieth-century Western literature
    revolutionary?
    4. What were some of the themes treated in modernist
    literary works?
    5. Who were the main exponents of literary modernism?
    6. What were some features of modernist drama, and who were
    some of the major dramatists of this period?

7. What did modernist poets consider to be the point of literature?

8. How was the work of T.S. Eliot typical of the mentality of the first quarter of the twentieth century?

9. What were dadaism and surrealism, and how were they expressed in twentieth-century literary works?

10. How did the Russian Revolution influence Russian culture in the 1920s?

11. What were some of the elements of "socialist realism"?

12. What is meant by "magical realism" and who were some of the writers associated with it?

13. What is meant by the theater of the absurd?

14. What is the difference between modernism and postmodernism?

15. Who were some of the pioneers of modernism in painting, and how would you describe their styles?

16. Who was Pablo Picasso?

17. What is meant by cubism, and who invented it?

18. What are the main characteristics of the paintings of Mondrian?

19. Who were the major modernist sculptures and in what ways did their work represent a departure from earlier styles?

20. Who was Frank Lloyd Wright and what were some of his architectural principles?

21. What is the most typical product of twentieth-century architecture?

22. How did the work of postmodernist architects differ from that of their predecessors?

23. Who were some of the revolutionary composers of music, and in what ways was their work revolutionary?

24. Who was Martha Graham?

25. How would you summarize the development of motion pictures in the twentieth century?

26. Who was Sergei Eisenstein and how did his political ideology affect his film making?

27. Who were some late twentieth-century film directors and what kind of films did they make?

28. How was the older Western view of science and natural laws challenged in the early twentieth century?

29. Who was Albert Einstein and what were some of his theories?

30. What is the big bang theory of how the universe began, and who proposed it?

31. What is DNA and what is the significance of its discovery?

32. How did the theories of Jung differ from those of Freud?

33. How would you characterize Pavlov's psychological theories?

34. What is behaviorism?

35. Who was Werner Heisenberg and what was his principle
    of indeterminacy?
36. What is meant by a paradigm?
37. In what ways did secularism pervade the twentieth-
    century mentality?
38. In what different ways did Christian commitment
    express itself at this time?
39. What are the main ideas of Christian neo-orthodoxy,
    and who were its main exponents?
40. Who were some major religious philosophers of this
    period?
41. What is logical positivism?
42. What is meant by pragmatism and who developed it?
43. How would you characterize the philosophy of
    existentialism?
44. How does structuralism represent a rebellion against
    existentialism?
45. How has poststructuralism been used by radical social
    critics in the late twentieth century?
46. What is meant by deconstruction?
47. How was traditional confidence in the existence of
    absolute truth eroded by twentieth-century thinkers?

Multiple-Choice Questions

1. Twentieth-century culture has been characterized by
    a. continuity and conservatism
    b. change and rebellion
    c. lack of social commitment
    d. ideological neutrality

2. Artistic modernism included all of the following
    elements except
    a. rebellious attitudes
    b. a cult of originality
    c. an emphasis on realism and naturalism
    d. a dedication to self-expression

3. Modernist writers
    a. sought to communicate their ideas clearly to masses
    of readers
    b. rarely criticized their own society and its values
    c. disdained the production of work that was
    intelligible to others
    d. sought inspiration in Enlightenment literature

4. Virginia Woolf, Franz Kafka, and James Joyce were all
   a. creators of often abstruse and tragic experimental fiction
   b. writers of humorous short stories
   c. famous dramatists
   d. British poets

5. Modernist poetry
   a. achieved wide popularity
   b. depended upon rhyme for its effect
   c. imitated medieval epic poetry
   d. expressed most clearly the modernist spirit in literature

6. Dadaism and surrealism both
   a. stressed the application of rationalism to art b. developed in art academies and universities
   c. avoided social criticism
   d. relied on nonrational forces to produce their work

7. Cultural experimentation in Russia
   a. lasted through the Stalinist period
   b. lacked modernist elements
   c. was totally dominated from the beginning by communist ideology
   d. flourished in the 1920s

8. Socialist realism involved
   a. the development of abstract Russian art
   b. the use of blank verse by Russian poets
   c. the utilization of art to promote communist goals
   d. the depiction of life as it really was in the Soviet Union

9. Later modernist painting included all of the following except
   a. paintings made up only of straight lines and colored rectangles
   b. recognizable objects
   c. interwoven patterns of lines
   d. blocks of color

10. One of the most famous architects of the twentieth century was
    a. Constantin Brancusi
    b. Frank Lloyd Wright
    c. Sergei Eisenstein
    d. David Smith

11. The most popular new music in the first half of the
    twentieth century was
    a. jazz
    b. twelve-tone scale music
    c. the work of Stravinsky
    d. the work of John Cage

12. The transformation of motion pictures into an art form
    was mainly due to
    a. new film making technology
    b. the popularity and talent of movie stars
    c. the invention of television
    d. film directors

13. All of the following were major figures in twentieth-
    century science except
    a. Marie Curie
    b. Albert Einstein
    c. Charles Darwin
    d. George Gamov

14. For both Freud and Pavlov, human beings
    a. are motivated by material, nonrational impulses
    b. are dominated by their rationality
    c. operate completely differently from animals
    d. are spiritual creatures imprisoned in illusory
    bodies

15. Major Christian thinkers in the twentieth century
    a. were impossible to find
    b. agreed that the anguish and unhappiness of modern
    people stemmed from their rejection of God
    c. had all become secularists by the end of the century
    d. were limited to "born-again" religious sects

16. Late twentieth-century philosophical schools
    a. showed a new confidence in the ability of the human
    mind to know reality
    b. denied the existence of outside reality
    c. rejected the view that the nature of things as they
    are should be studied by philosophers
    d. returned to the philosophical approach of the Greek
    philosophers

Answer Key

   1. b, 1038
   2. c, 1039

```
 3.  c, 1039
 4.  a, 1039-1041
 5.  d, 1043
 6.  d, 1043-1045
 7.  d, 1045
 8.  c, 1046
 9.  b, 1049-1051
10.  b, 1052
11.  a, 1052-1053
12.  d, 1054
13.  c, 1056-1059
14.  a, 1059
15.  b, 1061-1062
16.  c, 1062-1063
```

Essay Questions

1. What do you think of the emphasis placed by modern artists on self-expression rather than communication? If a work of painting or literature is unintelligible to everyone except the artist, and perhaps not to the artist either, what makes it art?

2. Painting and sculpture were traditionally supposed to imitate nature. Look at some examples of earlier Western art and compare them with pictures by Mondrian, Pollock, or other painters mentioned in the chapter. If the recent artists do not imitate nature, what do you think they are trying to reproduce on canvas? Do you like modern art? Why or why not?

3. Socialist realism was the subservience of art to ideology. Do you think there is an underlying ideology that has influenced the production of so many pessimistic and negative works in twentieth-century literature, art, music, and philosophy? What mentality or worldview is common to many of the artists discussed in the chapter?

4. Rock music has been criticized on many grounds, such as impairing the hearing of its fans, altering heartbeat rhythms, affecting brain cells so that the mind becomes receptive to messages conveyed by rock songs, and desensitizing spectators to obscenity, violence, and ugliness. Read some of these critiques, starting with the chapter on music in Allan Bloom's The Closing of the American Mind (1987). Discussions of the physical effects of rock rhythms are found in medical and psychiatric literature and books such as New Mind, New Body, by Dr. Barbara Brown (1974).

5.   What are the social consequences of the theory that human behavior is biologically determined? How many ramifications can you think of in fields such as education, welfare, criminal justice?

6.   What do you think of the principles of deconstruction as described at the end of the chapter? How could these principles be utilized by radical social critics (as they currently are by feminist deconstructionists)? Do we really need scientists or social science professionals to decode reality for us?

Chapter 35: The West and the World

Outline

    A.   Colonial Liberation
        1. independence of most Western colonies
           after World War II
        2. earlier independence movements
          a. isolated African revolts
          b. British India
            1) Congress party
            2) Mohandas K. Gandhi
              a) career
              b) principles
              c) achievements
        3. causes of disintegration of empires
          a. example of ease of Japanese victories over
            colonial powers
          b. war saps strength of imperial powers
          c. some postwar politicians oppose imperialism
          d. postwar dominance of two superpowers opposed
            to European colonial system
          e. Westernized, charismatic colonial leaders
          b. strong nationalistic organizations
          c. generally less violence than in earlier
            twentieth-century revolutions
        4. Asia
          a. India and Pakistan
            1) religious issues
            2) riots and mass migrations
            3) creation of Pakistan, 1947
            4) Ceylon
               a) independence, 1948
              b) changes name to Sri Lanka, 1972
            5) East Pakistan becomes Bangladesh
            6) postwar political history
               a) assassination of Gandhi, 1948
              b) Jawaharlal Nehru (1889-1964)
              c) Indira Gandhi (1917-1984)
              d) Rajiv Gandhi (1945-1991)
            7) economic problems
            8) India-Pakistan wars
            9) conflicts with China and Sikhs
          b. Southeast Asia
            1) Burma and Malaya freed by British

            2) Indonesia freed by Dutch
            3) Philippines freed by United States, 1946
            4) Indochina
                a) Vietnam war
                b) Khmer Rouge totalitarianism in
        Kampuchea (Cambodia)
            5) continued violence in Indonesia and
        Philippines
    5. Africa
        a. French colonies
            1) protectorates of Morocco and Tunisia
        granted independence
            2) Algeria
                a) considered province of France
                b) large number of Algerian-born
                    French settlers
                c) FLN terrorism and war with France
                e) De Gaulle grants independence, 1962
            3) freedom for French Equatorial and French
        West Africa
                a) awkward boundaries of new countries
                b) poverty of land
                c) French aid and progress in some states
        b. British West Africa
            1) Gold Coast
                a) Kwame Nkrumah and Convention Peoples
                    party
                b) campaign for immediate independence
                c) Gold Coast becomes Ghana in 1957;
                Nkrumah first president
             2) Nigeria and other British West African
        colonies gain independence
        c. British East Africa
            1) Kenya
                a) British settlers resist black rule
                b) Mau Mau terrorism
                c) leadership of Jomo Kenyatta
                d) independence 1963, Kenyatta president
            2) Tanganyika
                a) leadership of Julius Nyerere
                b) becomes Tanzania
            3) postindependence problems
        d. Belgian Congo
            1) lack of preparation for independence
            2) precipitate Belgian withdrawal
            3) civil war
            4) UN intervention and military takeover
            5) new nation of Zaire
        e. independence of Portuguese Angola and
Mozambique

  f. British Rhodesia
   1) Northern Rhodesia becomes Zambia
   2) white resistance in Southern Rhodesia;
  becomes Zimbabwe, 1980
 6. Israel and the Arab states
  a. British mandate of Palestine
  b. historical background of Zionism
  c. resistance of Palestinian Arabs to Jewish
   immigration
  d. formation of Israel, 1948
   1) Arab-Israeli War, 1948
   2) Israeli victory
   3) leadership of Ben-Gurion
   4) problem of Palestinian refugees
  e. later wars with Arabs
   2) 1956 war
   3) Six Day War, 1967
   4) Yom Kippur War, 1973
  f. agreement with Egypt, 1978
  g. formation of Palestine Liberation
   Organization
   1) PLO terrorism and international criticism
   of Israeli treatment of Arabs
   2) Israeli invasion of Lebanon, 1982
  h. continued Israeli-Palestinian friction
 7. South Africa
  a. Republic of South Africa
   a) historical background
   b) postwar apartheid policies of
    Afrikaaners
   c) African resistance
    1) African National Congress (ANC)
    2) neighboring states serve as bases
   for guerrilla and terrorist attacks
   d) South African reaction
   e) South African prosperity neutralizes
    threat of international boycott
   f) policies of new president, F.W. De
      Klerk, late 1980s
    1) offers peace to militants
    2) repeals apartheid laws
    3) legalizes ANC
    4) frees ANC leader Nelson Mandela
   g) black rivalries and violence
B. Nations of the Non-Western World
 1. definition of term non-Western
  a. application of term to developing countries
  b. includes developed non-Western countries
 2. characteristics of developing countries
  a. economic underdevelopment

      b. expanding populations
      c. political authoritarianism
      d. nonalignment in the cold war
      e. some ties to Western powers
      f. importance of religion, family, tribe, traditions in lives of people
3. problems
      a. shortage of modern education
      b. lack of economic infrastructure
      c. lack of resources
      d. inefficient agriculture
      e. inadequate industry
      f. widespread poverty and disease
4. agendas
      a. political ambitions
      b. international conflicts
      c. religious conflicts
      d. examples of conflicts
      e. desire for rapid economic and technological development
5. means of solving problems
      a. international organizations
         1) Organization of African Unity
         2) Arab League
         3) OPEC
      b. ties with West
         1) British Commonwealth
         2) French Community
         3) other contacts
      c. alliances with superpowers
         1) SEATO with United States
         2) treaties with USSR
      d. UN representation
      e. Western-style government bureaucracies
6. status of women
      a. lifestyle of upper-class women
      b. effects of outside jobs on working women
      c. life of women in villages
7. economic policies
      a. unsuccessful state socialism in many new nations
      b. trend in 1970s and 1980s to free-market measures
      c. problems with both approaches
      d. need for foreign currency
         1) sales of agricultural products and raw materials to West; imports of manufactured goods
         2) resulting neglect of subsistence agriculture, lack of control of profits and prices, industrial dependency

       e. need for Western investment
          1) foreign banks and government
          2) World Bank
          3) IMF and its conditions
          4) foreign aid
       f. theories of roots of economic problems
          1) leftist concept of Western policies as
          neoimperialism
          2) right-wing criticism of Western support
          as counterproductive
          3) theory that investment should be targeted
          to most needy groups and countries
  8. areas of growth in non-Western world
     a. Latin America
        1) historical background
        2) political situation
           a) Mexico
           b) Brazil
           c) Argentina
           d) Chile
        3) economic problems
           a) dependency
           b) foreign debt
           c) poverty and economic stagnation
           d) drugs and criminal cartels
        4) signs of hope
     b. the Middle East
        1) mostly Arab
        2) variety of authoritarian governments
        3) Muslim faith, nationalism, feuds among
        leaders
        4) Israel: most powerful state
        5) Egypt
           a) rule of Nassar
           b) nationalization of Suez Canal, 1956
           c) aid and advice from Soviet Union
           d) reversal of policies by Sadat until
        assassination, 1981
        6) Iran
           a) historical background of postwar
        period
           b) Shah Mohammed Reza Pahlavi: pro-
        Western
           c) overthrown by Islamic fundamentalists,
        1979
           d) rule of Ayatollah Ruhollah Khomeini
           e) seizure of U.S. embassy, war with Iraq
        7) Saudi Arabia
           a) conservative American ally
           b) world's largest oil reserves
           c) Islamic holy places

          8) importance of Middle East oil
               a) rise in oil prices in 1970s
               b) West curtails use of oil, causing
          oversupply
          c. Japan
               1) American postwar occupation of Japan
               2) rapid growth of political and economic
          stability
               3) alliance with United States
               4) spectacular economic development
               5) government role in business
               6) industrious and thrifty people
               7) achievements by 1990s
          d. the Pacific Rim
               1) South Korea
                    a) postwar political development
                    b) economic progress
               2) Taiwan
                    a) leadership of Chiang Kai-shek and
                    successors
                    b) great productivity and prosperity
               3) Hong Kong
               4) Singapore
     9. China
          a. communist political organization of country
          b. ideological campaigns
               1) Great Leap Forward
               2) Cultural Revolution
          c. reaction
               1) Deng Xiaoping and "pragmatism"
               2) closer ties with West
          d. massacre in Tiananmen Square, 1990
     10. India
          a. rapid economic development by end of century
          b. religious and nationalist divisions
          c. government regulation hampers economic
     growth
          d. free-market reforms under Prime Minister
     P.V. Narasimha Rao in 1990s
C.   The West and the World
     1. increasing globalization
     2. United States: only superpower left
          a. deployment of power under President Bush
               1) Panama
               2) Operation Desert Storm
               3) Somalia
     3. westernization
          a. political and military dominance of West
          b. Western science, technology, economics
          c. Western cultural and social patterns
          d. fashion and entertainment

4. the West and the world's problems
a. pollution
b. waste of resources
c. Western weapons scattered all over the world
d. economic exploitation by Western financial,
international, and multinational corporations
e. indigenous problems aggravated by Western
contacts
5. global solutions: must be joint ventures of
Westerners and non-Westerners

Read to Find Out

1. What were some factors involved in the growing
colonial discontent with Western rule?
2. What pattern was common to the postwar history of
most colonial nations?
3. What were the main imperial powers involved in the
colonial liberation movement?
4. What were some causes of the collapse of Western
imperialism?
5. How did World War II affect the imperialist powers?
6. What were some common features of the liberation
movements?
7. Who were some of the new leaders of these movements?
8. How did religion play a role in the postwar history
of India?
9. What became of the island of Ceylon?
10. How did Bangladesh come into existence?
11. Who were some of the leaders of India after
independence, and what problems did they face?
12. What new states emerged in Southeast Asia?
13. How would you summarize French problems with
Algeria, and how were they resolved?
14. What other French colonial territories in Africa
were granted independence, and what problems did they
have afterward?
15. What were some features of the process of liberation
in British West Africa?
16. What were the policies of Kwame Nkrumah?
17. What conditions prevailed in British East Africa?
18. What was the Mau Mau?
19. Who were Jomo Kenyatta and Julius Nyerere?
20. How did Belgium handle the transfer of power to the
Congolese?
21. What region attempted to secede from the newly
independent Congo, and what was the result of the Congo
crisis?
22. What Portuguese African colonies became independent,
and when?

23. What was the history of Rhodesia in the postwar period?
24. Why was the British mandate of Palestine the source of continuing conflict after World War II?
25. What is Zionism?
26. When was the state of Israel formed?
27. What were the causes and results of the 1948 Arab-Israeli War?
28. What other wars were fought by Israel after 1948?
29. What is the PLO?
30. What was the most recent Israeli military campaign?
31. What were some of the problems faced by the government and citizens of South Africa?
32. What is meant by apartheid?
33. What major changes in the relationship between the South African government and black South Africans took place in the late 1980s and 1990s?
34. Why is the term <u>non-Western</u> difficult to define? What further distinctions must be made among non-Western states?
35. What are some characteristics common to most developing countries?
36. What types of problems do they have, and what are some of their goals?
37. How do the developing countries obtain foreign aid?
38. What is the position of women in the developing countries?
39. What international organizations were set up to assist developing countries?
40. What is meant by neo-imperialism?
41. What differences of opinion exist as to the most effective way of helping developing countries economically?
42. What are some developed countries in the non-Western world?
43. In what ways do the problems facing the Latin American countries compare with those of Asia and Africa, and how do they differ?
44. Why did economic growth remain limited in some areas?
45. What political trend seemed to be developing in many Latin American nations in the 1980s and 1990s?
46. What were some features of the postwar history of Egypt?
47. What is the postwar historical background of Iran?
48. Who was the Ayatollah Khomeini and what were his policies?
49. What were the causes of the Iran-Iraq war, and what was its outcome?

50. How would you describe the situation of Saudi Arabia in the postwar period?
51. What is OPEC?
52. How would you describe and explain the extraordinary postwar economic growth of Japan?
53. What developed states exist on the Pacific rim, and what do they have in common?
54. How would you compare China and India at the end of the century?
55. How was China organized politically after World War II?
56. What was the Great Leap Forward?
57. What was the Cultural Revolution?
58. Who was Deng Xiaoping and what were his policies?
59. What and when was the Tiananmen massacre?
60. How would you describe the political and economic condition of India at the end of the century?
61. How did westernization appear to be a global phenomenon by the 1990s?
62. Where did President Bush send American troops in the 1980s and 1990s, and what were the results of those actions?
63. What problems, as well as benefits, have been brought to the rest of the world by Western science and technology?

Multiple-Choice Questions

1.   The causes of the collapse of the European empires were primarily
      a. religious
      b. financial
      c. political and ideological
      d. military

2.   After independence, India experienced
      a. peace and prosperity
      b. disastrous wars between Hindus and Muslims
      c. Soviet invasion
      d. conversion of the whole country to Islam

3.   All of the following are true of French Algeria except that
      a. it had a large French population that had lived there for generations
      b. France did not resist the Algerian rebellion
      c. it was the one African territory the French were determined to keep
      d. the Algerian National Liberation Front used urban terrorism

4. Kwame Nkrumah guided the Gold Coast to independence from Britain by
   a. using strikes and boycotts
   b. asking only for reform of the colonial administration
   c. declaring independence in 1945
   d. assassinating the British governor

5. Warfare in the Congo in the 1960s was due in part to all of the following except
   a. tribal rivalries
   b. a long preparation for self-government
   c. Katangan desire for independence
   d. struggle for control over the resources of Katanga

6. The state of Israel was
   a. set up by the British in 1948
   b. welcomed by the Arab League
   c. expanded to include the Mediterranean coast from Lebanon to the Suez Canal
   d. a source of continuing hostility and frequent wars with Palestinians and neighboring countries

7. A new development that occurred in the Republic of South Africa in the 1980s was
   a. the repeal of apartheid laws
   b. the execution of Nelson Mandela
   c. departure of the Afrikaaners
   d. election of a black African president

8. One basic economic problem of the developing countries is
   a. overproduction of consumer goods
   b. import and export dependency
   c. oil surpluses
   d. refusal to accept foreign loans

9. The most pressing national postwar goal for many Latin Americans was
   a. liberal democratic government
   b. economic development
   c. religious revival
   d. territorial conquest

10. The overthrow of the shah of Iran in 1979 was
    followed by
    a. the liberation of Iranian women
    b. a stable and peaceful republican regime
    c. the rule of a militant Shiite religious leader
    d. a communist takeover

11. The great importance of the Middle East to the
    rest of the world was due to its
    a. industrial technology
    b. business management techniques
    c. bauxite reserves
    d. oil

12. Japan's postwar economic growth was due to all of
    the following except
    a. its extensive natural resources, including oil
    b. U.S. support after the war
    c. the industriousness of the Japanese people
    d. cooperative business arrangements

13. On the Pacific Rim, the postwar era saw
    a. economic stagnation and political dictatorship
    b. great economic development in large countries
    only
    c. the rise of prosperous small nations and city-
    states
    d. communist regimes everywhere

14. Despite some liberalization in the 1970s, the
    history of communist China was generally marked by
    a. governmental terror and oppression
    b. weak leaders
    c. democratization
    d. renunciation of communist ideology

15. All of the following were features of postwar
    India except
    a. free-market reforms in the 1990s
    b. poverty
    c. ethnic, linguistic, and religious unity
    d. religious conflict

16. The end of the twentieth century seemed to be a
    time of
    a. domination of three superpowers
    b. renewal of the Cold War
    c. growth of global interdependence
    d. general rejection of globalism

17. Among the elements tending to unify world
     societies were
     a. industrialism and technology
     b. the spread of Christianity
     c. the new world government
     d. acceptance of the same political system

18. As a result of technological progress
     a. the environment was seriously threatened
     b. pollution was a thing of the past
     c. natural resources were unlimited
     d. global air and water quality improved

Answer Key

     1. c, 1071-1072
     2. b, 1074
     3. b, 1075
     4. a, 1076
     5. b, 1077
     6. d, 1078-1079
     7. a, 1080
     8. b, 1081
     9. b, 1087
    10. c, 1089
    11. d, 1090
    12. a, 1090
    13. c, 1090-1091
    14. a, 1092
    15. c, 1092
    16. c, 1092-1093
    17. a, 1093-1094
    18. a, 1094-1095

Map Exercises

1. On Map 35.1, page 1078, how many Western imperialist
powers are represented? Which were the first to liberate
their colonies and what are the current names of the first
new states? How many new states emerged from French West
Africa? Where is Algeria, and how did its historical
relationship with France differ from that of Morocco and
Tunisia? What new states developed from British colonies in
Asia? What southeast Asian state remained under British
control in the postwar period? Where is Katanga, and to what
new African nation was it forcibly reunited? Where is
Rhodesia, and into what new countries was it divided?

2. On Map 35.2, page 1085, locate the main developed and developing nations discussed in the chapter. Where are the most developed non-Western states located? Which of the Latin American countries are most developed? What are the two largest developing countries? What are the smallest, and where are they located?

3. On Map 35.3, page 1088, locate the countries that make up OPEC. Which country has the most oil and dominates the cartel? What countries are the biggest consumers of OPEC oil? What countries buy least from OPEC, and what reasons can you think of for this? Which developed countries have oil resources of their own, and which are totally dependent on foreign oil?

Essay Questions

1. Is there a revisionist view of Gandhi among recent historians, or is he still generally regarded as a "saint"? See what different interpretations you can find of his character and achievements.

2. White settlers in African territories such as Algeria, Rhodesia, and South Africa consider themselves "natives" because their families have been there for generations. In the Republic of South Africa, many black immigrants are more recent arrivals than many of the Europeans. In such a situation, is it right for the Europeans to consider themselves Africans, or should all whites leave Africa?

3. To what extent is the population problem a question of population distribution? There are huge tracts of arable, uninhabited land on all continents, including Australia. What difficulties and prejudices would need to be overcome in order to achieve a better distribution of people?

4. Develop an essay discussing the benefits and drawbacks of global westernization for non-Western peoples. Consider the effects of Western science, technology, political ideas, culture, fashion, and popular entertainment. Does the establishment of liberal democracy and fast food restaurants always represent progress, or can the undermining of traditional lifestyles and culture cause more anxiety than it relieves? Give examples and reasons for your arguments.